Eileen. Bur
10¹

C000151097

) 570 63|

AYRSHIRE MONOGRAPHS NO.25

The Street Names of Ayr

Rob Close

Published by
Ayrshire Archaeological and Natural History Society

First published 2001

Printed by
The Cromwell Press Ltd, Trowbridge, Wiltshire

•

Rob Close is the author of *Ayrshire and Arran: An Illustrated Architectural Guide* (1992), and is presently co-editor of *Ayrshire Notes*. He has also contributed articles to *Scottish Local History, Scottish Brewing Archive* and other journals. He lives near Drongan with his long-suffering partner, Joy. In 1995 he was one half of the Scottish Handicap Doubles Croquet Champions.

Cover design by David McClure.

ISBN 0 9527445 9 7

INTRODUCTION

Names have an important role in our lives: names of people, names of places, and names of things. In an enclosed, small community, these names remain informal, but as the community grows, and as travel and movement become commoner, then more formalised names are required, names which will prevent confusion. Formal and informal names can exist alongside one another. During the course of preparing this book, I agreed to meet some friends on the road between 'Nick's place' and 'the quarry': that we met successfully was due to the fact that we all recognised and understood these informal place names. However, to a different cohort of people, 'Nick's place' is known as 'the doctor's house', while had we been arranging this rendezvous with people unfamiliar with the area, we would have had to fall back upon more formal place names, names with a wider currency, names with 'public' approval, whether conferred by the local authority, the Post Office or the Ordnance Survey.

The requirement for a more formal pattern of names in Ayr began to become apparent in the early 19th Century. Although names such as High Street and Sandgate, usually prefaced with the definitive article, had been in use before 1800, a letter to a resident, addressed 'Ayr' (or 'Air'), would arrive safely. As the town grew in the years after 1800, and as the number of people receiving post increased, and as the number of strangers resorting to the town increased, the need to tackle the issue of nomeclature was recognised. On 11th October 1828 the Town Council "taking into their consideration the increasing state of the town, and the necessity thence arising of the streets and lanes being known to strangers, they resolve and agree to place the name of each street and lane in large painted capitals on the entries or corners thereof, and to number the houses, and they remit to the Magistrates and Dean of Guild to see this done and to report".[1] A list of names was presented to the Council the following month, which they amended, and on 19th November 1828 they authorised the Committee to proceed.[2]

The use of street names and house numbers becomes increasingly widespread as the century progresses. By September 1845, the Town Council had become involved in the formal naming of streets, when they agreed that Midsands Road should be renamed Midton Road. In 1894 the Council authorised the renaming of a number of roads, including Tollpark Road: an action which suggests that by then the Council believed that they had the power to confer or approve new names.

This is an issue which still engenders discussion, and to which there appears to be no satisfactory answer. As indicated earlier, the parties with the greatest interest in the naming of streets (apart from the householders themselves) were the Town Council, the Government-controlled Post Office, and the Ordnance Survey. The introduction of an organised postal system - the penny post - in 1840, and the increasing coverage of the country by the map-makers in the 1850s reinforced the need to establish a consensus. In rural areas especially, names became a particular interest of the Ordnance Survey, whose 'Name Books' detail various options for the individual farms, cottages, hills and other

---

[1]   South Ayrshire Libraries [SAL], B6/18/26, Ayr Council Book 1825-1828, 463.
[2]   *ibid*, 470.

features before finalising a formal pronouncement on the spelling to be adopted.[1] The Police & Improvement [Scotland] Act of 1861 empowered Councils to instruct householders to display and maintain road names and house numbers.

From the 1890s all new names appear to have been presented to Ayr Town Council for approval, though there are some which escaped their net. The records of the Council do not provide any indication as to whether consultation was involved. Occasionally, the Town Council minutes furnish some suggestion that the name had been proposed or suggested by the developer, but there is no evidence that any consultation was ever undertaken with, for instance, the Post Office. Evidence of some friction between the Council (perhaps prompted by the Post Office) and developers can be seen in the Council's action in curbing a tendency to give a different name to each new development. This was particularly prevalent north of the river, especially in streets such as McCall's Avenue, Hunter's Avenue and West Sanquhar Road.[2]

By and large, the developers seem to have co-operated with the Council. The lack of any overall naming pattern suggests that most names were proposed by the developers themselves and 'rubber-stamped' by the Council. From the 1920s the Council themselves became major developers, and the opportunity which this provided some ambitious councillors for self-advertisement was not missed.

In 1966 the Town Council decided to appoint a Sub-Committee to examine the process of street-naming. Their report was approved in February 1967, when they put forward a number of recommendations, including continuation of the established use of tree names in Castlehill and Masonhill;[3] that West Indian names be used at Rozelle;[4] and that established field names should also be used where appropriate. They also requested lists of the battle honours of the Ayrshire regiments - the Royal Scottish Fusiliers and the Ayrshire Yeomanry - but it appears that these lists, if ever completed, were not selected.

Since the 1980s the local authorities appear to have had less involvement in street naming. Such names as are brought before the Council are no longer 'approved', but are merely 'noted'. Since the establishment of South Ayrshire Council in 1996, even such 'noting' has disappeared from the public record.

The street names of Ayr offer a partial history of the town, a history approached in a different way than through the usual chronological pattern. They also demonstrate changing tastes and interests. It has been difficult to draw a line under this research,[5] and also not to

---

[1]   As may be imagined, this policy faced its biggest problems in Welsh-speaking parts of Wales and Gaelic-speaking areas of Scotland and Ireland, and the issue of 'correct' names remains a live political issue in Ireland

[2]   These were originally informal names for roads or tracks through the Common Lands of Newton. As they became urbanised, individual developers tended to give separate names to each development, usually a terrace of cottages or tenements, fronting these streets. Such a process led, naturally, to a proliferation of short 'streets', causing problems both for the Town Council and the postal authorities. A lengthy list of 'erased' terraces is given in the Ayr Directory for 1910-1911.

[3]   See ALDER BANK.

[4]   For the reason behind this, see PEMBERTON VALLEY.

[5]   For example, the date of BOSWELL PARK is known, and the reasons for the choice. This book does not however go into the meaning of the name Boswell. There are many other such examples.

stray too far into the philosophy of naming: Stuart Harris' 'The Place Names of Edinburgh' [Edinburgh, 1996] has a lengthy and thorough introduction to the subject, while standard works on place names and personal names can also be consulted for a fuller discussion of this subject than space permits here.

The physical expression of these names is of some interest. The 1828 Committee was to paint the names in capitals at corners and entries. Obviously such an exercise would have needed to be re-done regularly. At some untraced point, the Town Council must have decided to use the cast-iron name plates which now form an attractive part of Ayr's streetscape. In the Ayr Advertiser of 31st December 1874, the Town Council are advertising for a contractor to supply and erect 146 cast-iron name plates in the Newton and Wallacetown areas.[1] A further tranche was ordered in 1894, the contractor being John W Rodger, ironfounder, Ayr. 62 were ordered in August 1894, and a further 56 requested in October of that year. These 56 included 4 for Racecourse Road, as well as 3 each for Carrick Place, Barns Crescent, Racecourse View and Smith Street; also included were 2 each for Barrack Road and Skate Lane, but these were subsequently cancelled. In November 1894, John Eaglesham, the Burgh Engineer, ordered 3 'St Leonard's Road' from Rodger, as soon as possible.[2]

Most 20th Century signs are uninteresting, but there has been, in the town centre, a recent return to metal signs based on the original cast-iron signs.[3]

These signs apart, there is little of aesthetic quality in the presentation of Ayr's street names. Often overlooked, however, are the incised names of Fort Street and Wellington Square on the walls of 1 Wellington Square, of Park Circus on 3 Park Circus, and of Dalblair Quadrant on 10 Dalblair Road. Every effort has been made to ensure that the names in this book correspond with those in use. Names where this has been hardest to achieve have been those where word breaks have varied over time, such as Marlepark or Marle Park, Northpark Avenue or North Park Avenue. There is also the vexed issue of the apostrophe.

A map has not been included. For readers wishing to find contemporary street names, the street plan of Ayr produced by Nicolson Maps of Largs is excellent, and regularly updated. For lost names, I have tried to relate these to current names, so that they too can be identified by use of Nicolson's street plan. For those streets lost during the comprehensive redevelopment of Wallacetown, reference should be made to older street plans, such as that produced by Burrow of Cheltenham for Ayr Town Council, or Ordnance Survey plans. In the catalogue of names, current names are given in Roman type (e.g. HIGH STREET), while names which have been extinguished, or were never adopted, are given in Italic type (e.g. *MOIRA ANDERSON DRIVE*).

As always, the author owes a debt of thanks to many people. Foremost, on this occasion, is Sheila Penny, whose idea this was. The staff at South Ayrshire Libraries, Ayrshire Archives and North Ayrshire Libraries have been their usual cheerful and helpful selves. Joy

---

[1]   This is shortly after the amalgamation of the burghs of Ayr and Newton upon Ayr, so that it may represent a continuation of a policy already adopted south of the river.

[2]   Ayrshire Archives [AA], DIST 18/1/3/1/7, Ayr Burgh Engineer's Letter Book no.7, 1894-96, letters of John Eaglesham, Burgh Engineer, to J M Rodger, 10 August 1894, 23 October 1894 and 20 November 1894.

[3]   For example, New Bridge Street on the Town's Buildings. Compare also David McClure, Old Fingerposts in Ayrshire, Ayrshire Notes 18, Spring 2000, 12-20, especially 17-20.

Gladstone and members of the AANHS's Publications Committee have read the text at various stages, and made helpful comments which have improved the final text. Jean Kennedy also read and commented on the text, while her index to the 19th Century censuses was particularly useful, and eased the way considerably. David McClure sorted out the computer glitches. Joy Gladstone and Gavin Smith (some of whose driving practice was put to a higher purpose) did the driving for the survey. My thanks are due to them all.

Errors and omissions remain the author's alone. He is aware that the subject is far from exhausted, and would be grateful for any comments, corrections and additions.

Rob Close,
Drongan

THE STREET NAMES OF AYR

ABBOTS CRESCENT   See ABBOTS WAY

ABBOTS WAY
Abbots Way and EARLS WAY form the backbone of the late 1950s/1960s Doonfoot development of MacTaggart and Mickel. This is built on part of the lands of Greenan, which belonged for many years to the Kennedys of Dunure. These names recall one of the more dramatic incidents in the history of the Kennedys, the roasting in 1570 of Allan Steuart, Abbot (properly, the Commendator) of Crossraguel in Dunure Castle by Gilbert Kennedy, 4th Earl of Cassillis. Abbots Way and Earls Way were approved in May 1957;[1] a new road leading off Abbots Way has been named by association ABBOTS CRESCENT.[2]

ABERCROMBY DRIVE
This name was approved in December 1969.[3] It is derived from Abercromby Cottage which used to stand close to the right hand side of the mouth of the Doon.[4] This was built by, and occupied by, Charles Abercrombie (or Abercromby), a civil engineer (b.1756, d.1817), 'who flourished in Ayrshire many years ago, and who constructed the harbour at Dunure, as well as the new road to the ancient town of Maybole ... Mr Abercrombie was a man of some genius, but exceedingly eccentric, and his mode of life for a lengthened period was full of romance. After erecting the harbour at Dunure - a work of immense difficulty, as it is wholly scooped out of solid rock - he constructed a sloop which he dubbed the *Lady Isle*. .. This sloop he made his home, cruising about in the Clyde for weeks, although he had his marine dwelling drawn up to the beach on the Lord's Day, which he spent on land, and generally on the coast of Carrick, to which he was warmly attached. At length he disbanded the *Lady Isle*, and determined on erecting a cottage at the mouth of the Doon ... which he ordained to be built on the principle that, like a Turkish shopkeeper, he could sit in the centre of the chief apartment and reach any point of the room without rising'.[5]

ACADEMY LANE   See ACADEMY STREET

ACADEMY SQUARE   See ACADEMY STREET

---

[1]   South Ayrshire Libraries [SAL], Ayr Town Council Minutes 1957-58, 29, Works Committee 23rd May 1957.

[2]   Abbots Crescent was approved in October 1987. [SAL, Kyle and Carrick District Council Minutes 1987-88, 440, Planning & Building Control Committee 7th October 1987]

[3]   SAL, Ayr Town Council Minutes 1969-70, 256, Works Committee 15th December 1969.

[4]   In May 1937 Town Council agreed to demolish Abercrombie Cottage after it became vacant that Whitsunday. [SAL, Ayr Town Council Minutes 1936-37, 151, Finance Committee 6th May 1937]

[5]   W H Wylie, Ayrshire Museum, Kilmarnock, 1891, 71-72.

ACADEMY STREET

A street which is an improvement of one of the closes or vennels which led from Sandgate to the back lane (on the line of Fort Street). Ayr Academy opened on a new site in Fort Street in 1798-1800, and the name of this street reflects its rôle in connecting the Academy with the centre of the town. A house, adjoining the ACADEMY SQUARE, was advertised to let in 1809;[1] a house in Academy Street was advertised to let in January 1821.[2] Dillon[3] notes that 'any lane leading to the burgh school west of the Sandgate could be called School Vennel.[4] After the Academy was built the ways leading to it became Academy Street and ACADEMY LANE'. Gray refers to 'what was then called the Schule Vennel but now by the more refined and classical epithet of Academy Street',[5] while Howie refers to School Vennel, 'now named Academy Street'.[6]

AFTON COURT

Name approved in November 1966, 'as the other streets in the area were associated with Burns'.[7] The reference is to Burns's song "Sweet Afton" (referring to the Afton Water at New Cumnock).

AFTON PLACE

Obsolete name of 4-6 Carrick Road; the adjoining 2 Carrick Road was known as Afton Cottage. The land on which 2-14 Carrick Road were erected was acquired by the builder John Milligan in 1873.[8] See Afton Court for derivation.

AGNEW PLACE

Name given in the 1881 Census to two houses on the east side of Prestwick Road. They appear to have belonged to James Rodger, whose wife was Martha Agnew.

AILSA BUILDINGS

112-114 High Street, built in 1863-64 for Arthur, Currie & Co., drapers. For derivation see Ailsa Place.

AILSA PLACE

Street in the Victorian development of the Citadel of Ayr initiated by John Miller, the so-called *Baron* Miller. The name dates from c.1864: it originally applied only to the houses now 2-8 Ailsa Place (originally 1-4), but was ultimately used for the whole street. The names chosen reflect former owners of the Citadel, including the Kennedys, Marquises of

[1]   Air Advertiser, 21st December 1809, 4b. The house belonged to Mrs Crawford of Newfield, and was occupied by John Logan of Knockshinnoch.
[2]   Air Advertiser, 25th January 1821, 4a.
[3]   William J Dillon, The Streets in Early Times, in Annie I Dunlop, ed., The Royal Burgh of Ayr, Edinburgh, 1953, 72-73.
[4]   The Concise Scots Dictionary (Mairi Robinson, ed., Aberdeen, 1987 ed.) defines a vennel or vennal as "a narrow alley or lane between houses".
[5]   H C Gray's lecture on Old Ayr reported in the Ayr Advertiser, 25th January 1872, 5b.
[6]   James Howie, An Historical Account of the Town of Ayr, Kilmarnock, 1861, 14.
[7]   SAL, Ayr Town Council Minutes 1966-67, 219, Works Committee 21st November 1966.
[8]   Ayrshire Sasine Abridgement no.3084 of 1873.

Ailsa. They, in turn, took their title from Ailsa Craig, the prominent island in the Firth of Clyde which was part of their estate. Ailsa may mean 'isle of wings' or 'isle of cliffs'.[1]

AIRLIE COURT

Housing development, its name approved in September 1977,[2] within the former garden grounds of Airlie House, 5 Victoria Park, which was probably built c.1876 for Alice Cowan (d.1885), the relict of Charles Dalrymple Gairdner (b.1794, d.1867), banker. The name of the house was presumably derived from either the Angus parish and castle of this name, or from the title of the Ogilvys, Earls of Airlie, important and well-connected landowners in Angus. No connection between C D Gairdner and either place or family has been discovered, and the name was presumably chosen for its euphony.

ALBERT PLACE

Name given to the close or lane which ran between Loudoun Hall and 12 New Bridge Street. It is first recorded in the 1849-50 Directory: the honour is presumably for Prince Albert (see Albert Terrace, below) who had married Queen Victoria in 1840, and acquired his Scottish estate, Balmoral, in 1848.

ALBERT ROAD   See RONALDSHAW PARK

ALBERT TERRACE

The name is first found in the 1861-62 Directory. It appears to be a commemoration of Prince Albert, the Prince Consort (b.1819, d.1861).

ALDER BANK

Housing development, named in 1967. On the Masonhill estate; there are many similar tree names on this estate and neighbouring Castlehill, i.e. ASPEN COURT and DRIVE, BIRCH ROAD, BRIAR GROVE, CEDAR ROAD, CHESTNUT ROAD, FIR BANK, HAWTHORN DRIVE, HOLLY BANK, IVY PLACE, JUNIPER GREEN, LAUREL BANK, MAPLE DRIVE, PINE BRAE, POPLAR WAY, ROWAN CRESCENT, SPRUCE PARK, SYCAMORE CRESCENT and WILLOW PARK.[3] LARCHWOOD ROAD is a

---

[1] Ayrshire Post, 10th October 1924. More fanciful suggestions in J Kevan McDowall, Carrick Gallovidian, Ayr, 1947, 84, can be discounted.

[2] SAL, Kyle and Carrick District Council Minutes 1977-78, 223, Planning & Building Control Committee 7th September 1977.

[3] Fir Bank was approved in September 1959 [SAL, Ayr Town Council Minutes 1959-60, 118, Works Committee 24th September 1959]; Birch Road and Hawthorn Drive in February 1962 [SAL, Ayr Town Council Minutes 1961-62, 251, Works Committee 22nd February 1962]; Pine Brae and Rowan Crescent in January 1967 [SAL, Ayr Town Council Minutes 1966-67, 297, Works Committee 16th January 1967]; Alder Bank, Chestnut Road, Juniper Green and Sycamore Crescent in July 1967 [SAL, Ayr Town Council Minutes 1967-68, 105, Works Committee 17th July 1967]; and Briar Grove, Laurel Bank and Willow Park in July 1968 [SAL, Ayr Town Council Minutes 1968-69, 82, Works Committee 15th July 1968: powers were given to the Committee Convener and council officers to choose four from these three, POPLAR CRESCENT and LIME WALK]. In July 1973 the Town Council noted the use of Holly Bank, Ivy Place, Poplar Way and Spruce Park [SAL, Ayr Town Council Minutes 1973-74, 93, Works Committee 16th July 1973], and of Cedar Road in September 1974. [SAL, Ayr Town Council Minutes 1974-75, 131, Works Committee 16th September 1974]. In July 1994 Kyle and Carrick District Council approved Aspen Court, Aspen Road

variation on the theme, while FOREST WAY and GREENTREE PARK[1] exchange the specific for the general. That 'the use of the names of trees for streets in the Castlehill and Weir Housing Development at Masonhill be continued' was one of the recommendations from the Naming of Streets Sub-Committee that reported in January 1967.[2]

ALDERSTON AVENUE
Name dates from 1902.[3] This street was built on land feued from Alderston, 48 Prestwick Road, which first appears in the 1890-91 Directory as the home of Hugh Smith Walker (d.1919), of W G Walker & Sons, of the Hawkhill Chemical Works. Hugh Walker's wife, Lizzie Robb (d.1928), was the daughter of James Robb of Haddington, and the sister of James Robb, who had been manager for the Ayr Gas Co.[4] Alderston is an estate near Haddington, and the name presumably had pleasant associations for her. Alderston Avenue was first developed in 1902 by Robert Hutchison, builder, who then lived at Alderston, though 1-3 Alderston Avenue are TRAMWAY HOUSES, built by Ayr Town Council c.1903 for employees of the Burgh Tramways. ALDERSTON PARK (approved in December 1968)[5] and ALDERSTON PLACE (approved in November 1962)[6] are developments off Alderston Avenue.

ALDERSTON PARK   See ALDERSTON AVENUE

ALDERSTON PLACE   See ALDERSTON AVENUE

ALEXANDRIA TERRACE
Name dates from c.1893.[7]   Presumably in homage to either Alexandria, Egypt, or Alexandria, Dunbartonshire. Conspiracy theorists will consider that an intended honour to Princess Alexandra, wife of the Prince of Wales, later Edward VII, went awry between the initial concept and the iron founder's execution of an order for street signs.

ALLAN PLACE
This name honours (oddly using his forename) the Scots athlete Allan Wells (b.1952). Other names on this development are McCOLGAN PLACE, MURRAY PLACE and WHITTLE ROAD, which similarly honour other Scots athletes: Liz McColgan (b.1964),

---

[1]   and Maple Drive. [SAL, Kyle and Carrick District Council Minutes 1994-95, 83, Planning Applications Committee 12th July 1994]
      Forest Way and Greentree Park were approved in September 1959 [SAL, Ayr Town Council Minutes, 1959-60, 118, Works Committee 24th September 1959]; Larchwood Road in February 1962 [SAL, Ayr Town Council Minutes 1961-62, 251, Works Committee 22nd February 1962]

[2]   SAL, Ayr Town Council Minutes 1966-67, 340, Works Committee 20th February 1967.

[3]   Ayrshire Archives [AA], DIST18/1/3/1/12, Letter Books of Burgh and Water Engineer, no.12, May 1901 - February 1902, letter of 16th January 1902 of John Young, Burgh Engineer, to Robert Hutchison approving his suggestion of Alderston Avenue as the name for the new street. Approved by the Town Council at a meeting of the Works Committee on 22nd January 1902, the printed minutes of which use an erroneous spelling Alderstone.

[4]   Haddingtonshire Courier, 27th September 1889. The wedding was held at Gera in Germany. James Robb, junior, had emigrated from Ayr to Queensland in 1884.

[5]   SAL, Ayr Town Council Minutes 1968-69, 232, Works Committee 16th December 1968.

[6]   SAL, Ayr Town Council Minutes 1962-32, 167, Works Committee 22nd November 1962.

[7]   Originally applied to a terrace of 8 houses, numbers 1-8: c.1904 the road was renumbered, the original 1-8 becoming 6-20 Alexandria Terrace.

Yvonne Murray (b.1964) and Brian Whittle (b.1964). The names were approved by Kyle and Carrick District Council in April 1989.[1]

ALLEGHANY TERRACE

Unauthorised or obsolete name which was incorporated in the official names of streets as 31-41 Church Street;[2] it first appeared in the 1882-83 Directory. The Allegheny Mountains are part of the Appalachian Range in West Virginia, USA.

ALLENFIELD ROAD

Name approved in 1963.[3] A name of obscure derivation, though it may preserve the name of a field here.

ALLISON PLACE   See ALLISON STREET

ALLISON STREET

This name has existed from at least the 1820s, sometimes in the form Allison's Street.[4] It was built on land which belonged successively to William Allison, messenger in Ayr (d..c.1786), his daughters, and, from 1809, his grandson William Allison Smith. 52-64 Allison Street, built c.1864, were known as ALLISON PLACE. Allison Street was given a new lease of life in May 1974, when it was chosen as the name for part of the Inner Ring Road.[5]

ALLOWAY

This name first appears in a charter of 1236.[6] It has been, over the centuries, the name of the barony, the hamlet/village, and now of a substantial residential area. It also has a formal existence as a street name. In April 1958 the County Assessor asked the Town Council to look at the numbering and naming of streets in the Alloway area, and as a result of this the Burgh Surveyor, Thomas O'Beirne, recommended that that part of Monument Road between North Park Farm and the bridge over the Doon, inclusive, should be named 'Alloway'; this suggestion was approved by the Works Committee in June 1958.[7]

ALLOWAY PARK

As a street name dates from c.1873, but Alloway Park was the name from the early 19th Century of the field or park within the Laigh Sands on which Alloway Park, ALLOWAY PLACE and PARK TERRACE were built at different times. This field belonged to David Cathcart, Lord Alloway (b.1763, d.1829, created Lord Alloway 1813). Howie notes that 'about this time, or shortly after, Mr John Kinross purchased that field behind Wellington Square. This field was then popularly known as Provost Shaw's Park, but it in reality

---

[1] SAL, Kyle and Carrick District Council Minutes 1988-89, 995, Planning and Building Control Committee 5th April 1989.

[2] 1910-11 Directory, 246, List of Erased Terraces, Etc.

[3] SAL, Ayr Town Council Minutes 1963-64, 161, Works Committee 21st November 1963.

[4] See for instance Ayrshire Sasine Abridgement no.1763, of 1823, which refers to Allison's Street.

[5] SAL, Ayr Town Council Minutes 1974-75, 19, Works Committee 20th May 1974.

[6] Alastair Hendry, The Barony of Alloway 1324-1754, [Ayr], [1992], 3.

[7] SAL, Ayr Town Council Minutes 1957-58, 319, Works Committee 24th April 1958; ibid 1958-59, 20, Works Committee 22nd May 1958, and 50, Works Committee 26th June 1958.

belonged to Lord Alloway. The houses built on this ground were called ALLOWAY PLACE'.[1] Alloway Place replaces a square proposed by Cathcart,[2] while PARK TERRACE was developed from 1870.[3] ALLOWAY PLACE LANE is the lane at the back of Alloway Place. ALLOWAY ROW is used once, probably erroneously, instead of Alloway Place in Macarter's 1830 Directory.[4]

ALLOWAY PLACE	See ALLOWAY PARK
ALLOWAY PLACE LANE	See ALLOWAY PARK
ALLOWAY ROW	See ALLOWAY PARK
ALLOWAY SQUARE	See ALLOWAY PARK

ALLOWAY STREET
One of the main streets out of the centre of the town, leading to Alloway. Dillon says 'the COW VENNEL ... led off the High Street into the burgh moor. The built-up part of it is now appropriately named Alloway Street, for the original path led through Alloway to Maybole. The old name shows the reason for the route because it was the Cow Road along which cattle were herded to the communal pasture. Along this vennel were located the cattle markets known as the Fauldback'.[5] Gray notes that Cow Vennel 'was very narrow, and many of the houses were occupied by a low class of lodgers, who were of a migratory character. With the view of having a better access to the town the Road Trustees, about 30 years ago, purchased these houses and made the street what it now is'.[6] The Cow Vennel was also known as the COW WYND, and in 1997 this name was resurrected for a small commercial development off Alloway Street.

ALTRY PLACE
Name approved in January 1973.[7] No place or other feature with this name has been found.

---

[1] James Howie, An Historical Account of the Town of Ayr, Kilmarnock, 1861, 38. Howie is writing of the period around c.1810-c.1815.
[2] The proposed ALLOWAY SQUARE is shown on the "Plan of the Town and Part of the Parishes of Ayr, Newton upon Ayr and Saint Quivox, Surveyed by John Wood Edin[r] 1818" [Copy in SRO, RHP 2557: hereafter 'Wood's Plan, 1818']: John Strawhorn, The History of Ayr, Edinburgh, 1989, 134, suggests that it had been planned by David Cathcart in 1799. It is probably the 'square intended to be built at Ayr' in a drawing of 1799 by John Robertson, Edinburgh, architect [SRO, RHP 2555]. The middle terrace of Alloway Place dates from c.1824, and the southmost terrace from shortly after: the north terrace dates from c.1842.
[3] The land for the houses in Park Terrace was feued by Agnes Lennox or Watson in two blocks, in 1870 and 1872. See Ayrshire Sasine Abridgements no.859 of 1870 and no.2550 of 1872.
[4] 1830 Directory: entry for James Miller, ironmonger.
[5] William J Dillon, The Streets in Early Times, in Annie I Dunlop, ed., The Royal Burgh of Ayr, Edinburgh, 1953, 71.
[6] H C Gray's lecture on Old Ayr reported in Ayr Advertiser, 25th January 1872, 5cd. If Gray is accurate the widening of Cow Vennel and, perhaps, the change of name must have taken place c.1842.
[7] SAL, Ayr Town Council Minutes 1972-73, 264, Works Committee 15th January 1973.

ANDERSON CRESCENT
Name approved in October 1955, as ANDERSON PLACE.[1] Named after William M
Anderson (b. 1891, d. 1961), who was Provost of Ayr from 1955 to 1958. Born at
Gasswater near Lugar, Anderson was a partner in W & J Anderson, outfitters, 7 Alloway
Street, which he and his brother founded in 1919.[2]

ANDERSON PLACE   See ANDERSON CRESCENT

ANNFIELD GLEN ROAD
This name was approved in October 1955.[3] This street is close to the course of the Annfield
Burn, which appears to take its name from Annfield Farm, which was advertised to let in
1833.[4] The small valley through which the burn flows seems to have been known as the
Annfield Glen.[5]

ANNFIELD PLACE
First found in the 1888-89 Directory, but by 1896 this 4-house terrace had been absorbed
into Argyle Street as 4-10 Argyle Street. The origin of the name is obscure.

ANNPIT ROAD
Name approved in September 1957.[6] Ann Pit was the name of the stone quarry which was
here, which was part of the common property of the Freemen of Newton. Latterly, it
became the property of Ayr Town Council, and was used as a refuse tip, and had been filled
in by February 1904.

APNA PLACE
Original name for the houses, built c.1880, which became 18-20 Viewfield Road, and which
were approved for demolition in 1972.[7] The name has defied all attempts at explanation.

ARDLUI ROAD
Name aproved by Town Council in June 1903.[8] It appears to have been chosen purely for
its euphony and associations. Ardlui is an attractive village close to the head of Loch
Lomond.

ARGYLE PARK   See ARGYLE STREET

---

[1]   SAL, Ayr Town Council Minutes 1955-56, 167, Works Committee 27th October 1955.
[2]   Ayrshire Post, 15th September 1961, 17c. His brother was James McEwing Anderson
         (b.1896, d.1964), whose obituary is in Ayrshire Post, 6th November 1964, 16b.
[3]   SAL, Ayr Town Council Minutes 1955-56, 167, Works Committee 27th October 1955.
[4]   Ayr Observer, 1st January 1833, 1a.
[5]   In December 1916 a house in Annfield Glen for George P Templeton was approved by the
         County Council. [AA, CO 3/12/1/7, Ayr County Council, Ayr District Committee Minute
         Book 1914-1919, Building Bye-laws Committee, 12 December 1916]
[6]   SAL, Ayr Town Council Minutes 1957-58, 126, Works Committee 26th September 1957.
[7]   AA, Ayr Dean of Guild Court plans, box no.217, plan no.149.
[8]   SAL, Ayr Town Council Minutes 1902-03, 168, Works Committee 3rd June 1903. This
         name, spelt Ardluie in the minute, and Quail Road, were suggested by the solicitor David
         Fergusson.

ARGYLE STREET
Name first found in 1888-89 Directory: the street was adopted as a public road in August 1892.[1] It appears to have been chosen for its euphony and associations, either with the county or the dukedom (it ran parallel to Duke Street): the spelling is that which was generally accepted in the 19th Century, and retained when the street was demolished during the comprehensive redevelopment of Wallacetown, as part of the new development was given the name ARGYLE PARK (approved in February 1973).[2]

ARMOUR DRIVE
Name dates from c.1954: 'Armour' was one of four names approved for streets in Forehill in October 1954.[3] One of many Forehill names associated with Burns: in this case the reference is to Burns' long-suffering wife, Jean Armour (b.1767, d.1834).

ARMSTRONG CLOSE
Name used in the 1871 Census for 39-41 Main Street, which between 1862 and 1875 were the property of James Armstrong, shoemaker in Ayr.

ARNPRIOR PLACE
Name approved in April 1988 for a small development at Rozelle Nurseries.[4] Built on land attached to 'Arnprior', a house built c.1962 for James McKay, who had been born at Arnprior, Ontario, in 1911. This Canadian village was originally settled by emigrants from Arnprior, Stirlingshire.[5]

ARNSHEEN TERRACE
Unauthorised or obsolete name which was incorporated in the official names of streets as 12-24 Duke Street:[6] it first appears in the 1890-91 Directory, as 'Aranshean'. Arnsheen is a farm near Barrhill, and is also the formal name for the parish church at Barrhill.

ARRAN COURT   See RIVERSIDE PLACE

ARRAN MALL
Name bestowed in 1995 on the upgraded and improved DALBLAIR ARCADE.[7] For 'Arran', see Arran Terrace, below.

ARRAN TERRACE
Name dates from c.1868. Part of the development of the Citadel of Ayr. Most Citadel names are taken from previous owners, including Ailsa Place (q.v.). Arran Terrace leads

---

[1]   Ayr Advertiser, 11th August 1892, 6c.
[2]   SAL, Ayr Town Council Minutes 1972-73, 301, Works Committee 20th February 1973. Argyle Street in Glasgow, too, uses this now otherwise obsolete spelling.
[3]   SAL, Ayr Town Council Minutes 1954-55, 159, Finance Committee 6th October 1954.
[4]   SAL, Kyle and Carrick District Council Minutes 1987-88, 1032, Planning and Building Control Committee 20th April 1988.
[5]   Personal communication from James McKay.
[6]   1910-1911 Directory, 246, List of Erased Terraces, Etc.
[7]   SAL, Kyle and Carrick District Council Minutes 1995-96, 172, Planning Applications Committee 11th July 1995. On a vote 7 members of the Committee voted for Arran Mall, and 4 for retaining Dalblair Arcade.

from Ailsa Place and continues a short theme of Clyde islands. ARRANVIEW COURT, in the Heathfield area, was approved in February 1992,[1] and offers (as does much of Ayr) views across the Clyde towards Arran.

ARRAN VIEW
16 local authority houses in Low Road, Whitletts, built by Ayr County Council c.1927 (i.e., before Whitletts was incorporated into the Burgh), were initially known as 1-16 Arran View. c.1930 they were renumbered as 33-63 Low Road, and c.1960 renumbered again as 22-52 Low Road.

ARRANVIEW COURT   See ARRAN TERRACE

ARROL DRIVE
Name approved by Ayr Town Council in March 1933,[2] as part of the residential development of the Seafield estate. The best known previous owner of Seafield had been Sir William Arrol, (b.1839, d.1913), the celebrated engineeer and bridge-builder, best known for the Forth Bridge, and the name commemorates this association. Arrol acquired Seafield in 1888, and was MP for South Ayrshire from 1895 to 1903.

ARTHUR STREET
Name approved in 1908, at the request of Andrew Lang,[3] son of Arthur Lang (b.1802, d.1890, see Bellevue Crescent), who owned the Carrick Oval property on which the street had been developed. Carrick Oval was developed in association with the grounds of Sandgate House. See Boswell Park, and the plan on page 5 of the Ayr Advertiser for 14th March 1907.

ARTHURSLIE PLACE   See BELLEVUE CRESCENT

ASHGROVE STREET
Name dates from c.1889.[4] The street was built on part of the Castlehill estate, owned by the Ballantine Bowman family, who also owned the estate of Ashgrove near Kilwinning. This name, in turn, is a prettification of the estate's earlier name, Ashinyards. An earlier development on Castlehill land had taken as its names BALLANTINE DRIVE and BOWMAN ROAD, which first occurs as BOWMAN PLACE in 1880[5], honouring the family. In January 1884 it was reported to the Town Council that it was proposed to make a

---

[1]   SAL, Kyle and Carrick District Council Minutes 1991-92, 1814, Planning Applications Sub Committee 25th February 1992.
[2]   SAL, Ayr Town Council Minutes 1932-33, 110, Works Committee 8th March 1933.
[3]   SAL, Ayr Town Council Minutes 1908, 167, Works Committee 6th May 1908.
[4]   Ayrshire Sasine Abridgement, no.9337 of 17th May 1890 records the July 1889 sale of land bounded 'by a proposed new road to be called Ashgrove Street'. It is recorded in the 1894-95 Directory as the address of 'Mrs Hill', 'Robert McCreath' and 'William Wyllie'.
[5]   Ayrshire Sasine Abridgement, no.10524 of 14th December 1880: 'a new road to be formed called Bowman Place'.

new street on Castlehill grounds, to be known as Ballantine Drive;[1] in 1890 the Town Council agreed to adopt Ballantine Drive and Bowman Road as public roads.[2]

ASPEN COURT   See ALDER BANK

ASPEN DRIVE   See ALDER BANK

ATHOLE BUILDINGS
Unauthorised or obsolete name which was incorporated in the official names of streets as 9-15 Burns Statue Square.[3] This property was built in 1899-1900 for the publican Joseph Johnston (b.c.1850, d.1915) on the site of the Athole Arms Hotel, and included a new Athole Arms. This inn name is recorded in the 1873-74 Directory, when the publican is Mrs Andrew Hendrie. Athole (usually now spelt Atholl) is the name of a large area in north Perthshire, and of an important Scottish dukedom.

AUCHENBEG CRESCENT
The name is taken from the adjacent house in Maybole Road, built c.1899-1900 for Mrs Eliza Glen. The name is Gaelic, meaning 'little field'. The street name was approved in September 1959.[4]

AUCHENDOON CRESCENT
This name, together with AUCHENTRAE CRESCENT, dates from the 1930s. They are part of the residential development of Seafield estate, and are ersatz Gaelic, meaning 'field of the black water' and 'field by the beach or sea', indicative of the position of this estate close to the sea and the mouth of the Doon. These names were approved by Ayr Town Council in July 1934.[5]

AUCHENTRAE CRESCENT   See AUCHENDOON CRESCENT

AULD BRIG
Medieval stone bridge of four arches crossing the Ayr: Strawhorn records that in November 1491 James IV gave ten shillings to 'the massonis of the bryg off Air'.[6] Part of the bridge fell into the river in 1688, while the north arch collapsed in 1732, but despite repairs and rebuilding on both occasions, the bridge continued to give concern, and a proposal in 1784 to repair and widen the bridge was only dropped when the Council decided to build a new bridge (opened in 1788) and restrict the Auld Brig to pedestrian traffic.[7] It must have been considered quite a venerable structure even in the late 18th Century, but the name Auld Brig (almost never Old Bridge, except in very formal situations, though contrast. Old Bridge Street) presumably only came into use once the alternative, new, bridge was built and opened.

---

[1]   Ayr Advertiser, 17th January 1884, 6c. The suggestion that Ballantyne (sic) Drive is named after the late 18th Century Provost, John Ballantine, is clearly erroneous. [John M Short, Street Names in Annie I Dunlop, ed., The Royal Burgh of Ayr, Edinburgh, 1953, 87]
[2]   Ayr Advertiser, 16th October 1890, 6d.
[3]   1910-1911 Directory, 246, List of Erased Terraces, Etc.
[4]   SAL, Ayr Town Council Minutes 1959-60, 118, Works Committee 24th September 1959.
[5]   SAL, Ayr Town Council Minutes 1933-34, 230, Works Committee 4th July 1934.
[6]   John Strawhorn, The History of Ayr, Edinburgh, 1989, 32.
[7]   Ayrshire Post, 3rd November 1898, 5b.

AULD NICK'S VIEW
Name in use by 1999 for the road which runs alongside Alloway Parish Church. It is directly opposite Alloway Auld Kirk, where, in 'Tam o' Shanter', Auld Nick held court.

AVONDALE ROAD
Short lived, and possibly never used, name for part of SOUTHPARK ROAD, into which it was absorbed in 1894.[1] This is the name of the parish which includes Strathaven, but no direct connection has been discovered. Note also that Avondale Villas was the original name of 20-22 Carrick Road, built c.1874 by William Andrew, builder, and see also Avondale Terrace, below.

AVONDALE TERRACE
Unauthorised or obsolete name which was incorporated in the official names of streets as 14-24 Falkland Park Road.[2] It dated from c.1889, and appears to have been built by James Cuthill, builder (b.c1845, d.1921), who was born in Hamilton, Lanarkshire, and is called "of Springfield, Lanark" in his death notice.[3] See Avondale Road.

AVONDALE VILLAS	See AVONDALE ROAD
BACK HAWKHILL AVENUE	See HAWKHILL AVENUE
BACK HAWKHILL ROAD	See HAWKHILL AVENUE
BACK MAIN STREET	See MAIN STREET
BACK OF THE ISLE	See HOPE STREET
BACK PEEBLES STREET	See PEEBLES STREET
BACK ROW	See ELBA STREET
BACK STREET	See MAIN STREET

BAGGOT'S CLOSE
On the south-west side of High Street, close to the site of the modern 39 High Street.[4] As a surname, Baggot (or Baggat) is found in Roxburghshire from the 13th Century, and is thought to be a corruption of 'Bathgate'.[5] No connection with this property has yet been established.

BAIRD ROAD
This name was approved in November 1954:[6] it was objected to by the developer - Cambusdoon Feuing Co. - in September 1955, but the Town Council agree to abide by their decision.[7] The estate of Cambusdoon was owned from 1853 by James Baird (b.1803,

[1]   Ayr Advertiser, 19th April 1894, 5a.
[2]   1910-1911 Directory, 246, List of Erased Terraces, Etc.
[3]   Ayr Advertiser, 1st December 1921, 5g; 1891 Census, Registration District 578, Enumeration District 29, entry no.29.
[4]   Ayr Observer, 30th October 1832, 1a.
[5]   George F Black, The Surnames of Scotland, Edinburgh, 1993, 41 and 60.
[6]   SAL, Ayr Town Council Minutes 1954-55, 202, Works Committee 26th November 1954.
[7]   SAL, Ayr Town Council Minutes 1955-56, 133, Works Committee 22nd September 1955.

d.1876), a member of the famous family of iron and coal masters. It was reported to the Council in November 1959 that, due to changes in the proposed road layout, the stretch of road between Greenfield Avenue and Cambusdoon Road could be numbered as a continuation of Baird Road.[1]

BALLANTINE DRIVE   See ASHGROVE STREET

BALMINNOCH PARK
Name approved in January 1973.[2] Balminnoch is the name of two farms in South Ayrshire, one in Straiton and one in Ballantrae, appropriated purely for its pleasant sound.

BALMORAL TERRACE
Unauthorised or obsolete name which was incorporated in the official names of streets as 71-77 Prestwick Road;[3] warrant to build this terrace was given in November 1901.[4] Named after the Royal residence in Aberdeenshire, which was acquired by Prince Albert in 1848.

BANKFIELD PLACE
Name given in 1999 to a new development off Dalmellington Road. The development is on the site of Bankfield Caravan Park, which took its name from Bankfield House. This was built c.1927 for James Gibson: the name may have been given to the house as it was built on a field on Bank farm. Gibson was quickly succeeded by William Carlyle (b.c.1881, d.1933) who established a market garden here. The name has also been transferred to the roundabout where the Ayr to Dalmellington Road meets the Ayr By-pass, Bankfield Roundabout.

BARNFORD CRESCENT
Name approved in June 1969.[5] Barnford is the name of a farm in Kirkmichael: its name borrowed purely for its euphony.

BARNS CRESCENT   See BARNS STREET

BARNS PARK   See BARNS STREET

BARNS STREET
Also BARNS CRESCENT, BARNS PARK, BARNS TERRACE. Barns is the name of a long-established small estate on the south side of Ayr (Barns House can still be seen at 1 Barns Crescent). The name appears to mean 'barns' (cf. Barnes in Surrey), and may reflect a former location of town granaries, though probably not of the 'Barns of Ayr' in which William Wallace slaughtered an English garrison. The family most closely associated with Barns are the McNeights, who acquired the estate in the mid 18th Century: Lieutenant-Colonel Patrick McNeight died in 1840, and the estate was then broken up, though Barns House remained in the ownership of the family until 1915. Barns Street is part of Ayr's Georgian development, and dates from c.1800: Gray states that 'Barns House ... had a public

---

[1]   SAL, Ayr Town Council Minutes 1959-60, 174, Works Committee 26th November 1959.
[2]   SAL, Ayr Town Council Minutes 1972-73, 264, Works Committee 15th January 1973.
[3]   1910-1911 Directory, 246, List of Erased Terraces, Etc.
[4]   AA, Ayr Dean of Guild Court plans, box no.12, plan no.44. The developers were John and William Foggo, builders.
[5]   SAL, Ayr Town Council Minutes 1969-70, 68, Works Committee 16th June 1969.

road which passed it in a line with Carrick Street and joined the Racecourse Road ... The then proprietor was allowed to shut up this road on opening up a road now called Barns Street',[1] while Howie notes that 'the town by this time was rapidly increasing in population, and there was consequently a greater demand for accommodation for genteel families. Mr Mcnaughton (sic) of Barns, to meet the demand, feued out part of a field belonging to him, and which bordered the road leading from the head of Carrick Vennel to Sandgate Street. The row of houses, when built, took the name of Barns Street, deriving its title from the lands on which the houses were erected. It went long by the designation of Maidens' Row, because a number of the houses were tenanted by maiden ladies'.[2] Barns Terrace dates from c.1850, while Barns Park and Barns Crescent date from c.1875 and c.1878 respectively.

BARNS TERRACE   See BARNS STREET

BARRACK ROAD
Cast iron street names for Barrack Road were ordered in 1894, but the order was rescinded soon afterwards.[3] In 1906 Richard Gaffney, licensee of a pub in High Street, gave his address as BARRACKS SQUARE, Ayr, and the name was still current in 1936, when the Town Council considered a complaint as to its condition and use by fish lorries.[4] These names refer to the Army Barracks which formerly stood between South Harbour Street and the Citadel, and which had been built in 1794 by conversion of the former sugar warehouse.[5] The Barracks were demolished in 1964. Barracks Square may be a local name for that part of South Harbour Street at the Barracks entrance.

BARRACKS SQUARE   See BARRACK ROAD

BARTON AVENUE   See KIRKHOLM AVENUE

BATH PLACE
Name dates from c.1840s.[6] A public bath-house was established here c. 1840, and existed until c.1853: the keeper of the baths was one William Black. The property still exists as 6-12 Bath Place.

BATHURST DRIVE
Name approved in June 1969.[7] A widespread name, deriving ultimately from a village in Sussex: its global use due to Earl Bathurst's spell as Colonial Secretary between 1812 and 1828. It may be one of the names which derive from the short-lived decision to use names

---

[1] H C Gray's lecture on Old Ayr reported in Ayr Advertiser, 25th January 1872, 5c.
[2] James Howie, An Historical Account of the Town of Ayr, Kilmarnock, 1861, 37.
[3] AA, DIST 18/1/3/1/7, Letter Book of the Burgh and Water Engineer 15th July 1894 - 22nd February 1896, letter of John Eaglesham to J M Rodger, ironfounder, 23rd October 1894. Eaglesham requests 56 cast iron name plates for various streets throughout the burgh: in this copy letter book the names Barrack Road and Skate Lane have been crossed out.
[4] SAL, Ayr Town Council Minutes 1935-36, 117, Works Committee 4th March 1936.
[5] John Strawhorn, The History of Ayr, Edinburgh, 1989, 92.
[6] It is recorded in the 1851-52 Directory.
[7] SAL, Ayr Town Council Minutes 1969-70, 68, Works Committee 16th June 1969.

with West Indian associations for the residential development of Rozelle: see PEMBERTON VALLEY.[1]

BEAGLE CRESCENT
Name approved in May 1957.[2] The 3rd Marquis of Ailsa (b.1847, d.1938) was a noted yachtsman: one of his yachts was the Beagle, a 10-ton yacht built at Culzean. Shortly after it was launched the Beagle was run down and cut in two by a heavy schooner in the Kyles of Bute.[3]

BEAUFORT PLACE
Unauthorised or obsolete name which was incorporated in the official names of streets as 44-54 McCall's Avenue;[4] these houses were approved by the Dean of Guild Court in May 1900.[5] Beaufort is an English ducal title, first conferred in 1682, taken from a town and castle in France, near Angers, which from the late 14th Century belonged to the English royal house of Lancaster.

BEECH GROVE
Name approved in December 1950.[6] Reason for choice unknown: it is in the Craigie estate, while the majority of Ayr's 'tree' names are in Masonhill.

BELLEISLE
The lands which formed Belleisle were acquired in 1787 by Hugh Hamilton of Pinmore (b.1746, d.1829), for whom the house was built. He died without issue and the estate passed to a younger son of his cousin, John Hamilton of Sundrum. The estate was acquired by Ayr Town Council in 1925. BELLEISLE COTTAGES was the original name both of 21-31 Alloway, built c.1903 for George Coats of Belleisle, and of 61-67 Greenfield Avenue, built c.1899 or earlier, also by George Coats of Belleisle (later Lord Glentanar, b.1849, d.1918). Hugh Hamilton had spent time and made his fortune in Jamaica, Belleisle being the name of one of his plantations there.

BELLEISLE COTTAGES   See BELLEISLE

BELLEISLE VIEW   See MOUNT CHARLES CRESCENT

BELLESLEYHILL AVENUE
Also BELLESLEYHILL ROAD. Names date from c.1901 (Bellesleyhill Avenue)[7] and 1905 (Bellesleyhill Road).[1] Bellesleyhill was a farm on Prestwick Road, Newton, but the

---

[1]   Bathurst is said to have been the name of one of the Hamiltons' sugar estates in the West Indies.
[2]   SAL, Ayr Town Council Minutes 1957-58, 29, Works Committee 23rd May 1957.
[3]   Ardrossan and Saltcoats Herald, 9th June 1877, 5e; Ayrshire Post, 15th April 1938, 8b.
[4]   1910-1911 Directory, 246, List of Erased Terraces, Etc.
[5]   AA, Ayr Dean of Guild Court plans, box no.10, plan no.261. The applicant was Alexander Smith, builder, but the development may actually have been carried out by George D Fraser, painter.
[6]   SAL, Ayr Town Council Minutes 1950-51, 236, Works Committee 22nd December 1950.
[7]   A terrace of 8 cottages, now 13-23 Bellesleyhill Avenue, was approved by the Dean of Guild Court in October 1901. [AA, Ayr Dean of Guild Court plans, box no.12, plan no.39] The

origin of this name is obscure. Thomas McCreath, after whom Tam's Brig (q.v.) is named, farmed Bellesleyhill. The 1871 Census reference to BELLESLEYHILL PLACE seems to refer to the subdivided farmhouse.

BELLESLEYHILL PLACE   See BELLESLEYHILL AVENUE

BELLESLEYHILL ROAD   See BELLESLEYHILL AVENUE

BELLEVALE
In 1806, the liferent interest of Elizabeth Ballantine, the widow of Provost David Fergusson, in 6 acres called Betty's Park was advertised for sale.[2] It was acquired by Andrew Gemmell, merchant (b.c.1757, d.1843) who renamed it Belvale, and sold by his Trustees in 1855 to Robert Ewen of Ewenfield.[3] No house appears to have been built on the land. In the 1920s the name was borrowed for two roads built on this land: BELLEVALE AVENUE and BELLEVALE QUADRANT. These names date from c.1922 (Bellevale Quadrant) and c.1924 (Bellevale Avenue). The streets were taken over as public roads in 1931.[4] Presumably chosen by Gemmell for its pleasant sounding quality. Betty's Park presumably referred to Elizabeth Ballantine or Fergusson, who died in 1831.

BELLEVALE AVENUE   See BELLEVALE

BELLEVALE QUADRANT   See BELLEVALE

BELLEVUE COTTAGES   See BELLEVUE CRESCENT

BELLEVUE CRESCENT
Also BELLEVUE LANE, BELLEVUE ROAD and BELLEVUE STREET. Bellevue Crescent and Bellevue Road are two of the streets created during the late 19th Century development of the Bellevue estate, which had been acquired in 1860 by Arthur Lang, schoolteacher (b.1802, d.1890), and feued by him thereafter.[5] Bellevue Lane and Bellevue Street[6] are minor streets in the same area. BELLEVUE COTTAGES were built in 1896 by David Milligan, joiner (b.1852, d.1936).[7] 1-12 BELLEVUE TERRACE were built over a number of years from c.1882: c.1896 they were renumbered as 54-32 Bellevue Crescent. Bellevue (or Belview) House dates from the late 18th Century, and still can be seen in Marchmont Road. It is one of a number of villas which were built to the south of Ayr at this time: the name is derived from the French, meaning "beautiful view". The house seems to have been built for a member of the family of McNeight of Barns, and was occupied by James Donaldson, Esq., in 1830. According to Howie, Bellevue was "popularly known in bygone days as Batchelor (sic) Hall from the unmarried condition of the proprietor".[8] On

---

applicant was Robert Hutchison, builder.   Rose Cottage (1-3) and Beech Cottage (5-7 Bellesleyhill Avenue) existed by 1888.

[1]   SAL, Ayr Town Council Minutes 1904-05, 119, Works Committee 8th March 1905.
[2]   Air Advertiser, 3rd March 1806, 1b.
[3]   Ayrshire Sasine Abridgements, no. 8424 of 1807, and no.3653 of 1855.
[4]   SAL, Ayr Town Council Minutes 1930-31, 221, Works Committee 6th May 1931.
[5]   Ayr Advertiser, 14th February 1861, 1d. BELLEVUE CRESCENT appears in the 1894-95 Directory, and BELLEVUE ROAD in the Directory for 1896-97.
[6]   Ayr Advertiser, 19th April 1894, 5a.
[7]   AA, Ayr Dean of Guild Court plans, box no.4, plan no.224.
[8]   James Howie, An Historical Account of the Town of Ayr, Kilmarnock, 1861, 17.

the death of Lieutenant Colonel Patrick McNeight in 1840, the estate of Barns was split up, with Bellevue passing to his sister Marion McNeight (b.c.1772, d.1860). Lang acquired the estate from her executors. In Lang's original proposals different names were envisaged: ARTHURSLIE PLACE for Bellevue Street; HOUSTOUN CRESCENT or HOUSTOUN STREET for Bellevue Crescent; LANG STREET for Park Circus and BELLEVUE STREET for Bellevue Road. Arthurslie and Lang are self-promotional, while Houstoun is the maiden name of Lang's wife Eliza.[1]

BELLEVUE LANE   See BELLEVUE CRESCENT

BELLEVUE ROAD   See BELLEVUE CRESCENT

BELLEVUE STREET   See BELLEVUE CRESCENT

BELLEVUE TERRACE   See BELLEVUE CRESCENT

BELLROCK COTTAGES   see BELLROCK ROAD

BELLROCK ROAD
In 1911 the Works Committeee recommended 'that names Bellrock Road and Springbank Road respectively be given to the roads presently known by these names.[2] Bellrock Road is first found in the 1904-05 Directory: the original houses, known as BELLROCK COTTAGES, were built in the 1860s by the Glasgow and South Western Railway. There is also a Bellrock Avenue in Prestwick. The origin of the name appears to to the Bell Rock, an offshore rock close to the boundary between Newton and Prestwick. The name Bellrock was also used for the stone quarry still to be seen on Prestwick St Nicholas golf course, and transferred in turn to these neighbouring streets. The Ayr street leads into the golf course, while the Prestwick street may have been a more deliberately historical choice. It may be supposed, though there is no evidence, that the rock was considered a hazard to shipping, and a bell placed on it to warn mariners.

BELMONT AVENUE
Also BELMONT CRESCENT, BELMONT DRIVE, BELMONT PLACE EAST, BELMONT PLACE WEST and BELMONT ROAD. Names of various dates of various developments on the lands of Belmont, which was a small suburban estate, said by Paterson to have been built for Lady Cathcart, who lived here until she inherited Rozelle in 1809.[3] Belmont was sold in 1847 to James Morton, solicitor, (b.1777, d.1867), and was demolished in 1939.[4] The name, like Bellevue, appears to be an invention, based on French, and meaning 'beautiful hill'. A long poem by Jeannie Reid Harcus, 'Walks through Belmont, Ayr' begins 'I love to walk each summer eve/ Along our quiet Belmont road'.[5] Belmont

---

[1]   In some references LANG CIRCUS and LANG CRESCENT are also found. All these earlier names appear to have been dropped soon after Arthur Lang's death.

[2]   SAL, Ayr Town Council Minutes 1911, 284, Works Committee 9th August 1911.

[3]   James Paterson, History of the County of Ayr, Kyle, part I, Edinburgh, 1863, 133. He says it was built after 1779, but a date subsequent to the death in 1783 of her husband, Sir John Cathcart, seems more probable.

[4]   The application for demolition was approved by the Ayr Dean of Guild Court in June 1939. See Ayrshire Post, 30th June 1939, 8a.

[5]   Ayrshire Post, 19th September 1892, 3e.

Avenue dates from c.1897;[1] BELMONT ROAD from c.1900. BELMONT PLACE (sic) was approved by the Town Council in April 1935,[2] but by 1936 appeared in Valuation Rolls as BELMONT PLACE EAST and BELMONT PLACE WEST. BELMONT CRESCENT and BELMONT DRIVE were approved in January 1948.[3]

BELMONT CRESCENT	See BELMONT AVENUE
BELMONT DRIVE	See BELMONT AVENUE
BELMONT PLACE EAST	See BELMONT AVENUE
BELMONT PLACE WEST	See BELMONT AVENUE
BELMONT ROAD	See BELMONT AVENUE

BELVIDERE TERRACE
This name dates from c.1882. A belvedere or belvidere is usually a high viewpoint, often a landmark in a planned park or estate. Any association with this short Newton street is difficult to ascertain.

BENTFIELD AVENUE
This name was approved by the Town Council in April 1936.[4] Chambers Twentieth Century Dictionary, 1972 edition, defines a bent as 'any stiff or wiry grass'. A postcard, postmarked 8th August 1935, looking northwards from near here is entitled 'Ayr Beach and Esplanade from the Bents'.[5]

BENTINCK PLACE
Built c. 1879, and quickly absorbed into Russell Street as 19-23 Russell Street. Bentinck is the family name of the Dukes of Portland: the first of the family to make an impression in the United Kingdom was Hans William Bentinck, a Dutch advisor to William of Orange, who 'as a Lieutenant General took a distinguished part at the Battle of the Boyne, 1690', and was created Earl of Portland in 1689.[6] In the late 19th Century the Portland family were big landowners in Ayrshire, particularly in the Kilmarnock and Troon areas.

BERESFORD LANE   See BERESFORD TERRACE

BERESFORD TERRACE
This name can be traced back to the 1850s, and was built on part of the Horsemarket Park, a field belonging to the Barns estate, whose development potential was enhanced by the completion of Miller Road. The name was first used for Beresford Cottage, now 32-34 Beresford Terrace, built c.1856 by Samuel Galbraith (b.1815 d.1877), and subsequently transferred to the Terrace. BERESFORD LANE is its rear service lane. Beresford Terrace

---

[1] It is recorded twice in the 1898-99 Directory, at 'Girls' Industrial School', and 'William Muir. Muir's house is 8 Belmont Avenue, while the Girls' Industrial School was built in 1896 and demolished in 1983.

[2] SAL, Ayr Town Council Minutes 1934-35, 140, Works Committee 3rd April 1935.

[3] SAL, Ayr Town Council Minutes 1947-49, 88, Corporation 12th January 1948.

[4] SAL, Ayr Town Council Minutes 1935-36, 146, Works Committee 8th April 1936.

[5] Jean Kennedy collection.

[6] Debrett's Peerage and Baronetage, London, 1995, P1019.

has been renumbered c.1912, and again c.1932, when attempts to absorb Killoch Place were finally abandoned. Beresford is the family name of the Marquises of Waterford, and seems to have been chosen for its English and aristocratic sound and associations.

BERKLEY AVENUE   See ENGLEWOOD AVENUE

BERKLEY ROAD   See ENGLEWOOD AVENUE

BERWICK PLACE
Former name of 21/22 Montgomerie Terrace. They were built c.1869 for George Nisbet (b.c.1834, d.1881), wine and spirit merchant. Nisbet was a native of Banff, and no particular reason for the choice of name has been found.[1]

BIRCH ROAD   See ALDER BANK

BLACKBURN DRIVE
Also BLACKBURN PLACE and BLACKBURN ROAD. Blackburn was a small estate on the southern edge of Ayr, an area of land which appears to have been called in earlier times, Quaver and Windyhall.[2] It was sold in 1819 to John Robb.(b.c.1781, d.1845). Robb sold a number of feus for villas in the 1820s; these were known as BLACKBURN PLACE until Racecourse Road gained acceptance as a name. Blackburn Road dates from the late 19th Century, while Blackburn Drive dates from c.1924. A new BLACKBURN PLACE was approved by the Town Council in July 1937.[3] The name, which is self-explanatory, is found c.1600, at which time Ayr Town Council offered for let the common grass 'from the Kirkyard Dyke to the Blackburne'.[4]

BLACKBURN PLACE   See BLACKBURN DRIVE

BLACKBURN ROAD   See BLACKBURN DRIVE

BLACKFRIARS WALK
Name approved in October 1968,[5] given to a small local authority scheme built on the site of Turner's Ayr Brewery, which itself stood on part of the lands which formerly belonged to the Dominican or Black Friars. The Dominican Friary in Ayr was founded c.1242 and dissolved in 1567.

BLACKHILL STREET
A name which dates from 1990. "Street" has, from about that time, become acceptable as a name in new housing developments, having been an anathema since the mid 1960s. No particular reason can be found for the choice of Blackhill. Other streets in this development

1   Nisbet was landlord of the Alfred Hotel, now known as Bridge's Bar.
2   It is described in an Ayrshire Sasine Abridgement, no.8822 of 1808, as "3 acres of land called the Quaver on the south end of that portion of the sandy lands of Ayr near the sea, and part of the lands of Carnochan Burn commonly called Windyhall, otherwise called Blackburn, consisting in whole of 23½ acres".
3   SAL, Ayr Town Council Minutes 1936-37, 249, Works Committee 7th July 1937.
4   John H Pagan, Annals of Ayr in the Olden Time: 1560 - 1692, Ayr, 1897, 78. The Low Green is the remnant of this 'common grass'; the Kirkyard at that time was, of course, at the former church, now St John's Tower.
5   SAL, Ayr Town Council Minutes 1968-69, 156, Works Committee 21st October 1968.

close to Castlehill Church are CAMPHILL PLACE, FELLHILL STREET, LARGHILL LANE and STOBHILL CRESCENT; these names are equally obscure (though Stobhill is the name of a well-known hospital in Glasgow), though the -HILL suffix is a common thread, linking them to the pre-existing road through the estate, Hillfoot Road. All five names were approved in July 1990.[1]

BLACKHOUSE CRESCENT See BLACKHOUSE PLACE

BLACKHOUSE PLACE
This name was approved in May 1952.[2] It honours the memory of the Blackhouse estate which stood to the east of Ayr. Blackhouse itself was approximately where Western House (Craigie Road) now is, some distance from this street, which is built on land that belonged not to Blackhouse, but to Craigie. The family most closely associated with Blackhouse were the Taylors (see Taylor Street), who acquired it in 1787 and developed the industrial potential of the area, and encouraged residential expansion. In 1938 the Town Council had approved BLACKHOUSE ROAD for a proposed road to run from opposite Wills Road around the edge of the Racecourse to Mainholm Road.[3] The road was never built; the plans either modified or aborted by the war. 1 and 3 Gemmell Crescent appear to represent such of the road as was built.
In Whitletts, BLACKHOUSE CRESCENT was the name given to property belonging to the Oswalds of Auchincruive on the south side of Main Road. c.1924 they became 11-43 Main Road, and were demolished c.1957.

BLACKHOUSE ROAD See BLACKHOUSE PLACE

BOAR'S HEAD CLOSE
On the north side of High Street, close to modern 48 High Street. The Boar's Head Inn was acquired from its long-time landlord, David Campbell, between 1818 and 1827 by the Incorporation of Hammermen, and the property was rebuilt by them in 1879. The Roman Catholic congregation in Ayr worshipped in a hall in Boar's Head Close between 1822 and the construction of their church in John Street in 1826.[4]

BOAT VENNEL
One of the oldest streets (and street names) in Ayr; the name of the narrow street which ran from the heart of the town to the river side, a street that enabled townspeople quickly to reach the harbour and the boats. Public street lamps were introduced to Ayr in 1747, one being "sett up in the Boat Vennall".[5] Harbour improvements mean that Boat Vennel no longer ends at the river side.

---

[1] SAL, Kyle and Carrick District Council Minutes 1990-91, 208-209, Planning and Building Control Committee 11th July 1990.
[2] SAL, Ayr Town Council Minutes 1952-53, 25, Works Committee 23rd May 1952.
[3] SAL, Ayr Town Council Minutes 1937-38, 227, Housing Committee 23rd June 1938.
[4] James Howie, An Historical Account of the Town of Ayr, Kilmarnock, 1861, 51. See also James J Fowler and J Strathearn McNab, The Churches from 1800, in Annie I Dunlop, ed., The Royal Burgh of Ayr, Edinburgh, 1953, 138.
[5] David M Lyon, Ayr in the Olden Times, Ayr, 1928, 33, quoting from the minutes of Ayr Town Council.

BOGHALL ROW   See VICTORIA STREET

BOSWELL PARK
Name approved in 1908.[1] This street with the neighbouring Arthur Street (q.v.), DOUGLAS STREET and DOUGLAS LANE[2] were developed on the lands associated with Sandgate House and Carrick Oval. Sandgate House belonged to the family of Boswell of Garallan, near Cumnock. John Douglas Boswell of Garallan (b.1811, d.1863), was a writer in Ayr: his widow lived at Sandgate House until her death in 1901. A plan of the proposed new streets is on page 5 of the Ayr Advertiser of 14th March 1907. In 1942 it was reported that Douglas Lane was being used almost exclusively by Western SMT buses:[3] it has subsequently become, to all intents and purposes, part of Ayr Bus Station.

BOUNDARY ROAD
This name was approved in April 1973.[4] It crosses the boundary between Ayr and Prestwick.

BOURTREEPARK
Name approved in October 1967,[5] when this small development replaced the house of the same name. The house appears to have built c.1829, and the first owner was Robert Gemmell, 'M.D., late of Demerara' (b.c.1778, d.1851). A tender for the demolition of Bourtreepark was accepted in November 1966.[6] Bourtree is a Scots word for the elder tree.

BOWMAN PLACE   See ASHGROVE STREET

BOWMAN ROAD   See ASHGROVE STREET

BRABAZON WAY   See LIBERATOR DRIVE

BRACKEN PARK
In September 1973, the Town Council agreed that 'a theme of wild flowers [would] form the basis of naming the streets' in Kincaidston.[7] Of the wild flowers chosen, some one would be happy to see in a garden, others (such as bracken) are less desirable. The others are CAMPION COURT, CELANDINE BANK, CRANESBILL COURT, CROCUS BANK, FERN BRAE, FOXGLOVE PLACE, GORSE PARK, HAREBELL PLACE, HEATHER PARK, HONEYSUCKLE PARK, IRIS COURT, MARGUERITE PLACE, MARIGOLD SQUARE, PRIMROSE PARK, ROCKROSE PARK, ROSEBAY PARK, RUSH HILL, SNOWDROP SQUARE, SORREL DRIVE, SPEEDWELL SQUARE, STONECROP PLACE, THISTLE WALK and TREFOIL PLACE. It will be seen that the expression 'wild flowers' has been interpreted liberally.

---

[1]   SAL, Ayr Town Council Minutes 1908, 273, Works Committee 9th September 1908.
[2]   The names Douglas Lane and Douglas Street were approved in October 1929. [SAL, Ayr Town Council Minutes 1928-29, 389, Works Committee 9th October 1929]
[3]   SAL, Ayr Town Council Minutes 1941-42, 241, Works Committee 9th September 1942.
[4]   SAL, Ayr Town Council Minutes 1972-73, 374, Works Committee 16th April 1973.
[5]   SAL, Ayr Town Council Minutes 1967-68, 184, Works Committee 12th October 1967.
[6]   SAL, Ayr Town Council Minutes 1966-67, 213, Markets and Slaughterhouse Committee 21st November 1966.
[7]   SAL, Ayr Town Council Minutes 1973-74, 125, Works Committee 17th September 1973.

BRADAN DRIVE
Name dates from 1974.[1] Loch Bradan is a reservoir near Straiton, originally created in 1912 to supply water to Troon. It was extended between 1968 and 1972 and now supplies much of South Ayrshire, including Ayr.   Neighbouring streets, CARCLUIE CRESCENT, FINLAS AVENUE, GRANGE AVENUE, MILTON PARK and RECAWR PARK, also take their names from springs and reservoirs connected with Ayr's piped water supply.[2] These names, except Bradan Drive, were all approved in November 1964.[3]

BRAEHEAD AVENUE
Also BRAEHEAD CRESCENT.   The name Braehead Avenue was approved by the Town Council in June 1938, and Braehead Crescent in August 1938.[4]   These streets are built on part of the lands of the farm of Braehead. Braehead Farm, comprising 178 acres, was sold in 1875 by the Blackhouse estate to the Oswalds of Auchincruive. When the land was sold to the Town, it belonged to John Gemmell (see Gemmell Crescent). The farmhouse at 201 Whitletts Road became a hotel, but burnt down in 1999.

BRAEHEAD CRESCENT   See BRAEHEAD AVENUE

BRAEMAR SQUARE
Also BRAESIDE ROAD. These names were approved in November 1950,[5] and relate to streets in the Braehead housing scheme (cf Braehead Avenue).   Braeside is a common Scots farm name, while Braemar is a village in Aberdeenshire; its name dating from the 16th Century when the lands were acquired by the Earl of Mar. The names have been chosen to complement Braehead.

BRAESIDE ROAD   See BRAEMAR SQUARE

BRIAR GROVE   See ALDER BANK

BRIG VENNEL
Dillon says 'this was the passage connecting the High Street with the Auld Brig. It still exists'.[6]   It corresponds to the modern Old Bridge Street.

BRITANNIA PLACE
Name dates from c.1896. It reflects a patriotic streak in the developer.   It may not be coincidental that Union Avenue is nearby.

---

[1]   One house, no.5, is in the 1975 Electoral Register, for which the qualifying date was 10th October 1974.

[2]   A gravitation water supply was first introduced into Ayr in 1842, from springs at Grange and Milton on Carrick Hill. with a holding reservoir at Carcluie. Increasing need saw the creation of larger schemes at Loch Finlas, opened in 1886, and at Loch Recawr, opened in 1933 (both in Straiton parish), before the introduction of the enhanced Loch Bradan scheme.

[3]   SAL, Ayr Town Council Minutes 1964-65, 190, Works Committee 16th November 1964.

[4]   SAL, Ayr Town Council Minutes 1937-38, 227, Housing Committee 23rd June 1938; SAL, ibid, 258, Works Committee 3rd August 1938.

[5]   SAL, Ayr Town Council Minutes 1950-51, 200, Works Committee 24th November 1950.

[6]   William J Dillon, The Streets in Early Times, in Annie I Dunlop, ed., The Royal Burgh of Ayr, Edinburgh, 1953, 71.

BROADWAY   See HARTHALL

BROADWOOD PARK
Name approved in June 1969.[1] Presumably chosen for its pleasant sound.

BROOK COTTAGES
Named in the 1851 Census, and presumably close to what is now Monument Road, between Summerfield and Slaphouse. Not found on the 1857 Ordnance Survey map.

BROOMFIELD GARDENS   See BROOMFIELD ROAD

BROOMFIELD PLACE   See BROOMFIELD ROAD

BROOMFIELD ROAD
This name was approved by Ayr Town Council in September 1845,[2] for a road through the Mid Sands of the Town Common which they had contracted with Edward Neilson to make and complete in April 1842.[3] Broomfield appears to have been the name given to one of the fields into which the Mid Sands were divided: whins (gorse and broom) would have been common throughout the mid and laigh sands before they were developed. A development off Broomfield Road has been named BROOMFIELD GARDENS, the name being approved by the Works Committee in May 1959,[4] in preference to BROOMFIELD PLACE, an alternative suggested by the Burgh Surveyor.[5]

BROUGHAM PLACE
Unauthorised or obsolete name which was incorporated in the official names of streets as 1-3 Racecourse Road.[6] These houses were built c.1857 by James Paton & Sons, builders.[7] Henry Brougham, 1st Lord Brougham (b.1778, d.1868) was Lord Chancellor from 1830-1834: in 1820 he had led the defence of Queen Caroline: 'His eloquence and boldness, though they forfeited for him the favour of the crown, gained him that of the people, and for the ten years between 1820 and 1830 Brougham was the popular idol'.[8]

BROUN DRIVE
This road was adopted as a public road in December 1999.[9] Agnes Broun (b.1732, d.1820) was the mother of Robert Burns: she married William Burnes in 1757.

BROWNCARRICK DRIVE
Name approved in January 1973.[1] One of the streets in Ayr nearest to the Carrick Hills, of which Brown Carrick is one of the more prominent.

---

[1] SAL, Ayr Town Council Minutes 1969-70, 68, Works Committee 16th June 1969.
[2] SAL, B6/18/30, 431, Ayr Town Council Minutes 1841-1848, 11th September 1845.
[3] SAL, B6/18/30, 70, Ayr Town Council Minutes 1841-1848, 16th April 1842. The contract price was £37 10s.
[4] SAL, Ayr Town Council Minutes 1959-60, 20, Works Committee 21st May 1959.
[5] SAL, Ayr Town Council Minutes 1958-59, 339, Works Committee 30th April 1959.
[6] 1910-1911 Directory, 246, List of Erased Terraces, Etc.
[7] See Ayrshire Sasine Abridgement no.1048 of 1857 for the sale of the land, part of the estate of Barns, to the Patons.
[8] Chambers's Encyclopaedia, New Revised Edition, Vol II, London, 1970, 598.
[9] SAL, South Ayrshire Council Minutes 1999-2000 (unbound), 941, Strategic Services Committee 7th December 1999.

BROWN'S SQUARE
Name, used in 1861 Census, for houses on south east side of Church Street, built on land acquired in 1858 by Robert Brown, coalmaster (b.c.1814, d.1886), who at that time was lessee of Craigie Colliery.[2]

BRUCE CRESCENT
Name dates from the 1850s. Close to St John's Tower, where Robert Bruce held a Parliament, the first called after the Scots' victory at Bannockburn. The street commemorates this Ayrshire-born king.

BRUCE PLACE   See BRUCEFIELD PLACE

BRUCEFIELD PLACE
Cottages in Prestwick Road, listed in the 1871 Census and, as BRUCE PLACE, in that for 1881. Bruce's Land appears in the same vicinity on the 1857 Ordnance Survey map. Presumably named after the proprietor.

BRYDEN'S CLOSE
Erstwhile name for the close at 241 High Street, more usually known as Plough Inn Close. James Alexander Bryden, son of James Bryden, coachbuilder (d.1932), had a haulage business here from c.1929 to c.1964.

BUCHAN COURT
Name dates from 2000. Presumably in honour of the Scots author and politician, John Buchan (b.1875, d.1940).

BUCKINGHAM TERRACE
Original name of 19-37 Charlotte Street, built c.1871 by William McFadzean, builder (b.1827, d.1873). In 1933 Ayr Town Council were discussing the upgrading of BUCKINGHAM TERRACE LANE, the rear access lane, (which is named on contemporary Ordnance Survey Maps as Charlotte Street Lane), though Buckingham Terrace had appeared in the 1910 list of unauthorised or obsolete names.[3] The English town and county have given their name to a dukedom, and Buckingham House was built in London in 1705 for the 1st Duke; the house was acquired in 1762 by George III as a town house for Queen Charlotte, and conversion to a palace (Buckingham Palace) was begun in 1821 under George IV.

BURNBANK PLACE
Also BURNBANK ROAD. Names approved in October 1955.[4] Burnbank Road runs along the right hand bank of the Annfield Burn, while Burnbank Place is a short street leading from it.

---

[1]   SAL, Ayr Town Council Minutes 1972-73, 264, Works Committee 15th January 1973.
[2]   Ayrshire Sasine Abridgement no.1929 of 1858. After the Craigie Colliery was worked out, Brown moved to New Cumnock, where he developed new coalfields through the Lanemark Coal Company.
[3]   1910-1911 Directory, 246, List of Erased Terraces, Etc.
[4]   SAL, Ayr Town Council Minutes 1955-56, 167, Works Committee 27th October 1955.

BURNESS AVENUE
Name approved in January 1962.[1]   William Burnes (b.1721, d.1784), father of Robert
Burns, generally spelled his name so: the 'double s' in Burness, a variant found among the
poet's relations in Kincardineshire, more readily indicates the two syllable pronunciation
favoured there.

BURNETT TERRACE
Name first appears in the 1886-1887 Directory: the houses of Burnett Terrace were built by
John Drinnan (b.1861, d.1910) Obscure: the fact that Frances Hodgson Burnett's best
known book, 'Little Lord Fauntleroy', was published in 1886 is, surely, coincidental.

BURNS COURT   See RIVERSIDE PLACE

BURNS HOUSE
Opened in 1975.   One of the least appealing buildings in Ayr, it is perhaps not the most
fitting building to bear Robert Burns' name.

BURNS STATUE ARCADE   See BURNS STATUE SQUARE

BURNS STATUE SQUARE
George Lawson's statue of Burns was unveiled in 1892, giving focus to this area at the head
of the town. A rather amorphous area, home to Ayr's cattle and horse markets, and many
carriers, carters, and the like, known indiscriminately as the Townhead or the Fauldbacks
was transformed after 1850 by the opening of the new Ayr Station, the creation of Miller
Road, and the first stirrings of residential development in streets such as Beresford Terrace.
The renumbering of the upper part of Alloway Street as Burns Statue Square appears to have
happened c.1895.   The dog-legged lane which runs from Burns Statue Square to Smith
Street is known both as BURNS STATUE ARCADE and UNION ARCADE.

BURNS' WICKET
Name in use by 1998. This small road serves Ayr Cricket Club's ground, and pays homage
to Burns' connection with Alloway.

BURNSIDE STREET   See RUSSELL STREET

BUTE COURT   See RIVERSIDE PLACE

BUTTERMARKET BUILDINGS   See BUTTERMARKET CLOSE

BUTTERMARKET CLOSE
An old name which was resurrected in the 1980s.   Dillon notes that, in 1953, 'the Butter
Market is up the Butter Market Close in the High Street.   Here, in recent years, every
Tuesday, Ayrshire farmers did direct trading with local grocers and townspeople. In 1900
the town made a profit of £48 on this market and by 1911 the sum had risen to £75.   When
rationing was introduced it put an end to the activities of this marketing, but the town retains

---

[1]   SAL, Ayr Town Council Minutes 1961-62, 223, Works Committee 25th January 1962. See
            also Ayrshire Post, 2nd February 1962, 14d, which notes that the name was approved on the
            birthday of Robert Burns.

the power - restated in an act of 1873 - to charge dues on every pound of butter sold'.[1] The Butter Market appears to have moved to this site - formerly used as the Fleshmarket - in July 1869 from a site in Newmarket Street occupied since 1814.[2] The name was then applied to the close at 90 High Street, while the tenement at 92-98 High Street, built in 1882-83, was known as BUTTERMARKET BUILDINGS.

CAGE WALK
This name is included in the 3rd edition of Nicolson's Ayr Street Plan. It is, however, not a street, but the popular name for the pedestrian footbridge attached to the downstream side of the railway bridge which crosses the Ayr at Ayr Station. The name arises because the open mesh construction of the footbridge has a cage-like appearance. The bridge was rebuilt c.1878, and in 1880 a house in Gordon Terrace is described as being bounded 'by a proposed road adjoining the Cage Walk Road'.[3]

CAIRN CRESCENT
Name approved in October 1961.[4] There is, between nos. 5 and 7 Cairn Crescent, a small cairn, which was re-erected here in 1965, following the development of the area. Noted by John Smith,[5] this is probably the cairn mentioned by Burns in 'Tam o Shanter': 'And thro' the whins, and by the cairn/ Where hunters fand the murder'd bairn'.

CAIRNRYAN WAY   See SOUTHFIELD PARK

CAIRNSMORE DRIVE
Name approved in January 1973.[6] Cairnsmore is a frequent mountain name in south west Scotland, e.g. Cairnsmore of Fleet, or Cairnsmore of Kells, and the street name presumably derives from these, but which, if any, is specifically honoured is not known.

CAIRNSMUIR PLACE
Unauthorised or obsolete name which was incorporated in the official names of streets as 56-66 McCall's Avenue,[7] the plans for which were approved in May 1900. The developer was Alexander Smith, builder.[8] For the meaning of the name see Cairnsmore Drive.

CALEDONIA ROAD
Name dates from c.1955: 'Caledonia' was one of four Burns-related names approved for streets in Forehill in October 1954, the others being Armour, Cessnock and Cunningham. Caledonia is, of course, the Latin name for Scotland, and the line 'Hail, Caledonia! Name for ever dear!' appears in Burns' poem, 'Prologue'.

---

[1]   William J Dillon, Fairs and Markets, in Annie I Dunlop, ed., The Royal Burgh of Ayr, Edinburgh, 1953, 194.
[2]   Ardrossan and Saltcoats Herald, 24th July 1869, 5c.
[3]   Ayrshire Sasine Abridgement no.10215 of 1880. For the bridge see John R Hume, The Industrial Archaeology of Scotland. 1. The Lowlands and Borders, London, 1976, 47.
[4]   SAL, Ayr Town Council Minutes 1961-62, 142, Works Committee 26th October 1961.
[5]   John Smith, Prehistoric Man in Ayrshire, London, 1895, 158.
[6]   SAL, Ayr Town Council Minutes 1972-73, 264, Works Committee 15th January 1973.
[7]   1910-1911 Directory, 246, List of Erased Terraces, Etc.
[8]   AA, Ayr Dean of Guild Court plans, box no.10, plan no.258.

CALLENDAR PLACE
Name approved by Ayr Town Council in March 1958.[1] The derivation is from Callendar
Park near Falkirk, the estate of the Forbes family, who acquired in 1785 much of the lands
of the Barony of Newton,[2] and initiated much of the industrial and residential development
of Wallacetown.[3] The Callendar Estate still owns land in the Heathfield area; a fact
commemorated by the name FORBES DRIVE used for part of the industrial estate.
CALLENDAR ROAD, on the Heathfield Industrial Estate, was approved in February 1979:[4]
it is technically outwith the Ayr boundary, and in Prestwick.

CAMBUSDOON DRIVE
Name approved in September 1953.[5] Cambusdoon House, on whose lands this
development was built, was built in 1854 for James Baird of Cambusdoon [See Baird
Road]: the porch remains as a folly. The name appears to be a Victorian creation, ersatz
Gaelic, on the principle of names such as Cambuslang and Cambusnethan, and was
bestowed at a formal ceremony in April 1854:[6] the estate had previously been known as
Craigweil. Cambus is from the Gaelic *camas*, meaning a 'bend' or a 'bay'.

CAMBUSLEA ROAD
Name approved by Ayr Town Council in September 1904.[7] The major initial developer was
John Milliken, builder, (b.c1852, d.1912), whose home since 1891 had been a house called
Cambuslea on this site.[8] The name, however, is obscure, but compare Cambusdoon, above.

CAMPBELL COURT   See JAMES CAMPBELL ROAD

CAMPBELL STREET
Name dates from c.1893, when the first four houses were approved: William Drinnan
(b.c.1854, d.1895), joiner, was the developer.[9] Which, if any, of the many bearers of this
common Scots surname is honoured is not known. The street is not on Craigie land, so that
it is probably not that family. The equally unspecific Gordon Street runs parallel to
Campbell Street.

CAMPHILL PLACE   See BLACKHILL STREET

---

1   Ayrshire Post, 14th March 1958, 20a.
2   Ayrshire Sasine Abridgement no.1752 of 1787.
3   William Forbes of Callendar (b.1743, d.1815) was the architect of the family fortunes. He
        secured profitable contracts to supply the Navy with copper for lining ships's hulls, and was
        jocularly known as 'Copper-bottomed' Forbes. His first wife was a daughter of John
        Macadam of Craigengillan.
4   SAL, Kyle and Carrick District Council Minutes 1978-79, 461, Planning & Building
        Control Committee 14th February 1979.
5   SAL, Ayr Town Council Minutes 1953-54, 101, Works Committee 25th September 1953.
6   Ayr Advertiser, 4th May 1854, 4c.
7   SAL, Ayr Town Council Minutes 1903-04, 242, Corporation 12th September 1904.
8   Ayr Advertiser, 19th September 1912, 8h; AA, Ayr Dean of Guild Court plans, box no.14,
        plan no.60.
9   AA, Ayr Dean of Guild Court plans, box no.1, plan no.17. The first four houses are 2-8
        Campbell Street.

CAMPION COURT   See BRACKEN PARK

CARCLUIE CRESCENT   See BRADAN DRIVE

CARLETON TERRACE
Unauthorised or obsolete name, first noted in the 1896-97 Directory, which was incorporated in the official names of streets as 33-39 Bellevue Crescent.[1] Carleton is an estate and ruined tower house in Colmonell parish, near Lendalfoot. It should be noted, however, that contemporary Directories more often use the spelling CARLTON TERRACE, with its echoes of grand houses in the West End of London.

CARNELL'S VENNEL
'This lane cut off from Boat Vennal (sic) and ran north to the river. Probably it crossed Boat Vennal and proceeded south following a line represented by Fort Street. It received its name from Wallace of Carnell who had a tenement in it'.[2] In 1601-1602, during an outbreak of plague, Ayr Town Council paid £3 3s 4d to Bailie George Masoun for 17 carpollis [small pieces of timber] to close Carnell's Vennel.[3]

CARNOCHAN STREET
Name approved by Ayr Town Council in October 1933 for a road in Seafield.[4] In March 1934 it was agreed to take the name-plate down, and in July of that year, it was decided that this street should be numbered as part of Seafield Drive.[5] The name appears to be derived from Carrochan Burn or Carnochan Burn, an ancient name of the Seafield area.

CARRICK AVENUE
Also CARRICK GARDENS, CARRICK PARK, CARRICK ROAD, CARRICK ROAD LANE and CARRICK VIEW. The oldest name is CARRICK ROAD, which is of c.1883 and is a re-naming of Maybole Road. Although this is an old route the name does not appear to have a particularly long history, but compare Carrick Street. The other names are all of streets close to Carrick Road, and have merely borrowed the name. CARRICK GARDENS, approved in June 1984,[6] is the most recent: this is a wardened housing complex on the site of Carrick House (48 Carrick Road). This was a substantial suburban villa, originally built c.1847 by the Wallacetown builder, John Kay (b.1788, d.1860), and extended after it was acquired by the ironmaster Henry Houldsworth in 1871. In 1879, the Ayr Advertiser noted that 'what was known as the Horsemarket Field is pretty nearly all built upon, the latest erections being a number of neat cottages which go under the name of CARRICK PARK'.[7] CARRICK VIEW was the original name of 45-51 St Leonards Road,

[1]   1910-1911 Directory, 246, List of Erased Terraces, Etc.
[2]   William J Dillon, The Streets in Early Times, in Annie I Dunlop, ed., The Royal Burgh of Ayr, Edinburgh, 1953, 71.
[3]   George S Pryde, ed., Ayr Burgh Accounts 1534-1624, Edinburgh, 1937, 211.
[4]   SAL, Ayr Town Council Minutes 1932-33, 290, Works Committee, 4th October 1933.
[5]   SAL, Ayr Town Council Minutes 1933-34, 118, Works Committee, 7th March 1934; *ibid*, 230, Works Committee, 4th July 1934.
[6]   SAL, Kyle and Carrick District Council Minutes 1984-85, 95, Planning & Building Control Committee 20th June 1984.
[7]   Ayr Advertiser, 26th June 1879, 4e.

of c.1895, but had been officially suppressed by 1910;[1] while CARRICK AVENUE was adopted c.1905, superceding Doon Terrace as the road developed.

CARRICK GARDENS   See CARRICK AVENUE

CARRICK OVAL   See CARRICK STREET

CARRICK PARK   See CARRICK AVENUE

CARRICK PLACE   See CARRICK STREET

CARRICK ROAD   See CARRICK AVENUE

CARRICK ROAD LANE   See CARRICK AVENUE

CARRICK STREET
This is the remnant of the ancient road into Carrick, which left the High Street here, passed close to Barns House, kept close to the shore (roughly on the line of Racecourse Road) before crossing the Doon at Doonfoot. This section of the route in the town was also known as CARRICK VENNEL.[2] CARRICK PLACE was a house in Carrick Street, occupied for some years by the teacher/developer Arthur Lang (b.1802, d.1890), who also owned stables in CARRICK OVAL on the north side of Carrick Street.

CARRICK VENNEL   See CARRICK STREET

CARRICK VIEW   See CARRICK AVENUE

CARSELOCH ROAD
Name approved in October 1962.[3] No source for the name has been identified.

CARWINSHOCH VIEW
Name approved by Ayr Town Council in October 1933.[4] Carwinshoch is a farm on the seaward side of Brown Carrick Hill, just to the south of Ayr (cf Browncarrick Drive). It can, presumably, be seen from here, but so can many more notable features.

CASSILLIS STREET
Name dates from the 1830s.[5] Like neighbouring Ailsa Place (q.v.), the name honours the family of Kennedy of Cassillis, who were at one time proprietors of the Fort or Citadel of Ayr. Cassillis House is an ancient house in Kirkmichael parish, with a 15th Century core, and 19th Century additions. The property has been in the hands of the Kennedys since the 14th Century. Properly pronounced "cassels", the spelling pronunciation is gaining precedence.

[1]   1910-1911 Directory, 246, List of Erased Terraces, Etc.
[2]   William J Dillon, The Streets in Early Times, in Annie I Dunlop, ed., The Royal Burgh of Ayr, Edinburgh, 1953, 71.
[3]   SAL, Ayr Town Council Minutes 1962-63, 140, Works Committee 25th October 1962.
[4]   SAL, Ayr Town Council Minutes 1932-33, 290, Works Committee, 4th October 1933.
[5]   It is found in McCarter's 1832-33 Directory for Ayr as the address of James Murdoch, merchant.

CASTLE SQUARE
Also CASTLE VIEW and CASTLE WALK. The name Castle Walk was approved in May 1957,[1] the other two in 1982,[2] though Castle Square appears not to have been used until c.1997. They all take their name from their proximity to Greenan Castle, a prominent feature in the sea view south from Ayr.

CASTLE VIEW	See CASTLE SQUARE
CASTLE WALK	See CASTLE SQUARE
CASTLEHILL COURT	See CASTLEHILL ROAD
CASTLEHILL CRESCENT	See CASTLEHILL ROAD
CASTLEHILL GARDENS	See CASTLEHILL ROAD

CASTLEHILL ROAD
This name was adopted in 1894 for the first stretch of the road to Dalmellington, supplanting Dalmellington Road.[3] Castle Hill is a prominent eminence about 1½ miles south east of Ayr, now largely developed for housing purposes, which presumably had a prehistoric importance as a defensive site. It is also supposed to have been the site of a Roman camp. These features would have suggested the name 'Castle Hill'. Between 1799 and 1804 Patrick Ballantine (b.c.1751, d.1810) built a house here, called Castlehill. This part of the Dalmellington road passes through the Castlehill lands, and was developed for residential purposes when the estate began to make feus available in the 1880s and 1890s. A short street connecting it with Chalmers Road is called CASTLEHILL CRESCENT, this name being approved by Ayr Town Council in 1932, on a suggestion of Mr Wilson of Castlehill.[4] CASTLEHILL GARDENS is the formal name given to four Castlehill estate cottages erected in 1910.[5] CASTLEHILL COURT is the name given to the 1990s residential conversion of the former Castlehill Stables.

CATHCART PLACE	See CATHCART STREET

CATHCART STREET
Name dates from before 1830: the street is an improvement, from c.1822 and initially called CATHCART PLACE, of one of the vennels which led from Sandgate to the back dykes, and to the pre-1650s church of St John. That this is so is confirmed by an advertisement of 1831, selling a house in 'John Street now called Cathcart Street'.[6] Gray notes that c.1800

---

[1] SAL, Ayr Town Council Minutes 1957-58, 29, Works Committee 23rd May 1957.
[2] SAL, Kyle and Carrick District Council Minutes 1982-83, 343, Planning & Building Control Committee 13th October 1982.
[3] Ayr Advertiser, 19th April 1894, 5a.
[4] SAL, Ayr Town Council Minutes 1931-32, 158, Works Committee, 9 March 1932. For Wilson of Castlehill see LESLIE CRESCENT.
[5] AA, CO3/12/1/5, Ayr County Council, Ayr District Committee Minute Book 1907-1911, 703, Building Byelaws Committee, 4th October 1910.
[6] Air Advertiser, 3 February 1831, 1d. The original developer appears to have been Thomas King, builder: see National Archives of Scotland [NAS], B6/5/1, Ayr Burgh Register of Sasines, Minute Book 1809 - 1843.

'Cathcart Street had not been opened up, the whole ground behind being occupied as a garden in connection with [the house in Sandgate occupied by Lady Dumfries]'.[1] It is not named on the Armstrongs' map of 1775, and on Wood's map of 1818 it is marked as 'St Johns Street'. The name recalls Margaret, Lady Cathcart (b.c.1740, d.1817), the wife of Sir John Cathcart of Carleton, and daughter of Robert Hamilton of Bourtreehill. Widowed in 1783, she succeeded to Rozelle in 1809, and died there in April 1817. In 1804 she advertised for a gardener: applicants were to call 'at her house in Ayr'.[2]

CEDAR ROAD   See ALDER BANK

CELANDINE BANK   See BRACKEN PARK

CENTRAL ARCADE
Alternative name for LORNE ARCADE. Between High Street and Arthur Street, it is, indeed, close to the centre of Ayr. The name may have been adopted intentionally to imply closeness to the commercial centre.

CESSNOCK PLACE
Name dates from c.1954: 'Cessnock' was one of four names approved for streets in Forehill in October 1954. Cessnock is an estate and stream in Galston parish. It is one of the Burns names, for on its banks 'dwelt the lassie with sparkling rogueish een'.[3]

CHALMERS AVENUE
Also CHALMERS ROAD. These names date from c.1895 (Chalmers Road) and January 1948 (Chalmers Avenue). [4] These names recall James Chalmers (b.c.1801, d.1883), a nurseryman on whose nursery ground Chalmers Road was initially built.[5]

CHALMERS ROAD   See CHALMERS AVENUE

CHALMERS ROAD EAST   See INVERKAR ROAD

CHALMERS ROAD WEST   See CHALMERS AVENUE

CHAMBERGATE
In use by 1348 for the lower High Street, the street leading to the Chamber or Tolbooth. See reference under Sandgate.

CHAPEL BRAE   See ELBA STREET

---

1   Lecture by H C Gray on Old Ayr reported in Ayr Advertiser, 25th January 1872, 5c.
2   Air Advertiser, 9th February 1804, 4c.
3   Francis H Groome, Ordnance Gazetteer of Scotland, Vol 1., Edinburgh, 1882, 258.
4   SAL, Ayr Town Council Minutes 1947-49, 88, Corporation 12th January 1948.
5   Information on Chalmers is scanty. According to the 1881 Census he was born in Patna. His death on 11th June 1883 is recorded in the Ayr Advertiser of 21st June 1883, 5f, and in Confirmations and Inventories for 1883. From 1876 he lived at Roselea Cottage, 12 Carrick Road: the family name is regularly mis-spelled Chambers in contemporary Directories. Chalmers Road was originally Chalmers Road West; Inverkar Road was Chalmers Road East. They appear to have entered Chalmers' nursery from either side, both named Chalmers Road, and the suffixed added for differentiation. Chalmers Road lost its suffix when Chalmers Road East was renamed Inverkar Road in 1925.

CHAPEL STREET   See ELBA STREET

CHAPELPARK ROAD
This name was adopted in 1894.[1] The Chapel of St Leonard stood close to this road. It was a pre-reformation hospice or chapel, and the buildings have long vanished, though they were still to be seen when Timothy Pont made his survey in the late 16th Century.[2] Pagan says that 'it stood in meadowland, on a site near that which is at present occupied by the church of the same name. Its stones were eventually used in building part of the wall round the racecourse'.[3]

CHARLOTTE STREET
Name dates from c.1813. The honour is for Princess Charlotte (b.1796, d.1817), the daughter (and only child) of the Prince of Wales (who became in 1820 George IV) and his wife Princess Caroline of Brunswick. Had she lived, Charlotte would have succeeded to the throne.

CHERRY HILL ROAD
Name approved, as CHERRY HILL, in September 1961.[4] No derivation known: it has presumably been chosen for its pleasant associations.

CHESTNUT ROAD   See ALDER BANK

CHURCH COURT   See CHURCH STREET

CHURCH PLACE
Name dates from at least 1870s. It was given to that part of Cross Street (King Street) at the junction with Main Street, and which was opposite the (now demolished) Newton on Ayr Parish Church. The name is still visible on the red sandstone flats at the corner of King Street and Main Street, but had been officially suppressed by 1910.[5]

CHURCH STREET
Name dates from c.1860. The street ran north east from John Street at Wallacetown Parish Church. It was demolished in the redevelopment of Wallacetown: part of the new development, of c.1970, is called CHURCH COURT.

CHURCHILL CRESCENT
Name approved in December 1950.[6] The honour is undoubtedly for the country's wartime leader, Sir Winston Churchill (b.1874, d.1965). In 2000 the name CHURCHILL TOWER was bestowed on a new development at Ayr Harbour. It is close to the site of Ayr Barracks, known latterly as Churchill Barracks. See Barrack Road.

CHURCHILL TOWER   See CHURCHILL CRESCENT

---

[1]   Ayr Advertiser, 19th April 1894, 5a.
[2]   John M Short, Street Names, in Annie I Dunlop, ed., The Royal Burgh of Ayr, Edinburgh, 1953, 83.
[3]   John H Pagan, Annals of Ayr in the Olden Time: 1560-1692, Ayr, 1897, 4.
[4]   SAL, Ayr Town Council Minutes 1961-62, 110, Works Committee 21st September 1961. See also Whin Hill Road.
[5]   1910-1911 Directory, 246, List of Erased Terraces, Etc.
[6]   SAL, Ayr Town Council Minutes 1950-51, 236, Works Committee 22nd December 1950.

CITADEL PLACE
The Fort or Citadel of Ayr was built in the 1650s under the Commonwealth of Oliver Cromwell as part of his scheme to control Scotland. Subsequently, under successive owners, the Citadel remained somehow apart from the town, until it was acquired by John Miller in 1854; he commenced feuing it for residential purposes. Citadel Place is the main approach to the Citadel or Fort area from the town, and replaces the original entrance which can still be seen in a lane which runs from midway along Citadel Place, behind Ayr Academy. When first named, c.1857, Citadel Place was the name of one side of the street, Cromwell Place, q.v., that of the other. Citadel Place was renumbered in 1935 to include Cromwell Place. In 1994 Kyle and Carrick District Council approved the name Citadel Leisure Centre for the improved and extended Ayr Swimming Baths.[1]

CLAREMONT PLACE
Found in the 1888-89 Directory, as a part of Boghall Row, and presumably fell into disuse c.1896 when Boghall Row was renamed Victoria Street. Claremont is an estate near Esher, Surrey: the name is French-derived, with a meaning of 'unclouded hill'.

CLARENDON PLACE
Name approved in October 1955.[2] Clarendon was a hunting lodge near Salisbury, Wilts, enlarged into a palace by Henry II: long destroyed, but the name has often been used for titles. In the 19th Century, George Villiers, 4th Earl of Clarendon (b.1800, d.1870) was thrice foreign secretary, including during the Crimean War. However no particular reason, beyond its euphony and aristocratic associations, can be found for its choice here.

CLARKE AVENUE
Name approved in July 1916.[3] It was suggested by the developer, William Clarke, builder (b.1854, d.1934).[4]

CLARK'S CLOSE
A close or yard at or near 166 High Street. James Foulds Clark had refreshment rooms here in the early 1880s, but moved to 8 High Street when the area was redeveloped by the Town Council from 1885.

CLIMIE'S CLOSE
Close at 219-223 High Street, where in the mid 1880s Andrew Climie established a fleshing business which remained here until recent years.

CLOCHRANHILL ROAD
Name dates from c.1930, but as a farm name Clochranhill is considerably older. In 1829-1830 Clochranhill Farm was occupied by a Mrs McEwen. See also 1794 reference under Dumfriespark.

---

[1]   SAL, Kyle and Carrick District Council 1994-95, 205, Special District Council 21st September 1994.
[2]   SAL, Ayr Town Council Minutes 1955-56, 167, Works Committee 27th October 1955.
[3]   SAL, Ayr Town Council Minutes 1916, 246, Corporation 10th July 1916.
[4]   See Clarke's obituary in Ayrshire Post, 17th August 1934, 10d.

CLOVERHILL

Name approved in April 1972.[1] Cloverhill was a farm or cottage (and is now a house) on the road which led from Holmston past McNairston to the Dalrymple-Coylton road: it is on the opposite side of the by-pass from this street. See also Crofthead Road.

CLUNES STREET

Also known as CLUNES VENNAL.[2] Street leading from Main Street into Newton Green. The name was in use by 1830 (as Clune's Vennal), but the derivation is obscure. It looks like a surname, but remains to be explained. The street was renamed CROWN STREET in 1922, following a petition from residents in the street urging a change to 'Crown Street, Gilmour Street or some other suitable name' as 'at present they suffer in many ways from the street being named Clunes Vennal. Neither why the original name was such a problem, nor why the names Crown or Gilmour were 'suitable' was explained.[3] Clunes Vennal appears to have been called earlier Common Vennal, and appears on Wood's Plan, 1818, as EAST VENNAL.

CLUNES VENNAL   See CLUNES STREET

COLLECTORS VENNEL

A house in Collectors Vennel, occupied by Major Webster, was advertised for sale in 1806.[4] Wood's map of 1818 shows Collectors Vennel to be the street now known as St John Street, and this is confirmed by Howie:[5] a street in this position is shown on the Armstrongs' map of 1775, but not named. The name presumably recalls one of the Customs Collectors at Ayr, but which is not known.

---

[1]   SAL, Ayr Town Council Minutes 1971-72, 351, Works Committee 17th April 1972.
[2]   An advertisement in Air Advertiser, 19th April 1838, 1f, has Clunes' Vennal.
[3]   SAL, Ayr Town Council Minutes 1921-22, 157, Works Committee 8th March 1922. The initial decision to rename was overturned by the Corporation on 13th March (*ibid*, 169); adhered to by the Works Committee on 5th April (*ibid*, 191), and finally approved by the Corporation on 10th April, after an attempt to rename it Clunes Street was defeated in a close vote (*ibid*, 202). During the discussion on 13th March, Bailie Smith said that a year or two ago a murder had been committed in Clunes Vennal, and householders said that since then letting had suffered. Provost Mathie-Morton 'did not think that a change should be made in the name of the street. Anyone conversant with archaeology knew that Vennal was a very old word. He could not see how a murder should affect letting of houses or rooms in the street. A number of years ago they changed Cross Street to King Street, and still further back they altered Boghall Row to Victoria Street, but he did not know that their action had resulted in an improvement. In a matter of this kind they should not be guided by sentiment. If they were going to alter the names of streets they might change Wellington Square to Pavilion Avenue. (A member - Or Lawyers' Retreat)'. [Ayrshire Post, Friday 17th March 1922, 3a]
[4]   Air Advertiser, Thursday 17th April 1806, 4c.
[5]   James Howie, "An Historical Account of the Town of Ayr", Kilmarnock, 1861, 14. The St John Street on Wood's plan is modern Cathcart Street.

COMMON VENNEL, Ayr
An alternative name for Kirkport, presumably because this was a public or common passage; its upkeep a charge on the common or public funds. In 1535-36 Ayr Town Council paid £1 10s for the redding and calsying of the Common Vennel.[1]

COMMON VENNEL, Newton
Appears to be an alternative name for Clunes Street. For derivation, see Common Vennel, Ayr.

COMMONHEAD PLACE   See SOUTHFIELD PARK

CONTENT AVENUE
Also CONTENT STREET. Content Avenue dates from c.1890, and appears to have originally been planned to be called CONTENT PARK ROAD,[2] while Content Street dates from earlier in that century: it is on Wood's map of 1818. Content House, now demolished, seems to have been built c.1799 for Anthony Whiteside, wine merchant. The name Content-upon-Ayr is sometimes used for this part of Wallacetown.[3] The name is puzzling, but it is suggested that the name was given by Whiteside to his house, the name presumably meaning that it was a place of peace and contentment. The area became increasingly industrialised and the name adopted for the street and other developments, such as the Content Stone Quarry.

CONTENT STREET   See CONTENT AVENUE

CONTENT TERRACE   See DUCAT ROAD

CORANBAE PLACE
Name approved in January 1973.[4] Obscure: no place or other feature with this name has been found.

CORNHILL
Name of c.1976. In Kincaidston, but not quite compatible with the wild plant names (see Bracken Park) which prevail there. Cornhill is the estate's commercial centre, so a slight distinction was perhaps deliberately aimed for.

CORPSE AVENUE
In 1864 it was reported that the Glasgow and South Western Railway had commenced building a new station at Newtonhead (the present Newton on Ayr Station) 'at the head of the Corpse Avenue'.[5]

---

[1]   George S Pryde, ed., Ayr Burgh Accounts 1534-1624, Edinburgh, 1937, 75.
[2]   There is a reference to it under this name in a minute of the Roads & Footpaths Committee of 1st May 1905, corrected in the minutes of the same committee on 29th May 1905. [SAL, Ayr Town Council Minutes 1904-05, 169 and 205.]
[3]   The Air Advertiser of 27th June 1805, 4c, refers to a house 'lately built and neatly finished' at Far Content, while that of 22nd August 1805, 1c, carries an advert for the 'freestone quarry now opened at Content'.
[4]   SAL, Ayr Town Council Minutes 1972-73, 264, Works Committee 15th January 1973.
[5]   Ardrossan and Saltcoats Herald, 27th August 1864, 4d.

CORSEHILL PARK
Also CORSEHILL PLACE and CORSEHILL ROAD. These names date from July 1954,[1] and 1903[2] respectively. They are named from Corsehill House, which used to stand in Monument Road, and whose gardens are still maintained as a public garden. Corsehill may mean hill with a cross (its proximity to Chapel Park should be noted): the name also exists in Ayrshire as the name of a former estate and ruined castle near Stewarton. Corsehill House was probably built c.1818 for the banker William Cowan (b.1759, d.1841); in 1868 it was acquired by Margaret Hart, of Dalrymple, who had inherited £100,000 through the death of a relative in South America.[3] It was demolished in 1961.[4]

CORSEHILL PLACE	See CORSEHILL PARK
CORSEHILL ROAD	See CORSEHILL PARK

CORSERINE ROAD
Name approved in January 1973.[5] Corserine is a hill in the Southern Uplands, the highest peak in the Rhinns of Kells, close to the village of Carsphairn.

COW VENNEL	See ALLOWAY STREET

COW VENNEL
A Cow Vennel in Newton is recorded in 1887,[6] but has not been identified.

COW WYND	See ALLOWAY STREET
COWAN COURT	See COWAN CRESCENT

COWAN CRESCENT
This name was approved in December 1962, during William Cowan's period of office as Provost of Ayr.[7] Cowan (b.1904, d.1989), Provost from 1961-1964, owned a creamery and milk business in Ayr. In 1984 COWAN COURT was an alternative proposal for the street which became Limond's Court (q.v.). It is not apparent for whom this latter honour was intended.

CRAIGHALL PLACE
Name approved in June 1969.[8] Presumably chosen solely for its pleasant quality.

---

[1] SAL, Ayr Town Council Minutes 1954-55, 103, Works Committee 30th July 1954. Approval given to both Corsehill Park and Corsehill Place.
[2] Approved by Town Council in March 1903. [SAL, Ayr Town Council Minutes 1902-03, 114, Works Committee 23rd March 1903]
[3] Ardrossan and Saltcoats Herald, 16th May 1868, 5b.
[4] AA, Ayr Dean of Guild Court plans, box no.132, plan no.20.
[5] SAL, Ayr Town Council Minutes 1972-73, 264, Works Committee 15th January 1973.
[6] Ayrshire Sasine Abridgement no.2110 of 1887. The reference is to a piece of land bounded on the north by the Cow Vennel, Newton.
[7] SAL, Ayr Town Council Minutes 1962-63, 187, Corporation 10th December 1962. The name was adopted after Councillor W S Lanham declined having a street named in his honour. [Ayrshire Post, 14th December 1962, 20f]
[8] SAL, Ayr Town Council Minutes 1969-70, 68, Works Committee 16th June 1969.

CRAIGHOLM BRIDGE
Name given to the footbridge which crosses the river Ayr, linking Craigie Campus and
Holmston Road. The bridge was erected in 1974.[1] In 1988,[2] the name was approved as
CRAIGHOLM ROAD, for one of the main streets on an estate built on the lands of the
demolished Holmston Farm.

CRAIGHOLM ROAD   See CRAIGHOLM BRIDGE

CRAIGIE
The family of Wallace of Craigie held the estate of Craigie near Kilmarnock from at least the
15th Century; towards the end of the 16th century they were confirmed in proprietorship of
Newton Castle (see, inter alia, Garden Street), where they lived until c.1701. c.1730 the
family built Craigie House, a mile or so inland, as the main family residence. In the late 18th
Century the estate passed to the Campbell family, and was purchased from them by the
Town Council in 1939 for £12,500.[3] The house still exists - it reopened in 1998 as the
Ayrshire Business Centre - and the core of the estate has been developed as the Craigie
Campus of the University of Paisley (until 1993 Craigie College of Education). Being close
to Ayr, the estate has been subject to continual pressure for industrial and residential
development. The Craigie colliery was worked in the 1860s by Robert Brown.[4] The estate
has given its name to these streets: CRAIGIE AVENUE (which is referred to as CRAIGIE
STREET in a Town Council minute of December 1902)[5], CRAIGIE ROAD[6], CRAIGIE
WAY and CRAIGIE LEA.[7] See also Craigholm Bridge, Fothringham Road and James
Campbell Road.

CRAIGIE AVENUE   See CRAIGIE

CRAIGIE COTTAGES
Obsolete name for 73-75 John Street, now demolished: houses built c.1856 for James
Campbell of Craigie.

CRAIGIE LEA   See CRAIGIE

---

[1] Ken Andrew's Guide to the Kyle and Carrick District of Ayrshire, Ayr, 1981, 35.
[2] SAL, Kyle and Carrick District Council Minutes 1988-89, 421, Planning and Building
     Control Committee 5th October 1988.
[3] SAL, Ayr Town Council Minutes 1939-40, 26, Cleansing Committee 21st December 1939.
     The estate was acquired in 1783 by William Campbell "who, we believe, was the architect
     of his own fortune, which he acquired chiefly in India". [James Paterson, History of the
     County of Ayr, Vol. 1, Edinburgh, 1852, 341.]
[4] See BROWN'S SQUARE.
[5] SAL, Ayr Town Council Minutes 1902-03, 22, Works Committee 3rd December 1902. This
     may be a clerical error, as there is no other evidence that this name was used.
[6] Craigie Road was opened in 1897-98 as an approach road from Whitletts Road to the
     Victoria Bridge, q.v., and, according to the Ayr Advertiser of 21st May 1896, 4d, in which
     these proposals were first publicised, created "an extensive and valuable piece of feuing
     ground". See also Fothringham Road.
[7] Craigie Way and Craigielea were approved in December 1950. [SAL, Ayr Town Council
     Minutes 1950-51, 236. Works Committee 22nd December 1950].

CRAIGIE PARK TERRACE
Unauthorised or obsolete name which was incorporated in the official names of streets as 5-23 Fothringham Road.[1] Plans of these houses were approved in 1903: the developer was a Mrs Adam Fullarton.[2]

CRAIGIE ROAD See CRAIGIE

CRAIGIE STREET See CRAIGIE

CRAIGIE TERRACE
Original name of 55-71 and 64-90 John Street. These houses, now demolished, were built c.1860 on land feued from the Craigie estate.

CRAIGIE WAY See CRAIGIE

CRAIGLEUR TERRACE
Terrace of c.1878, which was subsequently incorporated in the official names of streets as 30-40 Carrick Road.[3] No particular reason for this name has been identified..

CRAIGMILLAR BUILDINGS
In King Street and Limond's Wynd: Built by Thomas Millar, licensed grocer (b.c.1854, d.1899), from 1897, to provide 'healthy dwellings for the working classes, at moderate rents'.[4] The name appears to be an informal one, obviously modelled on the proprietor's name. More formal names are MILLAR'S LAND and, for the flats at 65 King Street, FRONT BUILDINGS. their 'unfit' condition was noted by the Town Council in May 1953,[5] and they were acquired by the Town Council for demolition in 1954. By 1956 it was noted that 'there will be few regrets at the passing of Spion Kop. It is one of Ayr's well-known landmarks, but for many years it has been a sadly outmoded structure'.[6] Millar's Land was demolished c.1957, and Front Buildings followed c.1962.

CRAIGSHIEL PLACE
Name approved in April 1976.[7] No particular reason for this name has been identified.

CRAIGSTEWART CRESCENT
Name approved in January 1973.[8] No particular reason for this name has been identified.

---

[1]   1910-1911 Directory, 246, List of Erased Terraces, Etc.
[2]   AA, Ayr Dean of Guild Court plans, box no.14, plan no.29.
[3]   1910-1911 Directory, 246, List of Erased Terraces, Etc.
[4]   Ayr Advertiser, 13th May 1897, 7a. See also Millar's obituary in Ayr Advertiser, 31st August 1899, 4d, where it is said that he 'has left his mark on the district by erecting a few years ago large blocks of dwellinghouses for the working classes, at the junction of Cross Street and Limond's Wynd'.
[5]   SAL, Ayr Town Council Minutes 1953-54, 37, Health Committee 29th May 1953.
[6]   Ayrshire Post, 1st June 1956, 13c.
[7]   SAL, Kyle and Carrick District Council Minutes 1975-76, 608, Planning and Building Control Committee 14th April 1976.
[8]   SAL, Ayr Town Council Minutes 1972-73, 264, Works Committee 15th January 1973.

CRAIGSTON AVENUE
This name was approved by the Town Council in September 1937, on a suggestion of the developer, Edward Ecrepont.[1] It appears to be a purely fanciful invention.

CRAIGWEIL PLACE
Also CRAIGWEIL ROAD. Names date from 1920s; the formation of Craigweil Road being approved in April 1920;[2] The names are taken from the house, 2 Craigweil Road, (now Ayr Youth Hostel) which was known as 'Craigweil'. With Carleton Turrets and Westfield, this was one of a group of large villas erected by David Reid, upholsterer, in 1879. The names appear to have been chosen randomly by Reid. The first tenant of Craigweil was George Coats, who subsequently moved to Belleisle. The owner of Craigweil from c.1934 until his death in 1960 was the bus and plane pioneer, John Cuthill Sword.

CRAIGWEIL ROAD   See CRAIGWEIL PLACE

CRANESBILL COURT   See BRACKEN PARK

CRAWFORD'S CLOSE
In 1861 Census enumerators' books this name is applied to houses at 99 High Street: the proprietor at this period appears to have been William Crawford, smith and bellhanger. He was b.c.1830, and appears to have left Ayr in the early 1860s.

CROCUS BANK   See BRACKEN PARK

CROFTHEAD ROAD
Name approved in April 1965.[3] Crofthead was a farm on the road leading from Holmston to the Coylton-Dalrymple Road (cf Cloverhill): it is now the site of Masonhill Crematorium and a caravan park which occupies the site of an old smallpox hospital built in 1903.[4] Like Cloverhill it has presumably been borrowed on account of its local associations and pleasant sound.

CROMWELL LANE   See CROMWELL PLACE

CROMWELL PLACE
Name dates from c.1857. The derivation is identical to that of Cromwell Road, but while Cromwell Road is a renaming of a road with an 'unpleasant' name, the opposite process took place in Cromwell Place. In June 1935, the Town Council agreed to a request from the residents to renumber Cromwell Place as part of Citadel Place: the residents presumably did not wish to be associated with the Lord Protector, though the fact that Citadel Place and Cromwell Place were on opposite sides of the same piece of road may also have influenced

1   SAL, Ayr Town Council Minutes 1936-37, 267, Works Committee 8th September 1937.
2   SAL, Ayr Town Council Minutes 1919-20, 221, Works Committee 7th April 1920.
3   SAL, Ayr Town Council Minutes 1964-65, 358, Works Committee 19th April 1965.
4   John Strawhorn, The History of Ayr, Edinburgh, 1989, 191.

the request.[1] CROMWELL LANE is recorded as the name for the lane off Citadel Place which runs behind Ayr Academy.[2]

CROMWELL ROAD

While obviously associated with the Fort or Citadel, built under the orders of Oliver Cromwell, this is not one of the names adopted by John Miller for his development of the Fort (see, inter alia, Ailsa Place). Cromwell Road leads to the site of Ayr's first gas works and was, initially, in consequence, called GAS WORK ROAD: it is also recorded as GAS WORKS LANE. Unsurprisingly, pressure from the residents led the Town Council in April 1902 to agree to a name change.[3] One of the houses in Gas Work Road was Cromwell Cottage, and this appears to have suggested the new name.

CROOKSMOSS BOWLING GREEN

In 1949 the Town Council agreed that four old houses at Crooksmoss should be vacated and demolished.[4] Crooksmoss Bowling Green opened in 1955. Crooksmoss Drive was the name originally proposed in December 1977[5] for the road which eventually was named Whitfield Road. The origin of the name remains obscure.

CROOKSMOSS DRIVE   See CROOKSMOSS BOWLING GREEN

CROSBIE PLACE

Original name, from c.1860, for 21-27 Northfield Avenue, and probably named, for no particular reason, after Crosbie near Troon.

CROSS LANE   See LIMOND'S WYND

CROSS STREET

The main east-west street running from Newton Steeple through Wallacetown. It appears to have been so named because it ran 'across' Wallacetown, rather than from any cross that may have existed.[6] As one of the main streets of the Newton/Wallacetown area it had, in the late 19th Century, a bad reputation, as a haunt of thieves, beggars, prostitutes and other ne'er-do-wells, and in January 1905, Ayr Town Council agreed to rename it KING STREET, in response to a petition from the residents first presented in September 1904.[7] The name CROSS STREET was revived in May 1974 for the short street running between

---

[1]   SAL, Ayr Town Council Minutes 1934-35, 196, Works Committee 5th June 1935.
[2]   For example in SAL, Ayr Town Council Minutes 1954-55, 66, Works Committee 25th June 1954, where the Committee authorise the pointing of the archway in Cromwell Lane.
[3]   SAL, Ayr Town Council Minutes 1901-02, 109, Corporation, 14th April 1902. According to the Ayr Advertiser, 17th April 1902, 6b, the change was requested as the old name hindered letting of the houses. The proprietors had suggested ESPLANADE ROAD.
[4]   SAL, Ayr Town Council Minutes 1949-50, 238, Housing Committee 19th December 1949.
[5]   SAL, Kyle and Carrick District Council Minutes 1977-78, 476, Planning and Building Control Committee 21st December 1977.
[6]   John M Short, Street Names, in Annie I Dunlop, ed., The Royal Burgh of Ayr, Edinburgh, 1953, 79, suggests however that Newton Market Cross originally stood close to Newton Church, and gave the name to the street.
[7]   SAL, Ayr Town Council Minutes 1903-04, 228, Works Committee 7th September 1904.

Garden Street and John Street,[1] which separates the ASDA supermarket from its car park. See also Four Corners.

CROSSBURN
Name approved in January 1973.[2] This short street crosses the small burn which flows through the Burton development.

CROSSHILL PLACE
Short-lived name used in the 1891 Census, for houses at 56 Green Street. Probably named for the Ayrshire village, but no particular association has been established.

CROWN STREET
Name dates from 1922, when it was agreed to rename Clunes Vennal. Crown Street presumably chosen to give the street a tone not conveyed by the superceded name, but see Clunes Street.

CULZEAN ROAD
Name approved in December 1969.[3] Culzean Castle is the Ayrshire seat of the Kennedys, Marquises of Ailsa, and a nationally renowned attraction.

CUMBRAE COURT   See RIVERSIDE PLACE

CUMNOCK ROAD   See HOLMSTON ROAD

CUNNINGHAM CRESCENT
Also CUNNINGHAM DRIVE and CUNNINGHAM PLACE. Names date from c.1954: 'Cunningham' was one of four names approved for streets in Forehill in October 1954,[4] while Cunningham Place was specifically approved in November 1954.[5] James Cuninghame, 14th Earl of Glencairn (b.1749, d.1791) was, according to Burns, 'my best friend, my first and dearest patron and benefactor: the man to whom I owe that I am and have!'[6] Cunningham Drive leads off GLENCAIRN ROAD, which was approved - with the other Forehill 'Glen' names - in November 1952.[7]

CUNNINGHAM DRIVE   See CUNNINGHAM CRESCENT

CUNNINGHAM PLACE   See CUNNINGHAM CRESCENT

CUNNING PARK DRIVE
Name of street dates from 1965,[8] but it is derived from the house known as Cunning Park which lay between the Esplanade and Doonfoot Road. This name can be traced as far back

[1]   SAL, Ayr Town Council Minutes 1974-75, 19, Works Committee 20th May 1974.
[2]   SAL, Ayr Town Council Minutes 1972-73, 264, Works Committee 15th January 1973.
[3]   SAL, Ayr Town Council Minutes 1969-70, 256, Works Committee 15th December 1969.
[4]   SAL, Ayr Town Council Minutes 1954-55, 159, Finance Committee 6th October 1954.
[5]   SAL, Ayr Town Council Minutes 1954-55, 202, Works Committee 2th November 1954.
[6]   Quoted in James A Mackay, ed., The Complete Letters of Robert Burns, Ayr, 1987, 226.
[7]   SAL, Ayr Town Council Minutes 1952-53, 209, Works Committee 21st November 1952.
[8]   SAL, Ayr Town Council Minutes 1965-66, 335, Works Committee 19th April 1966.

as the mid 16th Century.[1] Although it is recorded in one source as Cunningham Park, with the inference that it is associated with a bearer of the common Ayrshire surname, it is probable that the derivation is from Coney Park, a park or field frequented by coneys or rabbits. Rabbits may have been warrened here as a source of meat.

CURTECAN PLACE
Short street off Chalmers Road, built in the grounds of the house called Curtecan, now 47 Carrick Road. The house was built c.1881 by Gavin Girdwood (b.c.1828, d.1901). The street name was approved by the Town Council in October 1935.[2] The name Curtecan however is much older: 'per Curtecan usque ad capud Curtecan' (... by Curtecan to the head of the Curtecan ...) being part of the description of the boundaries of Ayr in the Charter of Foundation granted by William the Lion in 1205. The meaning of the name, which is probably Gaelic in origin, is not known. The Curtecan Burn is usually, these days, known as the Belleisle or Slaphouse Burn, and is some way from Curtecan Place.

DAISY COTTAGES
Name dates from c.1887. Presumably a purely fanciful name.

DALBLAIR ARCADE	See DALBLAIR ROAD
DALBLAIR BUILDINGS	See DALBLAIR ROAD
DALBLAIR COURT	See DALBLAIR ROAD
DALBLAIR QUADRANT	See DALBLAIR ROAD

DALBLAIR ROAD
Dalblair Road dates from at least 1830, DALBLAIR ARCADE was approved in June 1966.[3] The latter is on the site of, and the road follows the back boundary of, Dalblair House, a grand house built by James Gibb, a local industrialist in the 1790s,[4] and demolished, after many years as the Hotel Dalblair, to make way for the shopping development, and the extension to Hourston's department store. Dalblair is a farm and small estate in the upland reaches of the parishes of Cumnock and Auchinleck. Gibb called his house Somerset House: it seems to have acquired the name Dalblair House in the 1820s, when it was owned by David Limond, town clerk of Ayr (b.c.1772, d.1854), who was also laird of Dalblair. DALBLAIR VILLAS, now 42-44 Dalblair Road, were built c.1858; DALBLAIR

---

[1]   Michael Wallace of Cunning Park was Provost of Ayr on three occasions between 1560 and 1575. [John Strawhorn, The History of Ayr, Edinburgh, 1989, 283], while Simon Simpson had a distillery here in the late 18th Century. [Michael S Moss & John R Hume, The Making of Scotch Whisky, Edinburgh, 1981, 237]

[2]   SAL, Ayr Town Council Minutes 1934-35, 293, Works Committee 8th October 1935.

[3]   SAL, Ayr Town Council Minutes 1966-67, 59, Works Committee 20th June 1966. A request from the developers that the name be DALBLAIR SHOPPING PRECINCT was rejected by the Town Council in July 1966 (*ibid*, 90, Corporation 11th July 1966).

[4]   '... Dalblair House, the property of a gentleman of the name of Gibb, who had amassed a little fortune by exercising the trade of a soap-boiler, by which he was enabled to build the elegant mansion near his works, in the hope, it was said, of attaining by a matrimonial alliance then in view a fortune equal to the requirements of a large establishment'. [James Morris, Recollections of Ayr Theatricals from 1809, Ayr, 1872, 4-5]

TERRACE, of c.1880, was an unauthorised or obsolete name which was incorporated in the official names of streets as 17-25 Dalblair Road,[1] while DALBLAIR BUILDINGS was the name given to 32-40 Alloway Street, single storey shops built c.1895.[2] DALBLAIR QUADRANT was the name given, c.1906, to 4-10 Dalblair Road. DALBLAIR COURT is the name given, c.1986, to the development at 47 Dalblair Road. Dalblair Aracde was upgraded and improved in 1997 and rechristened ARRAN MALL.

DALBLAIR SHOPPING PRECINCT   See DALBLAIR ROAD

DALBLAIR TERRACE   See DALBLAIR ROAD

DALBLAIR VILLAS   See DALBLAIR ROAD

DALMELLINGTON ROAD
As the road leading to Dalmellington, this is a name with a long history. The section nearest Ayr was renamed Castlehill Road in 1894.[3] The name is now formally used for the section between the roundabout at Castlehill Church and the by-pass at Bankfield Roundabout. Various more-or-less fanciful meanings are ascribed to Dalmellington, 'Dame Helen's Town' being the most persistent if least likely. It was called Dalmellingtoun in 1275, and Johnston[4] suggests this is the Gaelic, *dail meallan*, field among a cluster of knolls or hills (which would suit geographically), with the addition of an English, *ton*, a village or settlement. Cf also DALMILLING, below.

DALMILLING CRESCENT
The name is recorded, before 1214, as Dalmulin, from the Gaelic for the field of the mill.[5] According to Groome, 'Dalmullin or Dalmilling, a place in St Quivox Parish, Ayrshire, 1¾ miles E by N of Ayr. A Gilbertine priory was founded here in 1230 by Walter, Lord High Steward of Scotland; but in 1238 it became a cell of Paisley Abbey'.[6] No trace of the priory exists, and the name in the 1800s was restricted to a farm (spelled Dalmelling on the 1st edition Ordnance Survey map). This is turn gave its name to an Ayr Town Council housing development wherein may be found DALMILLING CRESCENT, DALMILLING DRIVE and DALMILLING ROAD.[7] Prior to the incorporation of Whitletts into Ayr in 1935, Ayr County Council built some houses there: among these was DALMILLING PLACE, of c.1929, which was incorporated into Main Road in 1957: the house numbers were unchanged.[8] Even earlier, DALMILLING ROW was the name given to a row of five houses which belonged to the Oswalds of Auchincruive, became 1-9 Main Road c.1924, and were demolished c.1957.

[1]   1910-1911 Directory, 246, List of Erased Terraces, Etc.
[2]   Illustrated in Ayr Advertiser, 30th May 1895, 5ef.
[3]   Ayr Advertiser, 19th April 1894, 5a.
[4]   James B Johnston, Place-Names of Scotland, London, 1934, 151.
[5]   James B Johnston, Place-Names of Scotland, London, 1934, 152.
[6]   Francis H Groome, Ordnance Gazetteer of Scotland, Vol II, Edinburgh, 1882, 340.
[7]   These three names were approved in February 1947. [SAL, Ayr Town Council Minutes 1946-47, 121, Housing & Town Planning Committee 24th February 1947]
[8]   SAL, Ayr Town Council Minutes 1956-57, 332, Works Committee 25th April 1957. 1-23 Dalmilling Place became 1-23 Main Road.

DALMILLING DRIVE	See DALMILLING CRESCENT
DALMILLING PLACE	See DALMILLING CRESCENT
DALMILLING ROAD	See DALMILLING CRESCENT
DALMILLING ROW	See DALMILLING CRESCENT

DAM PARK

Originally the informal name given to the field or park here, alongside the mill-dam of the Town or Nether Mills. Contractors to build a new Mill Dam Dyke at the Nether Mills were advertised for in 1816.[1] The public hall here, built in 1960 and demolished in 1997, was known as DAM PARK HALL. This name was chosen in October 1960; other suggestions at the time being RIVERSIDE HALL and CRAIGIE HALL.[2]

DAMFIELD ROAD

The cottages listed as Damfield Road in the 1891 Census appear subsequently to have been incorporated into Gordon Terrace. Damfield Road presumably led from Content towards the field (now Dam Park) alongside the mill dam.

DAMSIDE

Name dates from at least mid 19th Century. This road ran alongside the dam which controlled the flow of water out of Newton Loch, which provided the power for Newton Mill. See also Lochside Road and Main Street.

DANDER ROW — See DANER ROW

DANER ROW

Name which appears on nine occasions in the 1830 Directory. There is a reference in the Air Advertiser, 1834, to 'Green Street or Dander Row'.[3] The name may be derived from the Scots word meaning a stroll or leisurely walk, or from 'dander' or 'danders', meaning the refuse of a smith's fire or clinker.[4]

DARLINGTON PLACE — See DARLINGTON ROAD

DARLINGTON ROAD

Also DARLINGTON PLACE. It has been stated that towards the end of the 18th Century, Lottery Hall (q.v.) 'was occupied as the residence of the Earl of Darlington who at that period was in command of a troop of horsemen that was encamped in Newton Green'.[5] Hence the road to Lottery Hall was known as the Earl of Darlington's Road, becoming in time Darlington Road[6] and later Darlington Place. Darlington Place gave its name to the church at the junction with Main Street (now a theatre), whose manse in Miller Road became the Darlington Hotel. There appear to have been three Earls of Darlington: Henry

---

[1] Air Advertiser, 8th February 1816, 1a.
[2] SAL, Ayr Town Council Minutes 1960-61, 133, Parks Committee 2th October 1960.
[3] Air Advertiser, 9th October 1834, 3f.
[4] The Concise Scots Dictionary, Mairi Robinson, ed., Aberdeen, 1987 ed., 134.
[5] Ardrossan and Saltcoats Herald, 28th December 1867, 4f.
[6] For example on Wood's Plan, 1818; Ayr Observer, 1st May 1832, 3b; Air Advertiser, 9th October 1834, 3f.

Vane, created first Earl in 1754, and died in 1758; his son, also Henry, succeeded in 1758 and died in 1792; Henry II's son, William Harry, succeeded in 1792, and was raised to the marquisate as Marquis of Cleveland in 1827. He became Duke of Cleveland in 1833. Darlington Road in listed in the 1910-1911 Directory as the unauthorised or obsolete name for 2-12 North Harbour Street,[1] though the renaming appears to have taken place c.1881.

DAVIDSON PLACE
Street of c.1879-80, developed by Thomas Milliken, builder (b.1828, d.1880). It was demolished in the 1960s and the name re-used for part of the new development. The surname is presumably meant, but who, if anyone, is specifically honoured, remains obscure.

DEAN PLACE
Unauthorised or obsolete name which was incorporated in the official names of streets as 29-43 McCall's Avenue,[2] for which plans were approved in 1898. The developer was Alexander Smith, builder.[3] Perhaps a reference to Dean Castle, Kilmarnock.

DICK'S SQUARE
Name given to houses at the west end of the north side of Main Road, Whitletts. They were built c.1861, and demolished c.1937. Though Dick is an Ayrshire surname, the reference may be to Richard A Oswald of Auchincruive (b.1841, d.1921), of which estate Whitletts was part.

DONGOLA ROAD
In April 1902, Ayr Town Council agreed to the proposal by John Murdoch, architect, to name his new road Dongola Road.[4] Dongola is a town in Sudan which had been captured by a British Expeditionary Force under Sir Horatio Kitchener in 1896.

DONNINI COURT
Name dates from 2000. Fusilier Dennis Donnini (b.1925, d.1945), who served with the Royal Scottish Fusiliers, was awarded the Victoria Cross, posthumously, for his gallantry in attacking an enemy held village in the Netherlands. The Royal Scottish Fusiliers had their headquarters in Ayr Barracks, the site of which is nearby. Donnini came from Easington in Co. Durham.[5]

DOOCOT ROAD
In 1871 a piece of land is described as bounded on the north by DUCAT ROAD and on the west by CONTENT TERRACE.[6] Neither has yet been accurately identified, though this road presumably led to the Doocot Ford from the Wallacetown side of the river. 'Close to the [Blackfriars] monastery was a pigeon-house, as the old charters tell; and a reminiscence

---

[1]   1910-1911 Directory, 246, List of Erased Terraces, Etc.
[2]   1910-1911 Directory, 246, List of Erased Terraces, Etc.
[3]   AA, Ayr Dean of Guild Court plans, box no.8, plan no.97. See also Cairnsmuir Place and Ebenezer Place.
[4]   Ayr Advertiser, 17th April 1902, 6a.
[5]   [Anon], The Register of the Victoria Cross, Cheltenham, 1988 ed., 91.
[6]   Ayrshire Sasine Abridgement, no.87 of 1871.

of it lingers in the "Doo-cot Ford", the ford across the river to which a lane from Mill Street leads down'.[1] This ford was close to the position now occupied by Turner's Bridge.

DOON TERRACE
Unauthorised or obsolete name which was incorporated in the official names of streets as 1-7 Carrick Avenue.[2] Named for the river and/or loch. The four houses in Doon Terrace were built c.1882.

DOONBANK PARK
This name was approved in February 1953.[3] A small development close to the left hand bank of the Doon, and built on land which had been part of Doonbank Farm.

DOONFOOT ROAD
Old-established name, formally restricted to that part of the A719 road to Dunure and Doonfoot between the junction at Seafield Road and the bridge at Doonfoot. Doonfoot is at the mouth of the river Doon, where the river debouches into the sea.

DOONGATE
Name in use by 1348, and apparently an early name for the Sandgate: the road leading to the Doon. See reference under Sandgate.

DOONHOLM PARK	See DOONHOLM ROAD
DOONHOLM PLACE	See DOONHOLM ROAD

DOONHOLM ROAD
Also DOONHOLM PARK[4] and DOONHOLM PLACE.[5] Doonholm is a house of c.1760, built on lands formerly known as Berriesdam and Warlockholm, which were part of the lands of Alloway, sold by Ayr Town Council in 1754. Doonholm is a more refined name, reflecting its position close to the Doon, and retaining the -holm element (meaning 'meadow') from Warlockholm. Doonholm Road was so known by the mid 19th Century, while Doonholm Park and Doonholm Place are small developments off Doonholm Road.

DORNOCH PARK
Name approved in July 1957.[6] Small development to one side of, and behind, the house, 27 Racecourse Road, known at that time as Dornoch. The name is presumably taken from that of the county town of Sutherland, but a connection has not yet been determined. This house was originally known as Smith Villa, after Andrew Smith, miller, Alloway Mills (b.c.1779, d.1850), for whom it was built c.1833. It was apparently renamed Dornoch by David Wilson Paton, timber merchant (b.c.1861, d.1941), who tenanted the house between c.1890 and c.1900.

---

[1]   John H Pagan, Annals of Ayr in the Olden Time: 1560-1692, Ayr, 1897, 4-5.
[2]   1910-1911 Directory, 246, List of Erased Terraces, Etc.
[3]   SAL, Ayr Town Council Minutes 1952-53, 315, Works Committee 20th February 1953.
[4]   Approved in February 1976: SAL, Kyle and Carrick District Council Minutes 1975-76, 519, Planning and Building Control Committee 25th February 1976.
[5]   Approved in October 1962: SAL, Ayr Town Council Minutes 1962-63, 140, Works Committee 25th October 1962.
[6]   SAL, Ayr Town Council Minutes 1957-58, 92, Works Committee 25th July 1957.

DOUBLE DIKES ROAD   See SEAFIELD CRESCENT

DOUGLAS LANE   See BOSWELL PARK

DOUGLAS PLACE
Original name for 94-98 New Road, which date from c.1878. The derivation is obscure, but presumably influenced by the name of the noble Scots family.

DOUGLAS STREET   See BOSWELL PARK

DRUMBOWIE PLACE
This name appears twice in the 1892-93 Directory, and is part of Boghall Row. It was probably short-lived, and possibly finally dropped when Boghall Row became the more refined Victoria Street in 1896. Drumbowie is a farm in Ochiltree parish, but no connection has been established.

DRUMELLAN ROAD
Name approved in June 1969.[1] It is borrowed from a farm in Maybole parish. A number of other streets in this part of the Rozelle development borrow names from farms in southern Ayrshire. The original intention to use names associated with the West Indies is discussed under Pemberton Valley.

DRUMMOND CRESCENT
Name approved in February 1947, along with DRUMMOND STREET, which appears never to have been used.[2] Part of the Thornyflat estate; High Thornyflat farm was occupied by John Drummond (b.1892, d.1971) when it was acquired by the Town Council. An informal policy of so honouring the previous occupier of land developed by the Town Council has also led to Farrell Place and Gemmell Crescent.

DRUMMOND STREET   See DRUMMOND CRESCENT

DUCAT ROAD   See DOOCOT ROAD

DUKE STREET
Name dates from c.1885; taken over as a public road in August 1892.[3] It ran off Wellington Street, so may be in honour of the soldier-politician, Arthur Wellesley, Duke of Wellington (b.1769, d.1852), but also runs parallel to Argyle Street, so the honour may be intended for that family. These streets were demolished as part of the comprehensive redevelopment of Wallacetown. The name DUKE TERRACE, approved in February 1973,[4] was given to a street in the new development.

DUKE TERRACE   See DUKE STREET

---

[1]   SAL, Ayr Town Council Minutes 1969-70, 68, Works Committee 16th June 1969.
[2]   SAL, Ayr Town Council Minutes 1946-47, 121, Housing and Town Planning Committee 24th February 1947.
[3]   Ayr Advertiser, 11th August 1892, 6c.
[4]   SAL, Ayr Town Council Minutes 1972-73, 301, Works Committee 20th February 1973.

DUMFRIES PARK
Approved as a streetname in February 1976.[1] It is borrowed from the nearby farm known as Dumfries Park, but the derivation of this name is unknown. Dumfries Park was part of the burgh lands of Alloway, and was sold in 1754 to John Crawford of Doonside. 'Dumfries Park and Clockranehill' were offered for sale in 1794.[2]

DUNEDIN PLACE
Terrace of c.1890, which was subsequently incorporated in the official names of streets as 5-11 Falkland Road.[3] Dunedin is a Gaelic transliteration of 'Edinburgh', often used in a poetical or literary manner, and also of a town, settled and founded by Scots, in New Zealand.

DUNLOP CRESCENT
Also DUNLOP TERRACE, which was approved in December 1954.[4] Dunlop Crescent was approved in February 1983.[5] Dunlop Terrace was built on land acquired by the Town Council from the Western Meeting Club, the then proprietors of the Racecourse, and the name was given in honour of Colonel Thomas Charles Dunlop (b.1878, d.1960), who had 'acted as a negotiator between the Club and the Town Council'.[6]

DUNLOP TERRACE   See DUNLOP CRESCENT

DUNURE ROAD
Used formally for that part of the A719, the road to Dunure, which lies south of the bridge at Doonfoot, but as 'the Dunure road' will have been long in informal use.

DUTCH MILLS   See MILLBRAE

EARLS WAY   See ABBOTS WAY

EAST PARK ROAD
Approved by the Town Council in September 1904.[7] The street is built on part of the former lands of the Newton Freemen, and may refer to one of their parks or fields. It also lies to the east of the Newton Park, which circumstance had suggested the first name proposed by the developers, PARK ROAD, which was rejected by the Town Council in June 1904.[8] The road was not, however, developed until 1937.[9]

EAST VENNEL   See CLUNES STREET

---

[1]   SAL, Kyle and Carrick District Council Minutes 1975-76, 519, Planning and Building Control Committee 25th February 1976.
[2]   Glasgow Journal, 18th November 1794, 3c.
[3]   1910-1911 Directory, 246, List of Erased Terraces, Etc.
[4]   SAL, Ayr Town Council Minutes 1954-55, 240, Housing Committee 28th December 1954.
[5]   SAL, Kyle and Carrick District Council Minutes 1982-83, 650, Planning and Building Control Committee 16th February 1983.
[6]   Ayrshire Post, 14th January 1955, 14b. Dunlop, who was proprietor of the Ayr Advertiser as well as active in the horse-racing world, was knighted in 1955.
[7]   SAL, Ayr Town Council Minutes 1903-04, 242, Corporation 12th September 1904.
[8]   SAL, Ayr Town Council Minutes 1903-04, 172, Works Committee 8th June 1904.
[9]   AA, Ayr Dean of Guild Court plans, box no.68, plan no.152.

EASTWOOD
Terrace built c.1887; its name subsequently incorporated in the official names of streets as 18-26 Hawkhill Avenue.[1] Their appears to be no specific reason for the name.

EBENEZER PLACE
Terrace of c.1897, built for Alexander Smith,[2] which was subsequently incorporated in the official names of streets as 53-59 McCall's Avenue.[3] This Hebrew word meaning 'stone of help', referring to the stone raised by Samuel to commemorate a defeat of the Philistines, was adopted by Puritans in the 17th Century,[4] and has been frequently adopted as the name of dissenting chapels in Wales. It appears to have been a popular name in the 19th Century, but modern minds usually fail to get past the associations with Dickens' Ebenezer Scrooge.

EDENHALL ROAD
Name approved by Ayr Town Council in March 1958.[5] Edenhall was a house or cottage on Prestwick Road, close to this site, and occupied by a Captain Charles Campbell in 1851, and advertised to let in 1862 by its proprietor, Mathew Adam, shoemaker (b.c.1813, d.1884), who had acquired lands here in 1848.[6] The derivation is obscure.

EGLINTON LANE   See EGLINTON TERRACE

EGLINTON PLACE   See EGLINTON TERRACE

EGLINTON TERRACE
Eglinton Terrace is the centrepiece of the development of the Fort or Citadel, begun by John Miller shortly after he acquired the land in 1854. It commemorates one of the previous owners of the Fort, the Montgomeries, Earls of Eglinton, whose seat was Eglinton Castle near Kilwinning. The service lane behind Eglinton Terrace was known as EGLINTON LANE: in the 1930s some houses were built off the lane, and in 1936 the Town Council agreed to a request from the householders to rename the lane EGLINTON PLACE.[7] The Eglintons played a prominent part in the history of both Ayr and Ayrshire. MONTGOMERIE TERRACE, which was originally called MONTGOMERIESTOUN TERRACE, honours their family name.[8] See also Bruce Crescent, Ailsa Place and, for additional references to the Montgomeries, Winton Buildings.

ELBA COURT   See ELBA STREET

ELBA GARDENS   See ELBA STREET

---

[1]   1910-1911 Directory, 246, List of Erased Terraces, Etc.
[2]   AA, Ayr Dean of Guild Court plans, box no.6, plan no.320.
[3]   1910-1911 Directory, 246, List of Erased Terraces, Etc.
[4]   E G Withycombe, The Oxford Dictionary of English Christian Names, 2nd ed., Oxford, 1950, 87.
[5]   Ayrshire Post, 14th March 1958, 20a.
[6]   Ayr Advertiser, 20th February 1862, 1d.
[7]   SAL, Ayr Town Council Minutes 1935-36, 237, Works Committee 8th July 1936.
[8]   More particularly it recognises the fact that in 1663, following the Restoration, the Citadel was given to Hugh, Earl of Eglinton, with the status of a burgh of barony, known as Montgomeriestoun.

ELBA STREET

Also ELBA COURT[1] and ELBA GARDENS. The name dates from the early 19th Century. It appears to be a gloating reference to the defeat of Napoleon, and his first imprisonment on the Italian island of Elba from May 1814 to February 1815. It is occasionally seen in early deeds as ELBOW STREET.[2] The initial section of Elba Street, running alongside St Margaret's R.C. Church, appears to have been known as CHAPEL BRAE when first developed; it is also referred to as CHAPEL STREET in Macarter's 1830 Directory.[3] There was formerly a service lane called ELBA STREET LANE,[4] while ELBA STREET HOSTEL, a local authority wardened development, was built in 1934. See also William Street.

ELBA STREET HOSTEL	See ELBA STREET
ELBA STREET LANE	See ELBA STREET
ELBOW STREET	See ELBA STREET
ELLISLAND CRESCENT	See ELLISLAND PLACE

ELLISLAND PLACE

Also ELLISLAND SQUARE. These names were approved in September 1951,[5] and continue the Burns theme in Forehill. Robert Burns farmed at Ellisland, near Dumfries, from 1788 to 1791; while at Ellisland he wrote, among other works, Tam o' Shanter. Ellisland had, however, been part of the first proposals for Burns-related names in August 1948, as ELLISLAND CRESCENT, but after some debate, this proposed street had been numbered as part of Leslie Crescent,[6] and it was a further three years before Ellisland was re-used. The whole idea of using these names appears to have caused some discussion within the Town Council. Councillor Thomas Paterson,[7] for instance, said, rather obscurely, that 'he was well aware that there was a keen desire by the Burns fraternity to associate the poet with the names of some of the new streets and he thought they had to be careful in the manner in which they did it'.[8]

ELLISLAND ROAD	See ELLISLAND PLACE

---

[1] Approved in February 1980. [SAL, Kyle and Carrick District Council Minutes 1979-80, 687, Planning and Building Control Committee 20th February 1980]

[2] Elbow Lane and its Norse equivalent, Finkle Street, are relatively common names for streets with a dog-leg or elbow-like bend, for example in Kendal, Westmorland. Ayr's Elba Street is straight.

[3] Entry for Robert Paton, tailor.

[4] So named by 1881, but previously known as BACK ROW, under which name it appears in the 1861 and 1871 Censuses. See the area description for Enumeration District 25 in the 1881 Ayr (Registration District 578) Census.

[5] Initially both streets were to be called ELLISLAND ROAD, but it was subsequently decided to use two names. [SAL, Ayr Town Council Minutes 1951-52, 123, Corporation 10th September 1951; *ibid*, 136, Works Committee 21st September 1951]

[6] SAL, Ayr Town Council Minutes 1947-49, 333, Works Committee 27th August 1948; ibid, 365, Corporation 13th September 1948; ibid, 378, Works Committee 24th September 1948.

[7] See PATERSON STREET.

[8] Ayrshire Post, 17th September 1948, 8de.

ELLISLAND SQUARE	See ELLISLAND PLACE
ELMBANK PLACE	See ELMBANK STREET
ELMBANK ROAD	See ELMBANK STREET

ELMBANK STREET
Late Victorian name which appears in the 1888-89 Directory. In the 1890-91 Directory it is usually called ELMBANK ROAD. The adjacent property in New Road was known as ELMBANK PLACE, and also first appeared in the 1888-89 Directory. Elmbank House, occupied by William McColm, coal and shipping agent, (b.c.1830, d.1892), appears in the 1878-79 Directory, and presumably lent its name, which appears to have been chosen for its euphony, to the subsequently development. Occasional Directory references to Ellembank Street preserve the Ayrshire pronunciation.

ENGLEWOOD AVENUE
Name dates from 1904. In February 1904 the developers of this area, George Docherty and William Kirkland, suggested three names to the Council: BERKLEY ROAD, Englewood Avenue and OAKLEY AVENUE. The Council decided that one name was sufficient and suggested they choose between BERKLEY AVENUE and Englewood Avenue. The following month, the Council approved Englewood Avenue.[1] All three names appear to be fanciful inventions. Englewood Avenue is not a big street, and it must be assumed that the original proposals were for a larger development.

ESPLANADE
Name dates from late 19th Century, when the sea-wall and promenade alongside were progressively built and extended by Ayr Town Council, though a correspondent of the Ayr Advertiser in 1866 had suggested that the committee considering a memorial to Provost Primrose Kennedy (b.c.1803, d.1863) should make 'a carriage drive to the Doon foot', which might be called KENNEDY DRIVE.[2] Originally an esplanade was a level space between a citadel and a town; only later did it acquire the meaning of a level space for walking or driving in. 'The whole idea for the improvement was taken by Mr [John] Eaglesham, the Burgh Surveyor, from the Esplanades at Gibraltar and other Mediterranean resorts, and its adaptation to the circumstances existing at Ayr promises to be a great success'.[3] In 1902 when the householders of Gas Works Road petitioned for a new name, they suggested ESPLANADE ROAD, but the Town Council approved a change to Cromwell Road (q.v.).

| *ESPLANADE ROAD* | See ESPLANADE |

---

[1]   SAL, Ayr Town Council Minutes 1903-04, 64, Works Committee 3rd February 1904; ibid, 106, Corporation 14th March 1904.
[2]   Ayr Advertiser, 1st November 1866, 4e. The memorial to Kennedy was a drinking fountain at the Sandgate / Fort Street junction, now shorn of its purpose and resited in Wellington Square Gardens.
[3]   Ayr Advertiser, 19th July 1894, 4g.

ETTRICK PLACE
Name approved in October 1974.[1] Probably named from the river in the Borders, and, although later in date, continues the inter-war pattern set by TEVIOT STREET, approved in July 1925,[2] and TWEED STREET, approved in October 1935,[3] both well-known Border rivers.

EWENFIELD AVENUE
Also EWENFIELD GARDENS, EWENFIELD PARK and EWENFIELD ROAD. The earliest of these names, Ewenfield Road, was adopted in 1894.[4] In 1786 the Ayr merchant David Ewen (b.c.1744, d.1826) acquired a piece of land from Ayr Town Council, and built a house on the land which he called, with due modesty, Ewenfield: the house still stands in Ewenfield Road. EWENFIELD AVENUE was approved in June 1934,[5] and EWENFIELD PARK in March 1936 'at the request of the householders'.[6]   Finally, EWENFIELD GARDENS was approved in October 1939.[7]

EWENFIELD GARDENS	See EWENFIELD AVENUE
EWENFIELD PARK	See EWENFIELD AVENUE
EWENFIELD ROAD	See EWENFIELD AVENUE
FAIRFIELD PARK	See FAIRFIELD ROAD

FAIRFIELD ROAD
This name was adopted in 1894, the street having previously been called Tollpark Road.[8] At that time there was only one property in the street, the house known as Fairfield Lodge, presently the Fairfield House Hotel: this property was acquired in 1818 by William Gunning Campbell of Fairfield (in Monkton parish) (b.1784, d.1857), and the house was in existence by 1830. A subsequent development off Fairfield Road has the name FAIRFIELD PARK.[9] The name is borrowed from Campbell's estate in Monkton.

FALKLAND PARK ROAD
Also FALKLAND PLACE[10] and FALKLAND ROAD.[11]   Faulkland House,[1] occupied by Major William Baird, is recorded in the 1837 Directory for Ayrshire. William Baird appears

1   SAL, Ayr Town Council Minutes 1974-75, 174, Works Committee 22nd October 1974.
2   SAL, Ayr Town Council Minutes 1924-25, 366, Works Committee 8th July 1925.   In October 1925 the Council rejected a petition from the householders to rename the street TEVIOT DRIVE. [ibid, 475, Works Committee 7th October 1925]
3   SAL, Ayr Town Council Minutes 1934-35, 293, Works Committee 8th October 1935.
4   Ayr Advertiser, 19th April 1894, 5a.
5   SAL, Ayr Town Council Minutes 1933-34, 205, Works Committee 6th June 1934.
6   SAL, Ayr Town Council Minutes 1935-36, 119, Works Committee 4th March 1936.
7   SAL, Ayr Town Council Minutes 1938-39, 320, Works Committee 4th October 1939.
8   Ayr Advertiser, 19th April 1894, 5a.
9   These flats were built c.1971, and known as 1-101 Fairfield Road. They became 1-101 Fairfield Park c.1986.
10   Approved in May 1924. [SAL, Ayr Town Council Minutes 1923-24, 259, Works Committee 7th May 1924]
11   In use by 1888: it is found in Ayrshire Sasine Abridgement no.5476 of 11th July 1888.

to have acquired land in this part of Newton in 1833, and erected a house shortly after, which he called Falkland House. This was demolished in 1968,[2] but not before it had lent its name to various developments as the area became increasingly residential. Named either directly after the royal burgh in Fife, or indirectly through the Cary family, created Viscount Falkland in 1620. The Falkland Islands were named, in 1690, after the 5th Viscount, who was a navy treasurer; it may be worth noting that British occupation of the Falkland Islands took place 'in 1833, following the expulsion of an Argentinian garrison'.[3]

FALKLAND PLACE   See FALKLAND PARK ROAD

FALKLAND ROAD   See FALKLAND PARK ROAD

FARRELL PLACE
Name approved in November 1966, 'for the development at Farrell's nursery'.[4] This nursery at Lochside belonged to Patrick Farrell (b. c. 1870, d. 1952), for whom greenhouses were first built in 1933.[5]

FELLHILL STREET   See BLACKHILL STREET

FENWICKLAND AVENUE
Also FENWICKLAND PLACE. Names approved in October 1955 (Fenwickland Avenue) and September 1957 (Fenwickland Place).[6] Fenwickland is a former farm, which still exists on Maybole Road. Strawhorn records Ayr aldermen in the early 15th Century called Reginald de Fynvyk and Nicholas de Fynvyk, and supposes that Fenwickland is named after this family.[7] Neighbouring FINNICK GLEN[8] derives from the farm shown on Roy's Military Survey, of c.1750, as Finyglen, which is perhaps a poor transliteration of Fenwickland.

FENWICKLAND PLACE   See FENWICKLAND AVENUE

FERGUSON STREET
This name occurs in Sasine Abridgements in 1886,[9] and appears to refer to the road now known as Hawkhill Avenue. It appears never to have been adopted. Hawkhill belonged to, and was developed by, James Murray Ferguson (b.c.1837, d.1916), proprietor of the Ayr Observer, politician and land-owner.

1   The spelling with a 'u', i.e. 'Faulkland', appears to be an error.
2   AA, Ayr Dean of Guild Court plans, box no.187, plan no.88.
3   David Munro, The Oxford Dictionary of the World, Oxford, 1995, 211.
4   SAL, Ayr Town Council Minutes 1966-67, 219, Works Committee 21st November 1966.
5   AA, Ayr Dean of Guild Court plans, box no.57, plan no.6.
6   SAL, Ayr Town Council Minutes 1955-56, 167, Works Committee 27th October 1955;
     ibid, 1957-58, 126, Works Committee 26th September 1957.
7   John Strawhorn, The History of Ayr, Edinburgh, 1989, 31.
8   SAL, Ayr Town Council Minutes 1963-64, 139, Works Committee 24th October 1963.
9   e.g. in Ayrshire Sasine Abridgement no.765 of 21st May 1886.

FERGUSON STREET
This name was approved by the Town Council in May 1935.[1] Names approved at the same time honoured the Provost (Galloway) and a councillor (Murray), but no particular reason for this name has been found. It may be a belated honour for James M Ferguson (see previous entry).

FERN BRAE	See BRACKEN PARK
FIELD BANK	See MOUNT CHARLES CRESCENT
FINLAS AVENUE	See BRADAN DRIVE
FINNICK GLEN	See FENWICKLAND AVENUE
FIR BANK	See ALDER BANK

FISH CROSS
Semi-formal name for the widening of High Street at its junction with Hope Street and Old Bridge Street. Here stood a cross at which the fish salesmen, usually fishwives, gathering to ply their trade. Strawhorn quotes a 1547 decree that 'na kynd of stuff be sauld in tyme comyn at the fyshe cross but fysh',[2] while Dillon notes that much of the commerce of Ayr was centred here: 'here, from its pedestal, burghal proclamations were given forth and Kirk Session disciplines publicly carried out. It was the Town Cross of Ayr in all but name'.[3] The cross was taken down in 1854.[4]

FLAXTON COURT
Built in 1874, the house at 1 St Leonard's Road was originally known as Isalea. During the ownership, from 1922, of William Boyd Anderson (b.c.1850, d.1935) it was known as Flaxton House, and this name was transferred to this development in the grounds, approved in 1965. The developer was the Ayr builder Donald C McLean.[5] Flaxton is a small village north-east of York, and no reason for Anderson's choice of house name has been discovered.

FLESHMARKET CLOSE
In 1830 the Fleshmarket was at 98 High Street, and this close would have led from the High Street to the market. This market had been built in 1764: its importance declined when the town's trading privileges were abolished in 1848, and it is called the 'Old Fleshmarket' by 1858.

---

[1]   SAL, Ayr Town Council Minutes 1934-35, 179, Corporation 13th May 1935. An extension was approved in November 1945. [SAL, Ayr Town Council Minutes 1945-46, 16, Works Committee 26th November 1945]

[2]   John Strawhorn, The History of Ayr, Edinburgh, 1989, 39.

[3]   William J Dillon, Fairs and Markets, in Annie I Dunlop, ed., The Royal Burgh of Ayr, Edinburgh, 1953, 191.

[4]   The Ayr Advertiser, 23rd November 1854, 4a, reported that it had been removed about a fortnight previously.

[5]   AA, Ayr Dean of Guild Court plans, box no.165, no.3.

FLORIDA TERRACE
Three terraces forming the west side of Falkland Park Road, built c.1895, which were subsequently incorporated in the official names of streets as 3-25 Falkland Park Road.[1] Named for the American state, but no particular connection has been established.

FORBES DRIVE   See CALLENDAR PLACE

FOREHILL ROAD
While the formal street name dates only from 1937,[2] Forehill is a name of some antiquity. It was a farm on the outskirts of Ayr until subsumed in the steady residential growth. The name may be supposed to mean the near or townward side of the hill, that is the hill known as Castlehill.

FOREST WAY   See ALDER BANK

FORGE ROAD
Approved by Kyle and Carrick District Council in September 1995.[3] The road is on the site of Dickie's Stamp Works in Seaforth Road.

FORT COURT   See FORT STREET

FORT STREET
Fort Street runs parallel to Sandgate and roughly follows the line of the back dykes or outer defences of the town on the sea-ward side. The Citadel or Fort was built by Cromwell's forces outside this back lane, and would have remained a prominent feature long after it ceased to have any military function. When the back lane was developed the name Academy Street was used, but Fort Street was in use by 1830. For the celebrations of Victoria's coronation in June 1838 decorated arches were erected across the streets, 'but far the most valuable arch was stretched across Fort Street, opposite Mr Templeton's manufactory, being hung with beautiful imitation Brussels carpets of varied hues and patterns'.[4] The flatted housing development of c.1996 at the junction of Fort Street and South Harbour Street is called FORT COURT. The houses at 47-49 Fort Street, lying between the Theatre and the Wesleyan Chapel, were known jocularly in the 19th Century as PURGATORY.[5]

FOTHRINGHAM ROAD
This names dates from c.1898: as with Craigie Road, feuing and development in this area was made possible by the construction of the Victoria Bridge. As originally planned, a road paralleling the railway would have extended as far as Whitletts Road.[6] Richard Frederick

---

[1]   1910-1911 Directory, 246, List of Erased Terraces, Etc.
[2]   SAL, Ayr Town Council Minutes 1936-37, 267, Works Committee 8th September 1937.
[3]   SAL, Kyle and Carrick District Council Minutes 1995-96, 281, Planning Applications Committee 19th September 1995.
[4]   Air Advertiser, 28th June 1838, 4b.
[5]   Ayr Advertiser, 12th June 1851, 3f. The theatre is now the Baptist Church and the Wesleyan Chapel now the offices of the Ayr Advertiser.
[6]   Ayr Advertiser, 21st May 1896, 4d, discussing the proposals for the new bridge and road between Holmston and Whitletts Road.

Fothringham Campbell (b.1831, d.1888) was proprietor of Craigie from 1860, and the name has been chosen in his honour.[1] See also James Campbell Road.

FOUL VENNEL
'There is much perplexity as to the location of this lane and much conjecture as to the meaning of its title. Some authorities aver that Foul Calsay led from the Sandgate to the Kirk of St John the Baptist. Others maintain that it is the Carrick Vennel under an alternative name. There is a mention of a vennel leading from the Foul Vennel to St John's and the map of 1775 shows a lane from the Carrick Vennel to the Sandgaithead, and perhaps across to the church. Perhaps the name may help to solve the difficulty. The popular belief is that the name is brutally apt, and that the Foul Vennel led to the Foul Moor where plague-stricken persons were kept in compulsory isolation because of the foulness of their condition. But if the name is directional - and it should be - the word 'foul' may be a corruption of the noun 'fauld' meaning a fold. If so, any vennel leading to the faulds could bear the name Foul Vennel. The cattle market's appellation of 'Fauldbacks' seems to add some support for the suggestion'.[2] Pagan states categorically that 'on the other side of the street from the Old Tower was the Carrick Vennel or, as it was commonly called, the Foul Vennel. Its name was no doubt derived from the wet piece of ground in which it terminated, known as the Stank Acre'.[3] Pryde records that in 1552-53 Ayr Town Council paid 17s for calsay-mending in the Foul Vennel.[4]

FOUR CORNERS
Vernacular name for the junction of Cross (King) Street and Wallace Street, the heart of Wallacetown. In the late 19th Century it was, to the people of Ayr, synonymous with lawlessness and poverty, a land of brothels and shebeens. There is a photograph of the demolition of the last of the Four Corners in the Ayr Advertiser of 14th January 1960. Ironically, the main building at the junction nowadays is Ayr's Police Headquarters.

FOXGLOVE PLACE   See BRACKEN PARK

FRIARS' VENNEL
An alternative name for Kirkport (q.v.). The church, to which Kirkport leads, stands on the site of the Friary of the Fransiscans, or Greyfriars, established here in 1472-74.

FRONT BUILDINGS   See CRAIGMILLAR BUILDINGS

FRONT STREET
The name used in the 1841 Census for part of modern North Harbour Street, which fronts the river.

---

[1] Campbell spells his name without an 'e', and this should be regarded as the correct spelling. Many sources however adopt the correct-looking Fotheringham.
[2] William J Dillon, The Streets in Early Times, in Annie I Dunlop, ed., The Royal Burgh of Ayr, Edinburgh, 1953, 71-72.
[3] John H Pagan, Annals of Ayr in the Olden Time: 1560 - 1692, Ayr, 1897, 55.
[4] George S Pryde, ed., Ayr Burgh Accounts 1534 - 1624, Edimburgh, 1937, 118.

FULLARTON STREET
Fullarton Street is marked on Wood's Plan (1818), but not named. The name is in use by the 1830 Directory, which would tend to suggest that the honour is for Provost William Fullarton of Skeldon (b.c.1775, d.1835), the founder, in 1802, of the village of Patna.

FULSHAW CRESCENT
Name approved in September 1955.[1] It appears to have been derived from the nearby, and still extant, farm name, Fulshawwood.

GADGIRTH'S VENNEL
Pagan refers to the existence of a ford a little above the Auld Brig, 'which was reached by Gadgirth's Vennel'.[2] The vennel was at 68-70 High Street, and was known as the 'lairde of Gaitgirthis Vennel' in 1559. Gadgirth is an estate in the parish of Coylton.[3]

GALLOWAY AVENUE
Thomas Galloway (b.1859, d.1946) was Provost from 1933 to 1936, a position he held when this name was approved in May 1935.[4] He was a cabinetmaker; born in Glasgow, he worked for many years for the old-established Ayr cabinetmakers, Afflecks, before setting up his own firm, Galloway & Bowie.[5]

GALLOWAY CRESCENT
Terrace of c.1877 which was subsequently incorporated in the official names of streets as 49-79 Russell Street.[6] Probably named for the area of south-west Scotland. The developer was J. M. Ferguson (see Ferguson Street).[7]

GARDEN COURT   See GARDEN STREET

GARDEN PARK
Obsolete name for 34-36 Miller Road, built c.1871 on part of the Garden Park of Barns House.

GARDEN STREET
Also GARDEN COURT. Garden Street dates from the late 18th Century, and refers to the garden of Newton Castle, which stood here. From the late 16th Century, Newton Castle was the main residence of the Wallaces of Craigie: it appears to have been badly damaged in a storm c.1701, and its successor, Craigie House, was built c.1730. Titles of properties in

---

[1]   SAL, Ayr Town Council Minutes 1955-56, 134, Works Committee 22nd September 1955.
[2]   John H Pagan, Annals of Ayr in the Olden Time: 1560 - 1692, Ayr, 1897, 62.
[3]   See James Hunter, The House of John Blair of Adamton, in Allan Leach and John Strawhorn, eds., Ayrshire Collections, 2nd series, vol.11, [Ayr], 1976, 109-132. See also MCKILL'S CLOSE.
[4]   SAL, Ayr Town Council Minutes 1934-35, 179, Corporation 13th May 1935.
[5]   Ayr Advertiser, 11th April 1946, 7a.
[6]   1910-1911 Directory, 246, List of Erased Terraces, Etc.
[7]   Ayrshire Post, 6th November 1931, 14cd.

Garden Street refer to them being part of the Old Gardens of Newton Castle. The name Garden Court was approved in August 1979.[1]

GARLEFFIN PARK
This name was approved by the Town Council in January 1973,[2] but never adopted. Garleffin is a farm close to Glenalla, and Garleffin Park would have been on the same Doonfoot development as Glenalla Crescent.

GAS ROAD   See GAS WORK ROAD

GAS WORK ROAD
Former name for Cromwell Road, q.v. This road led, unsurprisingly, to the first Ayr Gas Works, which was begun in 1826 by the British Gas Light Co., and extended in 1848 by the Ayr Gas Co. There is an 1857 reference to 'Cromwell Cottage, GAS ROAD',[3] and the street was also known as GAS WORKS LANE. Two houses at the gas works are listed in the 1881 Census as GAS WORKS SQUARE.

GAS WORKS LANE   See GAS WORK ROAD

GAS WORKS SQUARE   See GAS WORK ROAD

GAVIN HAMILTON COURT
This name was approved in 1985,[4] and is another of the Burns-related names in Forehill. Gavin Hamilton (b.1751, d.1805) was a writer in Mauchline, and one of Burns' early patrons.

GEARHOLM ROAD
Name approved in April 1964.[5] It derives from the adjacent mansion house, Gearholm or Gairholm, now 4 Abercromby Drive. The name is recorded as 'ye Zairholm of Alloway' in 1586, which suggests that this was a holm close to a yair or fish-weir.[6]

GEMMELL CRESCENT
Name approved by the Town Council in August 1938.[7] John Gemmell was the proprietor of Braehead Farm, some of which he sold to the Town Council. He also developed part of the farm on his own account.

GEMMELL'S CLOSE
Name used in 1919 to refer to the close at 207 High Street.[1] A posting and carriage hire business was established here c.1860 by Alexander Gemmell (b.1836, d.1892) and continued into the 20th Century under his son, John Dick Gemmell.

---

[1]   SAL, Kyle and Carrick District Council Minutes 1979-80, 207, Planning and Building Control Committee 1st August 1979.
[2]   SAL, Ayr Town Council Minutes 1972-73, 264, Works Committee 15th January 1973.
[3]   Ayrshire Sasine Abridgement no.1006 of 1857.
[4]   SAL, Kyle and Carrick District Council Minutes 1984-85, 898, Planning and Building Control Committee 27th March 1985.
[5]   SAL, Ayr Town Council Minutes 1963-64, 305, Works Committee 23rd April 1964.
[6]   David M Lyon, Ayr in the Olden Times, Ayr, 1928, 52-53.
[7]   SAL, Ayr Town Council Minutes 1937-38, 258, Works Committee 3rd August 1938.

GEORGE PLACE   See GEORGE STREET

GEORGE SQUARE   See GEORGE STREET

GEORGE STREET
Also GEORGE SQUARE, which was in use by 1977.   George Street is not on the
Armstrongs' map (1775), but does appear on Wood's Plan (1818): it was probably
developed in the 1780s and 1790s.   The name honours King George III, who reigned from
1760 to 1820.   GEORGE PLACE is used in the 1861 Census for part of the south-east side
of George Street between Content Street and James Street.

GEORGE'S AVENUE
Name approved in 1908, but only after a narrow vote (7 to 6) in the Council.   The
alternative name proposed was QUEEN MARY'S AVENUE.[2]   The first development in the
street was by George Wyllie, builder (b.c.1860, d.1931).

GILMOUR STREET   See CLUNES VENNEL

GLEBE CRESCENT   See GLEBE ROAD

GLEBE ROAD
Also GLEBE CRESCENT, which was approved in October 1930.[3]   Glebe Road was in
formal use by 1931, but may have had an earlier informal existence.   The streets constitute
the main part of a local authority housing development built on the site of the manse and
glebe of Newton upon Ayr.   Newton became a separate parish in 1779, a glebe was provided
in 1780, and a manse was built in 1787.[4]

GLENAFTON ROAD   See GLENCONNER ROAD

GLENALLA CRESCENT
Name approved in January 1973.[5]   Glenalla is a farm three miles south of Crosshill,
Ayrshire, whose name has been appropriated for its pleasant sound.

GLENCAIRN ROAD   See CUNNINGHAM CRESCENT

GLENCONNER PLACE   See GLENCONNER ROAD

GLENCONNER ROAD
Name approved in November 1952;[6] also GLENCONNER PLACE, which was in use by
1953.   Glenconner is a farm near Ochiltree.   In the late 18th Century it was tenanted by John

1	SAL, Ayr Town Council Minutes 1918-19, 252, Public Health Sub (Insanitary Houses) Committee 29th May 1919.
2	SAL, Ayr Town Council Minutes 1908, 225, Works Committee 8th July 1908; ibid, 233, Corporation 13th July 1908.
3	SAL, Ayr Town Council Minutes 1929-30, 442, Works Committee 31st October 1930.
4	John Strawhorn, The History of Ayr, Edinburgh, 1989, 112.
5	SAL, Ayr Town Council Minutes 1972-73, 264, Works Committee 15th January 1973.
6	SAL, Ayr Town Council Minutes 1952-53, 209, Works Committee 21st November 1952. The same meeting also approved Glencairn Road and Glenriddel Road, as well as GLENAFTON ROAD, which was not used. These four names form an interesting Burns sub-group.

Tennant (b.1725, d.1810), factor to Lady Glencairn, and a friend both to Burns' father and to the poet.[1]

GLENDALE CRESCENT
Also GLENDALE PLACE. These names were approved in October 1955,[2] and are close to Annfield Glen Road. The name has presumably been based on that name, as no local connections have been discovered.

GLENDALE PLACE   See GLENDALE CRESCENT

GLENIFFER PLACE
Unauthorised or obsolete name, in use from c.1880, which was incorporated in the official names of streets as 3-5 Miller Road.[3] Gleniffer Braes are a well-known beauty spot with views across Paisley and Glasgow.

GLENMOUNT PLACE
Name approved in January 1973.[4] No particular reason for the choice of this name has been established.

GLENMUIR COURT
Approved in January 1985.[5] Also GLENMUIR PLACE (name given by Ayr County Council to houses it built from the late 1920s) and GLENMUIR ROAD (approved in November 1945).[6] Presumably chosen for its pleasant sound. Glenmuir Place was renumbered c.1952, when many houses were given new addresses in Glenmuir Road and Main Road.[7]

GLENMUIR PLACE   See GLENMUIR COURT

GLENMUIR ROAD   See GLENMUIR COURT

GLENPARK PLACE
Name approved in October 1962.[8] No particular reason for the choice of name has been established.

GLENRIDDEL ROAD
This name was approved in November 1952.[9] Robert Riddell of Glenriddell (2 'l's) (b.1755, d.1794/95) was a friend of Burns, especially while Burns was at Ellisland, and for

[1] James Mackay, ed., The Complete Letters of Robert Burns, 2nd ed., Ayr, 1990, 222.
[2] SAL, Ayr Town Council Minutes 1955-56, 167, Works Committee 27th October 1955.
[3] 1910-1911 Directory, 246, List of Erased Terraces, Etc.
[4] SAL, Ayr Town Council Minutes 1972-73, 264, Works Committee 15th January 1973.
[5] SAL, Kyle and Carrick District Council Minutes 1984-85, 652, Planning and Building Control Committee 9th January 1985.
[6] SAL, Ayr Town Council Minutes 1945-46, 16, Works Committee 26th November 1945.
[7] 2-32 Glenmuir Place became 4-34 Main Road and 34-56 Glenmuir Place became 1-23 Glenmuir Place, while 58-72 Glenmuir Place became, respectively, 56,58,52,54,48,50,44 and 46 Glenmuir Road.
[8] SAL, Ayr Town Council Minutes 1962-63, 140, Works Committee 25th October 1962.
[9] SAL, Ayr Town Council Minutes 1952-53, 209, Works Committee 21st November 1952. See also Glenconner Road.

him Burns compiled two volumes of poems and prose in manuscript, which became known as the Glenriddell Manuscripts.[1]

GORDON PLACE
Unauthorised or obsolete name which was incorporated in the official names of streets as 2-20 George Street.[2] These properties were built on land feued from John Taylor Gordon of Blackhouse in 1851 and 1853: the name is obviously in recognition of this fact. J T Gordon (b.c.1802, d.1884) was an entrepreneur who played a substantial part in the development of the coal field and industries of Wallacetown, Annbank and elsewhere. Originally from Aberdeenshire, he inherited Blackhouse from his mother, Jane Taylor.[3] See also Taylor Street.

GORDON STREET
This name dates from the 1890s. The honour is obscure: it is close to Campbell Street.

GORDON TERRACE
This name dates from c.1860. The honour is probably meant for J T Gordon of Blackhouse. See Gordon Place.

GORDON'S ROW
Name given in 1861 to the bulk of the south side of Main Road, Whitletts. It is no doubt again a reference to J T Gordon of Blackhouse (see Gordon Place); these houses appear to have become known later as Blackhouse Crescent.

GORSE PARK   See BRACKEN PARK

GOSCHEN TERRACE
Name dates from c.1898. George, Viscount Goschen, (b.1831, d.1907) was a British politician who held various cabinet posts; he was Chancellor of the Exchequer, 1887-1892. A Liberal, he disagreed with his party (and its leader, Gladstone) over proposals to extend the franchise and to give home rule to Ireland; as a result he was one of the founders of the Liberal Unionist party. His politics were presumably to the taste of the builder of the street, Alexander Smith.

GOUKSCROFT COURT
Also GOUKSCROFT PARK. These names date from the 1960s,[4] and derive from a farm-cum-nursery that formerly stood here. Presumably a croft or parcel of land frequented by

---

[1] James Mackay, ed., The Complete Letters of Robert Burns, 2nd ed., Ayr, 1990, 480.
[2] 1910-1911 Directory, 246, List of Erased Terraces, Etc.
[3] J T Gordon's obituary is in Ayr Advertiser, 26th June 1884, 4d.
[4] In April 1964 the Town Council approved the name GOWKSCROFT, rather than the GOWKSCROFT PARK suggested by the developer, but this decision was reconsidered in June 1964, and Gowkscroft Park approved. [See SAL, Ayr Town Council Minutes 1963-64, 305, Works Committee 23rd April 1964, and *ibid* 1964-65, 56, Works Committee 25th June 1964]. The change from Gowkscroft to Goukscroft happened almost immediately: certainly by March 1967 the Council agreed to take no action in response to a request for a name change from four residents in Goukscroft Park who felt the name 'is not pleasant and poses difficulties in spelling and pronunciation'. [SAL, Ayr Town Council Minutes 1966-67, 385, Works Committee 20th March 1967].

cuckoos, rather than by fools. In January 1851 the Ayr Advertiser carried an advert from 'John Smith, Goukscroft Nursery, successor to the late Patrick McKenna'.[1]

GOUKSCROFT PARK   See GOUKSCROFT COURT

GOULD STREET
Name approved in February 1932.[2] James Robertson Gould (b.c.1865, d.1938) was Provost of Ayr from 1924 to 1927, and a Councillor from 1905 to 1933. Gould was born in Edinburgh, and brought up in Glasgow. The 'rags-to-riches' story which took him from a lodging house at the Four Corners (q.v.) to a position as a draper and house-furnisher, and Ayr's first citizen, earned Jimmy Gould the soubriquet 'Ayr's Dick Whittington'.[3]

GOWANBANK ROAD
Name approved in October 1961,[4] and presumably chosen for its pleasant associations: a 'bank of daisies'.

GOWER PLACE
Name approved in November 1968.[5] With Linfern Place (q.v.) continues the loch theme in this area. Loch Gower is near Drumlamford House on the road between Barrhill and Newton Stewart.

GOWKSCROFT   See GOUKSCROFT COURT

GOWKSCROFT PARK   See GOUKSCROFT COURT

GRANGE AVENUE   See BRADAN DRIVE

GREEN STREET
Also GREEN STREET LANE. Name dates from the early 19th Century: Wood's Plan, 1818, perhaps in error, attaches the name Green Street to what appears to be York Street Lane, calling modern Green Street, John Street. Green Street is the central street through a 'new town' laid out from 1803 by the Freemen of Newton on part of the Newton Green.[6] This is part of the Newton Freedom lands which had, until then, been held in common and used for grazing livestock and the collection of fuel and sea-wrack. Green Street Lane runs behind Green Street: it is called GREEN STREET VENNEL in the 1841 Census. See also Daner Row.

GREEN STREET LANE   See GREEN STREET

GREEN STREET VENNEL   See GREEN STREET

GREENAN GROVE   See GREENAN ROAD

GREENAN PARK   See GREENAN ROAD

---

[1]   Ayr Advertiser, 30th January 1851, 1f.
[2]   SAL, Ayr Town Council Minutes 1931-32, 115, Works Committee 3rd February 1932.
[3]   See his obituaries in Ayrshire Post, 6th May 1938, 8cde, and ibid, 13th May 1938, 8a.
[4]   SAL, Ayr Town Council Minutes 1961-62, 142, Works Committee 26th October 1961.
[5]   SAL, Ayr Town Council Minutes 1968-69, 200, Works Committee 18th November 1968.
[6]   SAL, B6/27/6, Newton Community Minute Book 1802 - 1819, 30-31.

GREENAN PLACE   See GREENAN ROAD

GREENAN ROAD
Also GREENAN GROVE, GREENAN PARK, GREENAN PLACE and GREENAN
WAY. Names adopted at various dates for roads in the Doonfoot-Greenan area, part of the
old barony of Greenan. Greenan Castle is still a prominent landmark on the nearby clifftop.
Johnston[1] suggests that Grenan in Bute, and Grennan in Penpont are derived from the Gaelic
'grianan', meaning 'a sunny spot, a summer house, a mountain peak', and a similar meaning
would seem appropriate here. Greenan Road was approved in May 1954,[2] Greenan Place in
June 1954,[3] the other three names in October 1982.[4]

GREENAN WAY   See GREENAN ROAD

GREENBANK TERRACE
Terrace of c.1863 which was subsequently incorporated in the official names of streets as
108-118 New Road.[5] The name seems fanciful and euphonious.

GREENFIELD AVENUE
Greenfield was one of the estates created after the sale of the barony lands of Alloway: it
was renamed Cambusdoon in 1854.[6] Greenfield Avenue was laid out by the Town Council
in 1755: the contractor was William Burnes, father of Robert Burns.[7] The name was in use
by 1851.

GREENTREE PARK   See ALDER BANK

GRIFFIN DOCK ROAD
One of the roads on the north side of Ayr Harbour. A modern name adopted by the harbour
authorities for both the road, and the adjacent wet dock. It commemorates the steam yacht
Griffin, belonging to John Baird of Knoydart (b.1852, d.1900), which was the first vessel
into the wet dock when it was officially opened in 1878.[8]

GROSVENOR TERRACE
Terrace of c.1901 which was subsequently incorporated, c.1910, in the official names of
streets as 2-20 Fothringham Road.[9] The proprietor, Samuel Hill (b.1856, d.1936),
complained unavailingly to the Council about the obliteration of his terrace.[10] Grosvenor is

---

1   James B Johnston, Place-Names of Scotland, London, 1934, 197.
2   SAL, Ayr Town Council Minutes 1954-55, 28, Works Committee 28th May 1954.
3   SAL, Ayr Town Council Minutes 1954-55, 64, Works Committee 25th June 1954.
4   SAL, Kyle and Carrick District Council Minutes 1982-83, 343, Planning and Building
     Control Committee 13th October 1982.
5   1910-1911 Directory, 246, List of Erased Terraces, Etc.
6   Ayr Advertiser, 4th May 1854, 4c.
7   See Thomas Limond, The Roup of the Lands of Alloway, in John Strawhorn, ed., Ayrshire
     at the Time of Burns, [Ayr], 1959, 188-189.
8   Ayrshire Post, 7th May 1886, 3b. Baird was a nephew of James Baird of Cambusdoon
     (b.1802, d.1876) who made a major financial contribution to the costs of the construction of
     the dock, but who died before it was completed.
9   1910-1911 Directory, 246, List of Erased Terraces, Etc.
10   SAL, Ayr Town Council Minutes 1910, 126, Works Committee 9th March 1910.

the family name of the Dukes of Westminster, and is frequently used to give pretension to streets, hotels and the like.

GUILTREEHILL
Name approved in June 1969.[1] Guiltreehill is a farm in Kirkmichael parish; the guil-tree is the berberis or wild barberry. The name has been borrowed for its euphonious quality.

HALL'S VENNEL
Name dates from at least 1822, when it was called MATHEW HALL'S VENNEL.[2] It is named NORTH VENNEL on Wood's Plan, 1818. There have been a number of Mathew Halls in Newton on Ayr. The best known was probably the musician - a fiddler and 'cello player - who died on 6th September 1847 in Peebles Street, aged 87. Hall was patronised by the 12th Earl of Eglinton and was frequently engaged at Eglinton Castle and Coilsfield.[3] In June 1906 it was proposed that Hall's Vennel be renumbered as part of Taylor Street,[4] but this appears never to have been carried out, for an identical proposal was approved by the Town Council in February 1975.[5]

HAMILTON CRESCENT
Name approved by Ayr Town Council in October 1933.[6] One of a set of names suggested by Leslie Hamilton Wilson, proprietor of Castlehill, (see Leslie Crescent). Hamilton may have been his mother's maiden name.

HARBOUR STREET   See SOUTH HARBOUR STREET

HAREBELL PLACE   See BRACKEN PARK

HARTFIELD ROAD
Name approved in 1907.[7] It was built on land that belonged to George Hart of Corsehill (b.1818, d.1903).

HARTHALL
This name was approved in December 1954: the original proposal was to call this street BROADWAY.[8] Broadway is presumably a reflection of the street's width, while Harthall incorporates a nod in the direction of the then Provost, Adam Hart.[9]

---

[1]   SAL, Ayr Town Council Minutes 1969-70, 68, Works Committee 16th June 1969.
[2]   It is so called in Ayrshire Sasine Abridgement no.979 of 1822, which records the sale of a piece of land to John Taylor.
[3]   Ayr Advertiser, 9th September 1847, 4g. A note on Hall in Ayrshire Post, 22nd March 1935, 3b, states that his elbow had been shattered while playing shinty, so that he could no longer play the fiddle, and was forced to take up the 'cello.
[4]   SAL, Ayr Town Council Minutes 1905-06, 220-221, Works Committee 22nd June 1906.
[5]   SAL, Ayr Town Council Minutes 1974-75, 310, Works Committee 18th February 1975.
[6]   SAL, Ayr Town Council Minutes 1932-33, 290, Works Committee 4th October 1933.
[7]   SAL, Ayr Town Council Minutes 1907, 321, Works Committee 9th October 1907.
[8]   SAL, Ayr Town Council Minutes 1954-55, 240, Housing Committee 28th December 1954. Broadway had been approved in February 1947. [SAL, Ayr Town Council Minutes 1946-47, 121, Housing and Town Planning Committee 24th February 1947]
[9]   Ayrshire Post, 14th January 1955, 14b. Hart (b.1885, d.1966) was Provost from 1952 to 1955, and a partner in the joinery business of Hart & Cumming. His obituary is in Ayrshire Post, 16th September 1966, 16ab.

HAVANNAH PLACE
Terrace of 1879 which was subsequently incorporated in the official names of streets as 1-7 Viewfield Road.[1] Transatlantic name, being the contemporary spelling of Havana in Cuba, a port with which Ayr had frequent trading links. The developer was the Ayr tobacco importer James Murray Ferguson, (see Ferguson Street).[2]

HAVELOCK TERRACE
Terrace of c.1858 which was subsequently incorporated in the official names of streets as 8-26 Miller Road.[3] Sir Henry Havelock (b.1795, d.1857) was a British soldier, a hero of the 1857 Indian mutiny: 'a close student of military affairs, a stern disciplinarian, austere though courteous in disposition, he won the confidence of his men and was regarded by the public as a hero'.[4]

HAWKHILL AVENUE
Name dates from 1894,[5] and is a 'prettification' of the earlier BACK HAWKHILL ROAD; see also Ferguson Street. A residential development roughly on the line of the lane which led to the farm of Hawkhill. BACK HAWKHILL AVENUE[6] more accurately follows the line of the old lane, while HAWKHILL LANE is a formal name for the back service lane to Hawkhill Avenue. The farm name presumably means a hill frequented by hawks.

HAWKHILL LANE   See HAWKHILL AVENUE

HAWTHORN DRIVE   See ALDER BANK

HAY HILL
Name approved in December 1950.[7] The derivation is not known, but it is probably based on the name of a field here prior to development.

HAZELWOOD ROAD
Name suggested by the Trustees of the Ayr Industrial School, on whose land it was built, and approved by Ayr Town Council on 14th July 1902. The house at 9 St Leonard's Road was built c.1895 for Robert Harvey, and named Brochdhu: he sold it c.1901 to James Gray, potato merchant, who renamed the house Hazelwood. The street presumably borrowed the name of this house at its corner, but no specific reason for the house name has been established.

HEATH PARK   See HEATHFIELD ROAD

HEATHER PARK   See BRACKEN PARK

---

[1]   1910-1911 Directory, 246, List of Erased Terraces, Etc.
[2]   SAL, B6/22/1, Committees of the Ayr Police Commissioners 1877-80, Plans Committee 24th April 1879.
[3]   1910-1911 Directory, 247, List of Erased Terraces, Etc.
[4]   Patrick Cadall, in Chamber's Encyclopaedia, New Revised Edition, London, 1970, vol VI, 777.
[5]   Ayr Advertiser, 19th April 1894, 5a.
[6]   Used in the 1925-26 Valuation Roll, replacing the earlier, more prosaic, 'Back of Hawkhill'.
[7]   SAL, Ayr Town Council Minutes 1950-51, 236, Works Committee 22nd December 1950.

HEATHFIELD ROAD
A name in formal use by the 1900s: a road which represents one of the tracks through the Newton Freedom Lands. Heathfield is a name of long standing, and suggests a field or park of a heathy nature. Heathfield Cottage existed in this area in the mid 19th Century, and the name was also used for the isolation hospital built here from 1900. (cf. Ward Court). HEATH PARK, in use from 1923, is a small street off Heathfield Road; its name is derived from its proximity to Heathfield Road.

HIGH ROAD
Name formally adopted in the 1920s. Two of the main routes from Ayr diverge at Whitletts, where a toll was established in the late 18th Century. One, the LOW ROAD, takes the lower ground, leading via Galston and Strathaven to Hamilton; the other, the High Road, keeps to a higher contour and leads to Mauchline, Muirkirk and beyond. 22-52 Low Road were the first local authority houses built by Ayr County Council in Whitletts, and were originally known as 1-16 Arran View.

HIGH STREET
The use of High Street as the name for the main street of a burgh or town is widespread, meaning the 'highest' of 'chiefest' street in the place. In 1585/86 Ayr Town Council paid 5s for 15 horses to take the gravel and rubbish off the High Street.[1] In Glasgow the present stature of High Street shows how the commercial heart of the city has shifted westwards, and in Edinburghit defines the Old Town: in Ayr the heart of the town has remained unchanged.

HIGHFIELD ROAD
This name was approved in October 1955.[2] On the Belmont South estate, and presumably the highest part of that scheme.

HIGH MAYBOLE ROAD   See MAYBOLE ROAD

HILARY CRESCENT
Name approved in September 1925.[3] Named at the same time as the adjacent Inverkar Road. Both names remain unexplained.

HILLFOOT CRESCENT
This name was approved in June 1958.[4] It is close to HILLFOOT ROAD, a long-established informal name for the road which runs along the lower slopes of Castle Hill. In 1990 part of Hillfoot Road was realigned during new residential development, and the bypassed stretch given the name OLD HILLFOOT ROAD, while retaining the same house numbers (1-27).[5]

HILLFOOT ROAD   See HILLFOOT CRESCENT

---

[1]   George S Pryde, ed., Ayr Burgh Accounts 1534 - 1624, Edinburgh, 1937, 155.
[2]   SAL, Ayr Town Council Minutes 1955-56, 167, Works Committee 27th October 1955.
[3]   SAL, Ayr Town Council Minutes 1924-25, 434, Works Committee 9th September 1925.
[4]   SAL, Ayr Town Council Minutes 1958-59, 50, Works Committee 26th June 1958.
[5]   SAL, Kyle and Carrick District Council Minutes 1990-91, 209, Planning and Building Control Committee 11th July 1990.

HILLTOP PLACE
Name adopted in April 1974.[1] This short street is at the very top of Castle Hill, a position which gives rise to the name.

HILLVIEW PLACE
This name was used from c.1866 to c.1884 for the houses at 78 Elba Street, which were probably built c.1850. The houses presumably had a view of hills.

HOLLOW PARK
Also HOLLOW PARK COURT. Hollow Park was approved in December 1967,[2] and Hollow Park Court was in use by late 1976. Obscure, but may be a result of the January 1967 decision that 'so far as applicable names of fields and places listed on the Ordnance Survey Maps be taken for the names of streets in the respective localities'.[3]

HOLLOW PARK COURT	See HOLLOW PARK
HOLLY BANK	See ALDER BANK
HOLMSTON CRESCENT	See HOLMSTON ROAD
HOLMSTON DRIVE	See HOLMSTON ROAD

HOLMSTON ROAD
Name adopted in 1894 for the main road to Cumnock and Edinburgh, previously known as the CUMNOCK ROAD.[4] It had been used earlier in the 1867/68 Directory as the address of Hugh Wyllie, miller, Over Mills. Holmston was a small estate alongside the road, which belonged to the Wallaces, and was sold to Oswald of Auchincruive in 1781. Two residential streets leading off Holmston Road have been named HOLMSTON CRESCENT and HOLMSTON DRIVE - these names were approved by the Town Council in April 1936.[5]

HOME FARM ROAD
Name approved in September 1977.[6] The street leads to the Home Farm of Rozelle. A home farm was a farm managed for the direct benefit - in terms of produce and financial gain - of the proprietor of an estate.

HONEYSUCKLE PARK	See BRACKEN PARK

HOPE STREET
Name used from c.1855 for the street which passes behind Winton Buildings and the site of the Tolbooth. Traditionally known to the people of Ayr as the BACK OF THE ISLE, in acknowledgement of this position. See also Isle Lane.

---

[1]   SAL, Ayr Town Council Minutes 1973-74, 373, Works Committee 15th April 1974.
[2]   SAL, Ayr Town Council Minutes 1967-68, 261, Works Committee 18th December 1967.
[3]   SAL, Ayr Town Council Minutes 1966-67, 340, Works Committee 20th February 1967.
[4]   Ayr Advertiser, 19th April 1894, 5a.
[5]   SAL, Ayr Town Council Minutes 1935-36, 154, Corporation 13th April 1936.
[6]   SAL, Kyle and Carrick District Council Minutes 1977-78, 223, Planning and Building Control Committee 7th September 1977.

HOUSTON'S CLOSE
Name used in the 1871 Census for houses at c.43 Main Street. It is probably a reference to William Houston, (b.c.1817, d.1879), engine driver and spirit dealer.

HOUSTOUN CRESCENT   See BELLEVUE CRESCENT

HOUSTOUN STREET   See BELLEVUE CRESCENT

HUNTER'S AVENUE
The present street replicates one of the lanes or paths through the Common Lands of the Freemen of Newton, known as Newlands Road (q.v.), and also informally known as Hunter's Avenue as it led to the property known as Hunter's Place, on the boundary between Newton and Prestwick. Hunter was a common surname among the Freemen, and the name presumably derives from one or more of these Freemen, but it has not been possible to determine which. In 1905 the Town Council fixed Hunter's Avenue as the name of the entire (and then developing) road between Northfield Avenue and Heathfield Road,[1] in an attempt to stamp out and prevent fragmentary naming in terraces, a tendency which they had also to address in McCall's Avenue, West Sanquhar Road and elsewhere.

HUNTER'S CLOSE
Name used for houses at c.21 Main Street in the 1871 Census. As noted above, Hunter is a common Newton surname, and no specific attribution has been established.

HUNTER'S PLACE
Name used initially for a property on the boundary with Prestwick, in existence by the 1850s. It is on the site now occupied by Heath Park. The name was also used for properties at 83-131 New Road, where land belonging to David Hunter, an Ayr solicitor, was sold for development from 1841. Thirdly, the name was used, from c.1884, for houses at 54-62 Viewfield Road, built by Hugh Hunter, builder (b.c.1858, d.1924).

INVERKAR ROAD
Name approved in September 1925[2] as a renaming of Chalmers Road East; the meaning is obscure. The original name dates from c.1896; for its meaning see Chalmers Avenue. The 1925 name change was to prevent confusion with Chalmers Road West, which became Chalmers Road.

IRIS COURT   See BRACKEN PARK

IRONWELL CLOSE
Mentioned in 1864,[3] in 1893[4] and again in 1987, when it is said to be the close at 160 High Street.[5] Perhaps a close with a water pump in it.

---

[1]   SAL, Ayr Town Council Minutes 1904-05, 176, Works Committee 3rd May 1905.
[2]   SAL, Ayr Town Council Minutes 1924-25, 434, Works Committee 9th September 1925.
[3]   Kilmarnock Weekly Post, 4th June 1864, 8e.
[4]   SAL, B6/19/13, Ayr Town Council, Committee Minutes 1892-94, 201-202, Street Improvements Committee 13th September 1893.
[5]   SAL, Kyle and Carrick District Council Minutes 1987-88, 494, General Purposes Committee 29th October 1987.

ISLE LANE

Obsolete name for Hope Street, which replaced it from c.1855. Hope Street is still informally called the Back of the Isle, i.e. behind the island of buildings in the width of High Street.[1] Isle Lane had a fairly poor reputation, and the new name may have been conferred in the hope of improving that image.

IVY PLACE   See ALDER BANK

JAIL GREEN

Semi-formal name for that part of the Low Green that lay between the Jail and the shore. It now parades as Place de St.Germain-en-Laye (q.v.). The Jail was built in 1817, and demolished in 1930, when it was replaced by an extension to the County Buildings.

JAMES STREET

Name dates from early 19th Century, appearing on Wood's Plan of 1818. It appears to have originally been called ST JAMES STREET and, in part, ST JAMES SQUARE, while a sasine reference of 1817 refers to JAMES'S STREET.[2] Who is honoured is unknown. Following the construction in 1826 of the Roman Catholic Church, St Margaret's, in John Street, 'the gap between the chapel and the brewery was soon filled up by buildings. Thence James Street was formed and built'.[3]

JAMES BROWN AVENUE

Name approved in April 1938,[4] given to one of the main streets through the estate built on Dalmilling Farm, Whitletts. James Brown (b.1862, d.1939) was an Ayrshire miner who became an MP and the first member of the 'working classes' to become His Majesty's Commissioner to the General Assembly of the Church of Scotland. His father was a weaver who rose to become a colliery manager, while Brown himself worked in the pits from the age of 12 until he was 43. He was born in Whitletts, and lived for much of his life in Annbank.[5] A true 'lad o' pairts', Brown was a hero and role model for many in Ayr.

JAMES CAMPBELL ROAD

Name approved in December 1950.[6] Part of a Town Council development on the Craigie estate. Named for James Archibald Campbell (b.1872, d.1939), son of R F F Campbell (see Fothringham Road), from whom he inherited Craigie in 1888. He was the last laird of Craigie prior to its sale to Ayr Town Council. CAMPBELL COURT is a short street off James Campbell Road: its name approved in October 1955.[7]

---

[1]   The 1837-38 Cess Roll distinguishes between ISLE (from Fish Cross to Newmarket Street) and ISLE LANE (Newmarket Street to High Street). SAL, B6/29/14, Valuation Rolls of Ayr 1789-1839.

[2]   Ayrshire Sasine Abridgement no.13506 of 1818. St James Street and St James Square are referred to in Air Advertiser, 9th October 1834, 3f.

[3]   James Howie, An Historical Account of the Town of Ayr, Kilmarnock, 1861, 52.

[4]   SAL, Ayr Town Council Minutes 1937-38, 167, Housing Committee 22nd April 1938.

[5]   Ayrshire Post, 24th March 1939, 10de.

[6]   SAL, Ayr Town Council Minutes 1950-51, 236, Works Committee 22nd December 1950.

[7]   SAL, Ayr Town Council Minutes 1955-56, 167, Works Committee 27th October 1955.

JOHN STREET
This name probably dates from at least 1787: in 1801 it is described as 'John's Street, proposed to be made'.[1] It is in the 1830 Directory as John Street.[2] This street, through Wallacetown and Content, is built in large part on land which belonged to the estate of Blackhouse, which was owned by a succession of John Taylors, and is presumably named in their honour. The name was given a new lease of life in May 1974, when it was approved as the name for part of the inner ring road.[3]

JOHN STREET   See CATHCART STREET

JUNIPER GREEN   See ALDER BANK

KATE'S AVENUE
Former informal name for Longhill Avenue. It is said that there was at one time a leper colony in this area, and that 'Kate' was the last leper. There appears to be no documentary evidence to support this.

KENNEDY DRIVE   See ESPLANADE

KENSAL TERRACE
Terrace of 1903-04 which was subsequently incorporated in the official names of streets as 1-19 Quail Road.[4] The name appears to be taken, perhaps oddly, from Kensal Green Cemetery in west London. 'Opened in 1833, the first of the eight new cemeteries started on a commercial scale, and with standards of mortuary hygience in contrast to the horrid conditions then general in inner London graveyards. Kensal Green is the largest of them and the one favoured by the most generous patrons'.[5]

KENSINGTON TERRACE
Built c.1858-59 by James Paton & Sons, builders, this terrace was incorporated in the official names of streets as 33-43 Miller Road.[6] Named after the royal palace and residential and museum district in west London.

KERSEPARK
Name approved in June 1969.[7] Kerse Park is a farm in Dalrymple parish, and its name has presumably been chosen for its euphonious quality.

---

[1]   Ayrshire Sasine Abridgement no.846 of 1881.
[2]   Note however that on Wood's Plan, 1818, 'John Street' is applied to the modern Elba Street, while John Street itself is marked as 'proposed street'.
[3]   SAL, Ayr Town Council Minutes 1974-75, 19, Works Committee 20th May 1974.
[4]   1910-1911 Directory, 247, List of Erased Terraces, Etc. The terrace was built for Matthew Smith, joiner. [AA, Dean of Guild Court plans, box no.14, plan no.5, and box no.15, plan no.65]
[5]   Bridget Cherry and Nikolaus Pevsner, The Buildings of England. London 3: North West, Harmondsworth, 1991, 468.
[6]   1910-1911 Directory, 247, List of Erased Terraces, Etc.
[7]   SAL, Ayr Town Council Minutes 1969-70, 68, Works Committee 16th June 1969.

KILBRANDON CRESCENT
Name approved in October 1989,[1] while KILBRANDON WAY was approved in March 1991.[2] Named, for no particular reason, after either the Argyll parish which includes Seil Island, or the sound between Arran and Kintyre.

KILBRANDON WAY   See KILBRANDON CRESCENT

KILLOCH PLACE
A name of c.1857, which has survived various attempts to absorb it into Beresford Terrace. Killoch, or Killauch, was part of the Burrowfield of Ayr,[3] and Killoch Cottage (now 1 Midton Road) was in existence by 1845.

KILMARNOCK STREET
Obsolete name, its meaning self-explanatory. It appears on Wood's Plan, 1818, and is named in the 1841 Census Enumerators' Returns. It was renamed as part of Wallace Street thereafter: the change was presumably partly caused by the creation of New Road, and the consequent reduction of importance of this road as a northern entrance to Ayr.

KILNBANK CRESCENT
Name approved in June 1979.[4] The street is close to the left bank of the river Ayr at a point where the River Ayr Walk passes a disused lime-kiln: this circumstance has presumably suggested the name.

KINCAIDSTON DRIVE
Name dates from 1970s: it is the main street through the traffic-segregated Kincaidston estate (see Bracken Park). The estate has been built on the site of Kincaidston Farm, a name which means a farm occupied by a family of the name Kincaid.

KINCAIDSTON ROAD
Name approved in November 1965 for what had been part of the farm road leading to Kincaidston Farm.[5] It was renamed Linfern Place, q.v., in 1979, presumably to avoid confusion with the substantial development on Kincaidston Farm on the opposite side of the railway.

KING STREET
In 1905 Ayr Town Council agreed to rename Cross Street (q.v.), which had a poor reputation, King Street.[6] The name presumably honours the former Prince of Wales, King

[1]   SAL, Kyle and Carrick District Council Minutes 1989-90, 512, Planning and Building Control Committee 18th October 1989.

[2]   SAL, Kyle and Carrick District Council Minutes 1990-91, 821, Planning Applications Sub-Committee 5th March 1991.

[3]   John Strawhorn, The History of Ayr, Edinburgh 1989, Map C7.

[4]   SAL, Kyle and Carrick District Council Minutes 1979-80, 149, Planning and Building Control Committee 20th June 1979.

[5]   SAL, Ayr Town Council Minutes 1965-66, 172, Works Committee 15th November 1965.

[6]   Ayr Advertiser, 19th January 1905, 5g. A petition had first been presented to the Council in September 1904, and was discussed by the Works Committee on 23rd December 1904. The Committee decided not to authorise the change, but this decision was reversed at the

Edward VII, who had ascended the throne in 1901. On 21st May 1959 the Town Council's Works Committee agreed to take no action with regard to a further proposed change of name.

KING GEORGE V PLAYING FIELD
A playing field was part of the proposals for the development of Dalmilling Farm between Whitletts and Heathfield Road. In March 1939 the Town Council agreed to accept a grant of £1000 from the King George's Fields Foundation towards the cost of the playing field, subject to adopting this name and erecting a formal entrance, with heraldic panels provided by the Foundation.[1] Due to delays, the playing field was not completed and opened until 1957.[2]

KING'S COURT
Street of flats close to King Street, which has obviously influenced the name. The name was approved in July 1959.[3]

KIRKHOLM AVENUE
The house now known as 2 Kirkholm Avenue was built c.1913,[4] but no further development took place until c.1930. When 'the building of the [United Free] Church opened up the surrounding ground for building purposes and a name had to be found for the road created, the name Barton Avenue was suggested in honour of Mrs Barton, but she declined and proposed instead Kirkholm Avenue, a name which was acceptable to the local authorities, and was adopted'.[5]

KIRKPORT
Long-established name for the port or street leading to the kirk. It has presumably been in use since the 1650s, when the Auld Kirk of Ayr was built on its present site. It was widened in 1723, as this would 'tend much to the conveniency of the inhabitants while they issue from the church'.[6] 'It was called in the old days the Friars' Vennel, and led to the Water of Ayr'.[7] A further alternative name is Common Vennel, q.v.

KNOLL PARK
This name was approved in October 1963,[8] and presumably refers to some local but unidentified landmark.

---

[1] Corporation meeting on 16th January 1905. [SAL, Ayr Town Council Minutes 1904-05, 40 (Works Committee) and 60 (Corporation)]

SAL, Ayr Town Council Minutes 1938-39, 106-107, Parks Committee 2nd March 1939.

[2] See Ayrshire Post, 12th July 1957, 15cd. At the formal opening it was noted that this was one of 506 memorial playing fields grant-aided by the King George's Fields Foundation, of which 86 were in Scotland.

[3] SAL, Ayr Town Council Minutes 1959-60, 83, Works Committee 23rd July 1959.

[4] AA, Ayr Dean of Guild Court plans, box no.27, plan no.10. The house is subsequently listed in Valuation Rolls as 'Kilberry, off Prestwick Road'.

[5] Ayr Advertiser, 22nd September 1955, 10b, quoting Thomas A Wilson's History of the Ayr U.F. Church. Mrs Barton has not been identified.

[6] David M Lyon, Ayr in the Olden Times, Ayr, 1928, 34, quoting from the minutes of Ayr Town Council.

[7] John H Pagan, Annals of Ayr in the Olden Time: 1560 - 1692, Ayr, 1897, 60.

[8] SAL, Ayr Town Council Minutes 1963-64, 139, Works Committee 24th October 1963.

KNOWE, THE
Properly known as 94-104 Midton Road. The Knowe is a villa of c.1842 built for James Heron of Dalmore (b.c.1811, d.1849), which has now been subdivided, and further houses have been built in the grounds. It is commonly supposed that the piece of land on which the house was built included the knowe, or raised hillock, on which the gallows were traditionally erected.[1]

KNOWEHOLM
This name was approved in May 1957,[2] and appears to have been chosen purely for its pleasant sound.

KYLE CENTRE   See KYLE STREET

KYLE COURT   See KYLE STREET

KYLE STREET
Long established road which is the continuation of High Street towards the hinterland of Ayr, that is, to the province of Kyle, of which Ayr is the head town. Now something of a backwater, but a glance at a street plan will show the relationship between High Street, Kyle Street, Castlehill Road and Holmston Road, a relationship which was destroyed when the railway was driven through in 1856. Kyle Street, as a name, seems to have first come into use in the 1850s, perhaps as a direct consequence of the changes wrought by the arrival of the railway. KYLE CENTRE, a shopping development off the High Street, opened in 1988, while KYLE COURT is a sheltered housing complex of c.1992 at the head of Kyle Street.

LABURNUM ROAD
Name approved in 1963.[3] A 'tree' name close to, but earlier than the Masonhill-Castlehill names (see Alder Bank), and presumably chosen for its pleasant sound.

LADYBANK COTTAGES
In use in Censuses from 1841 to 1881 for cottages which appear to be near Gordon Terrace and the head of Content Street. They have not been properly identified, and the name remains unexplained.

LAIGH MOUNT
Name approved in October 1962.[4] It probably continues a previous field name, but no corroborative evidence has yet been found.

LAMFORD DRIVE
Name approved in January 1973.[5] Lamford is a farm on the Dalmellington to Carsphairn Road: its name presumably borrowed for its pleasant sound.

[1]   Alex F Young, The Encyclopedia of Scottish Executions 1750 to 1963, Orpington, 1998, 12.
[2]   SAL, Ayr Town Council Minutes 1957-58, 29, Works Committee 23rd May 1957.
[3]   SAL, Ayr Town Council Minutes 1963-64, 161, Works Committee 21st November 1963.
[4]   SAL, Ayr Town Council Minutes 1962-63, 140, Works Committee 25th October 1962.
[5]   SAL, Ayr Town Council Minutes 1972-73, 264, Works Committee 15th January 1972.

LAMLASH CLOSE
Off New Bridge Street. Presumably named after the Arran village, and indicative of the close links that once existed between Ayr and Arran. The name was in use by 1851.[1]

LANCASTER TERRACE
Terrace built c.1893 by William Clarke, builder.[2] It was subsequently incorporated in the official names of streets as 45-63 Bellevue Crescent.[3] No particular reason for the choice of name has been established.

LANDAU BUILDINGS
Unauthorised or obsolete name which was incorporated in the official names of streets as 17-23 Burns Statue Square.[4] A landau is a carriage with a folding top, allegedly first made at Landau in the Rhine Valley: these properties were built in 1894 for John Mains, coachbuilder.

LANDSBURGH HOUSE
A hostel for the homeless, in South Harbour Street, was formally opened on 12th March 1992, and named for Councillor James Landsburgh (b.1936, d.1991) 'in recognition of [his] work for the people of Kyle and Carrick'.[5] It was replaced in 1995 by this purpose-built hostel in Wallacetown, to which the name was transferred.

LANG STREET   See BELLEVUE CRESCENT

LANHAM CRESCENT
In 1962 the Town Council approved this name for the houses at Braehead being built to replace the temporary aluminium houses there. It was to honour William Lanham (b.1899, d.1980), Provost between 1958 and 1961.[6]

LANSDOWNE ROAD
This name was approved in 1905.[7] A name which, in various spellings, offers pretension, and is thus popular as a name for residential streets. The origin of the name seems to be Lansdown near Bath, which gave its name to the Fitzmaurices, Marquises of Lansdowne. Henry, the 5th Marquis (b.1845, d.1929) was successively Governor-General of Canada, Viceroy of India and, from 1900 to 1905, Foreign Secretary.

LARCHWOOD ROAD   See ALDER BANK

LARGHILL LANE   See BLACKHILL STREET

---

[1]   Ayr Advertiser, 12th June 1851, 4b. The Ayr Advertiser, 7th February 1850, 4c, refers to Lamlash Corner.
[2]   AA, Ayr Dean of Guild Court plans, box no.1, plan no.36.
[3]   1910-1911 Directory, 247, List of Erased Terraces, Etc.
[4]   1910-1911 Directory, 247, List of Erased Terraces, Etc.
[5]   SAL, Kyle and Carrick District Council Minutes 1991-92, 1737, Housing Committee 6th February 1992.
[6]   Ayrshire Post, 30th November 1962, 15c. However Lanham, whose professional life had been as an insurance official, refused the honour, and the name Cowan Crescent substituted.
[7]   SAL, Ayr Town Council Minutes 1904-05, 119, Works Committee 8th March 1905.

LAUGHLANGLEN ROAD
This name was approved in September 1959.[1] The name presumably continues an older name for the land here, but no corroborative evidence has yet been found.

LAUREL BANK   See ALDER BANK

LAWSON STREET
Name approved by Ayr Town Council in February 1932.[2] For whom the honour is intended has not been discovered.

LEEWARD PARK   See PEMBERTON VALLEY

LESLIE CRESCENT
Name approved by Ayr Town Council in October 1933.[3] It is on Castlehill property, owned at that time by Leslie Hamilton Wilson of Castlehill (b.1884, d.1968).[4] See also Hamilton Crescent, Lothian Road and St. Phillans Avenue.

LIBERATOR DRIVE
Name approved initially as LIBERATOR ROAD in November 1993, with Drive substituted for Road by March 1994.[5] It commemorates the Liberator aircraft of the Return Ferry Service which used Heathfield Aerodrome from 1941, and in particular honours the 22 men who were killed when a Liberator crashed at Whitletts on 14th August 1941.[6] This development is built on part of the Aerodrome.

LIBERATOR ROAD   See LIBERATOR DRIVE

LILYBANK TERRACE
Terrace built c.1901.[7] It was subsequently incorporated in the official names of streets as 98-108 Hunter's Avenue.[8] A fanciful name, borrowed from Lilybank (later 96 Hunter's Avenue), the adjoining house.

LIME WALK   See ALDER BANK

---

1   SAL, Ayr Town Council Minutes 1959-60, 118, Works Committee 24th September 1959.
2   SAL, Ayr Town Council Minutes 1931-32, 115, Works Committee 3rd February 1932.
3   SAL, Ayr Town Council Minutes 1932-33, 290, Works Committee 4th October 1933.
4   Wilson was the son of a muslin manufacturer in Paisley; he himself was a stockbroker in Glasgow. He gave the land on which Castlehill Church was built, partly in memory of his son, Larry, killed in the Prestwick air crash of Christmas Day 1954.
5   SAL, Kyle and Carrick District Council Minutes 1993-94, 366, Planning Applications Committee 30th November 1993; *ibid*, 579, Planning Applications Committee 29th March 1994.
6   Personal communication from Stanley Sarsfield, Ayr. The developers of the retail park had initially suggested a name such as BRABAZON WAY, after the Bristol Brabazon, an airliner of the 1950s, until it was realised that the Brabazon, though big and impressive (attributes with which they wished their park to be associated) was also an expensive flop and something of a white elephant.
7   AA, Ayr Dean of Guild Court plans, box no.12, plans nos. 31 and 46. The developer was John Buchanan from Govan.
8   1910-1911 Directory, 247, List of Erased Terraces, Etc.

LIMEKILN ROAD
In 1881 the Ayr Police Commissioners approved a plan of a limekiln which was to be built by Richard Anderson near the works of Weir & Co (see Weir Road).[1] This road name presumably came into use thereafter.

LIMOND'S COURT   See LIMOND'S WYND

LIMONDS WYND
Also LIMONDS COURT.[2] Limonds Wynd is a long-established name, first recorded in 1837.[3] In the late 19th Century it is often found as Lymond's Wynd, while what appears to be Limond's Wynd is named on Wood's Plan, 1818, as CROSS LANE. A property in this area was owned from 1776 to 1778 by David Limond (b.c.1744, d.1819), who was for many years Town Clerk of Ayr.[4] The street signs to the north of King Street give the name as Limonds Wynd; those to the south as Lymonds Wynd.

LINDSAY ROAD   See LINDSAY STREET

LINDSAY STREET
Name approved in November 1945, as LINDSAY ROAD.[5] Named in honour of Thomas Lindsay Robb (b.1881, d.1960), who retired in May 1946 after 32 years service as Town Chamberlain of Ayr. He was the son of James Robb, a farmer from Hindsward Farm, Skares, and his wife Hannah Lindsay. T L Robb was a kind and pleasant man, and an unassuming gentleman: 'if more people had been like him the world would have been a better place'.[6] Robb had presumably been consulted about the name: his natural modesty perhaps causing him to suggest his mother's maiden name rather than his own surname, though the potential for confusion with Robsland Avenue may also have been a consideration.

LINDSTON PLACE
Name approved in June 1969.[7] The name, chosen for its pleasant sound, has been borrowed from a farm in the parish of Dalrymple.

---

[1] SAL, B6/22/2, Ayr Burgh Police Commissioners, Minutes of Committees 1880-82, 63, Works Committee 7th January 1881. Anderson is listed as 'Limekiln, Newtonhead' in the Directory for 1882-83.

[2] Approved in November 1984, defeating the alternative proposal Cowan Court, 4-2. [SAL, Kyle and Carrick District Council Minutes 1984-85, 491, Planning and Building Control Committee 7th November 1984]

[3] As 'Limont's Lane' in Pigot's Directory of Ayrshire, 1837: the address of William Hunter, blanket, flannel and plaid manufacturer.

[4] Ayrshire Sasine Abridgement no.3771 of 1837.

[5] SAL, Ayr Town Council Minutes 1945-46, 16, Works Committee 26th November 1945.

[6] See Robb's obituary in Ayrshire Post, 1st April 1960, 13ef. P A Thomson, the Town Clerk, was honoured at the same time as Robb, while the Burgh Surveyor, John Young, had been honoured in the 1930s. Between them these three officials ran Ayr Town Council for over thirty years. See THOMSON STREET and YOUNG STREET.

[7] SAL, Ayr Town Council Minutes 1969-70, 68, Works Committee 16th June 1969.

LINFERN PLACE
The former Kincaidston Road was renamed Linfern Place in October 1979.[1] The name continues the loch and reservoir theme in this area, as Linfern Loch is about four miles south of Straiton.

LISBURN ROAD
Name dates from c.1907,[2] and is presumably borrowed from the town in County Antrim. The reason for this isolated choice is unclear.

LOANING, THE
This name was approved in October 1962,[3] and 'will perpetuate the ancient right of way between the clachan of Alloway and the old-time Ayr to Dalrymple road'.[4] Lot 7 at the roup of the Barony Lands of Alloway in 1754 is described as 'Alloway Loanings and Glebe'.[5] A small development off The Loaning is named UPPER LOANING, this name being approved in March 1972.[6]

LOCHLEA DRIVE
Name approved in August 1948.[7] It is one of the Burns-related names in Forehill: Burns' father tenanted Lochlea, a farm in Tarbolton parish, from 1777 until his death in 1784.

LOCHPARK
Name approved in May 1957 as Loch Park.[8] It is in the Doonfoot-Greenan area, remote from any loch.

LOCHSIDE COURT   See LOCHSIDE ROAD

LOCHSIDE ROAD
Also LOCHSIDE COURT.[9] Lochside Road was an informal name, now used formally, dating from the 19th Century for the road which originally ran alongside Newton Loch. The loch provided the water supply for Newton Mill, and was drained in the late 19th Century. See also Damside.

---

[1]   SAL, Kyle and Carrick District Council Minutes 1979-80, 363, Planning and Building Control.Committee 3rd October 1979.
[2]   AA, Ayr Dean of Guild Court plans, box no.19, plan no.69. The first developers were Alexander Smith & Sons, builders.
[3]   SAL, Ayr Town Council Minutes 1962-63, 140, Works Committee 25th October 1962.
[4]   Ayrshire Post, 16th November 1962, 16f.
[5]   Thomas Limond, The Roup of the Lands of Alloway, in John Strawhorn, ed., Ayrshire at the Time of Burns, [Ayr], 1959, 192.
[6]   SAL, Ayr Town Council Minutes 1971-72, 316, Works Committee 20th March 1972.
[7]   SAL, Ayr Town Council Minutes 1947-49, 333, Works Committee 27th August 1948.
[8]   SAL, Ayr Town Council Minutes 1957-58, 29, Works Committee 23rd May 1957.
[9]   Approved in February 1986. [SAL, Kyle and Carrick District Council Minutes 1985-86, 821, Planning and Building Control Committee 26th February 1986]

LONGACRE TERRACE
Terrace dated 1906, which was subsequently incorporated, c.1910, in the official names of streets as 1-17 West Sanquhar Road.[1] The proprietor, Robert Stewart, complained unavailingly to the Town Council about the obliteration of his terrace.[2] The name may have been a local name for one of the fields here.

LONGBANK DRIVE
Also LONGBANK ROAD. Names which date from the 1930s,[3] and which presumably recall some former feature on the Rozelle estate. See also the neighbouring Longlands Park.

LONGBANK ROAD   See LONGBANK DRIVE

LONGHILL AVENUE
Also LONGHILL PLACE. A long-established name for the lane or path, now a more-or-less residential road, linking the Dunure and Culroy roads, south of the Doon. Longhill was a farm close to the Dunure Road end. The trees that made Longhill Avenue a popular subject of early 20th Century picture postcards were felled in 1962.[4] See also Kate's Avenue.

LONGHILL PLACE   See LONGHILL AVENUE

LONGLANDS PARK
As a modern street name approved in 1963.[5] It is however an old field name as, in 1806, 'the Park of Longlands, in the parish of Air, lying east of Rozelle policy and most conveniently situated with regard to roads, water and shelter, [consisting] of near 40 acres of arable land, long rested, the lower part of which, along Slaphouse Burn, is of a deep, rich and fertile soil' was advertised for rent.[6]

LORNE ARCADE
Also known as Central Arcade (q.v.). This arcade dates from c.1904. On the site of the Lorne Temperance Hotel, which was an 'old established and well-known' hotel in the late 19th Century.[7]

LOTHIAN ROAD
Name approved by Ayr Town Council in October 1933.[8] It was suggested by Leslie Wilson of Castlehill (see Leslie Crescent), whose elder brother, George Lothian Wilson (b.1877) had died in 1930.

---

[1]   1910-1911 Directory, 247, List of Erased Terraces, Etc, which gives the new address as 19-35 West Sanquhar Road. The developer was John Stewart, builder. [AA, Ayr Dean of Guild Court plans, box no.16, plan no.67 (1904)]
[2]   SAL, Ayr Town Council Minutes 1910, 126, Works Committee 9th March 1910.
[3]   These names were adopted before this area was incorporated into the Burgh in 1935.
[4]   Ayrshire Post, 16th February 1962, 14ab.
[5]   SAL, Ayr Town Council Minutes 1963-64, 139, Works Committee 24th October 1963.
[6]   Air Advertiser, 15th May 1806, 1a.
[7]   Ayr Advertiser, 29th August 1878, 1b.
[8]   SAL, Ayr Town Council Minutes 1932-33, 290, Works Committee 4th October 1933.

LOTTERY HALL
Name of a house which used to stand in North Harbour Street, demolished in the winter of 1867-68 to make way for harbour improvements. It is said to have been built c.1787 by a Mr Vallance with 'the proceeds of a lucky speculation in the State Lottery'.[1]

LOVERS' LANE
A newspaper report in April 1868 refers to 'the corner of the Lovers' Lane, opposite Blackhouse'.[2] In 1875, when Hawkhill had changed hands, and was being developed for housing, a feuing plan was prepared and 'a road which was at one time much used by the public known by the name of Lovers' Lane, but which was shut up by the late proprietor, will be re-opened'.[3] This appears to be the lane running south-east from Hawkhill Bridge, shown on the 1st edition Ordnance Survey plan, though no modern street exactly replicates its position.

LOW ROAD   See HIGH ROAD

LYMBURN PLACE
Name approved in March 1954.[4] It honours the memory of Robert Lymburn (b.1858, d.1936), who had been the farm manager at Craigie, having worked there for more than 55 years. 'Mr Lymburn was a good farmer, and reared much stock that was a credit to the district'.[5]

LYMOND'S WYND   See LIMOND'S WYND

MACADAM PLACE
Also MACADAM SQUARE. Names approved in January 1968,[6] for part of the first phase of the redevelopment of Wallacetown, begun in January 1967 and completed during 1969. These names, however, are not re-workings of previous names, as is, for example, Church Court. Are they intended to honour John Loudon McAdam (b.1756, d.1836), the reputedly Ayr-born road surveyor?

MACADAM SQUARE   See MACADAM PLACE

McCALL'S AVENUE
Name dates from the late 19th Century.[7] The street is a development of one of the lanes or paths through the common lands belonging to the Freemen of Newton. Several members of the McCall family, many of them carters or carriers, were successively Freemen of Newton, and the name recalls this long-standing Newton family. The particular honour may be for Alexander McCall (b.1785, d.1860), whose wife was Elizabeth Twinningham (see

---

1   Ardrossan and Saltcoats Herald, 28th December 1867, 4f. No corroborative evidence has yet been found.
2   Ardrossan and Saltcoats Herald, 25th April 1868, 5c.
3   Ardrossan and Saltcoats Herald, 13th November 1875, 5d.
4   SAL, Ayr Town Council Minutes 1953-54, 355, Works Committee 26th March 1954.
5   Ayrshire Post, 21st August 1936, 11c. See also SAL, Ayr Town Council Minutes 1953-54, 316, Works Committee 19th February 1954.
6   SAL, Ayr Town Council Minutes 1967-68, 295, Works Committee 15th January 1968.
7   In use by 1883: it is recorded in Ayrshire Sasine Abridgement no.4899 of July 1883.

Twinningham Place). He was one of the leading carriers between Ayr and Glasgow in the pre-railway days.

McCOLGAN PLACE   See ALLAN PLACE

MACKIE STREET
Name approved by the Town Council in November 1935, at which time Hugh Mackie (b.1886, d.1958) was a Councillor and a member of the Housing Committee.[1] By profession a dentist, the Glasgow-born Mackie served as a Councillor from 1932 until 1936.[2]

McKILL'S CLOSE
An 1887 engraving by Robert Bryden of back properties at 68-70 High Street is entitled 'McKill's Close'. McKill is William McKill (b.1820, d.1898), who was in business here from c.1856.[3]

McLEAN STREET
Name approved by the Town Council in November 1935, at which time William McLean (b. 1871, d.1946) was a Councillor and a member of the Housing Committee.[4] An insurance agent, he served on the Town Council from 1932 until 1946.[5]

McMILLAN'S CLOSE
Name used in 1871 Census for houses at 3-5 Main Street. To date, McMillan has not been identified.

MACNAIRSTON ROAD
Shown on Nicolson's Street Plan as the name for the by-road which leads past Ayr Crematorium towards the farm of MacNairston. This road originally left the Cumnock road near Holmston farm: part of it on the town side of the Ayr By-pass was developed residentially, but was renamed Shavin Brae, q.v.

MACNEILLE BUILDINGS
30-38 Newmarket Street. A property built in 1869 by Ayr Town Council on the site of the Butter Market of 1814. The name honours the then provost, John Macneille (b.1803, d.1878), who was a tanner and leather merchant in the town.

MAIDENS' ROW   See BARNS STREET

MAIN ROAD
Name, rather unimaginative if descriptively accurate, of the road through Whitletts, the main road to Mauchline and Galston. At Whitletts Toll it divides into High Road and Low Road.

---

[1]   SAL, Ayr Town Council Minutes 1935-36, 33, Housing Committee 16th November 1935.
[2]   See Mackie's obituary in Ayrshire Post, 11th April 1958, 11de. It is noteworthy that Mackie only served as a councillor for four years but, in terms of getting this honour, happened to be on the right committee at the right time.
[3]   See James Hunter, The House of John Blair of Adamton, in Allan Leach and John Strawhorn, eds., Ayrshire Collections, 2nd series, vol.11, [Ayr], 1976, 110-111.
[4]   SAL, Ayr Town Council Minutes 1935-36, 33, Housing Committee 16th November 1935.
[5]   See McLean's obituary in Ayrshire Post, 7th June 1946, 5c.

MAIN STREET
The wide main street of the old burgh of Newton upon Ayr: the name is self-explanatory, and is used formally from early in the 19th Century. Until the middle of that century a mill lade, 'open, but neither clean nor sweet',[1] ran down the middle of the street, accounting for its width. This lade ran from the Newton Loch (see Damside and Lochside Road) to the Malt Mill of Newton, which stood close to the New Bridge. A back lane has the formal name BACK MAIN STREET: it and Back Peebles Street have also been known as BACK STREET.[2]

MAINHOLM CRESCENT   See MAINHOLM ROAD

MAINHOLM ROAD
This is a long-established, informal name for the road leading to the farm at Mainholm. An advert was placed in the Air Advertiser in 1806 for contractors to make a road, 26 feet wide, 14 inches deep, from a point at or near the Stanerel-head Engine, in St. Quivox, through part of Mr Taylor's lands, and lands of Braehead, towards Mainholm Ford.[3] MAINHOLM CRESCENT is first found in the 1961-62 Valuation Roll.

MANDELA GARDENS   See PLACE DE St. GERMAIN-EN-LAYE

MAPLE DRIVE   See ALDER BANK

MARCHFIELD QUADRANT   See MARCHFIELD ROAD

MARCHFIELD ROAD
Also MARCHFIELD QUADRANT. Names date from 1905 (Marchfield Road)[4] and 1924 (Marchfield Quadrant).[5] Housing development on part of the old Newton Common alongside the march or boundary between the parishes of Prestwick and Newton upon Ayr, hence this was the 'march field'.

MARCHMONT ROAD
Name approved in May 1910.[6] No particular reason for the name has been discovered. 5-11 Marchmont Road, built in 1900,[7] were originally known as MARCHMONT TERRACE.

MARCHMONT TERRACE   See MARCHMONT ROAD

MARGUERITE PLACE   See BRACKEN PARK

MARIGOLD SQUARE   See BRACKEN PARK

MARLBOROUGH COURT
Name from 2000. Close to the site of Ayr (Churchill) Barracks, it perhaps honours the English soldier-politician, John Churchill, Duke of Marlborough (b.1650, d.1722).

[1] Ayr Advertiser, 25th September 1873, 4d.
[2] Back Street is found in the Census Enumerators' Returns of 1881 and 1891.
[3] Air Advertiser, 13th March 1806, 1c.
[4] SAL, Ayr Town Council Minutes 1904-05, 201, Works Committee 17th May 1905.
[5] SAL, Ayr Town Council Minutes 1924-25, 64, Housing Committee 22nd December 1924.
[6] SAL, Ayr Town Council Minutes 1910, 191, Works Committee 4th May 1910.
[7] AA, Ayr Dean of Guild Court plans, box.no.11, plan no.24.

MARLE PARK
The name was approved by the Town Council in 1959.[1] It may continue an informal name
for the field over which this road was built.

MARSH BANK   See MOUNT CHARLES CRESCENT

MARY BOYD'S CLOSE
Recorded in 1583 as being near the town house of the Kennedys of Cassillis in that part of
the High Street now called Hope Street.[2]

MARYFIELD PLACE   See MARYFIELD ROAD

MARYFIELD ROAD
This name was approved by the Town Council in September 1957.[3] It is close to Prestwick
Road where cottages called Maryfield, or Maryfield Place, stood from the mid 19th Century
until 1958, when they were demolished prior to the construction of the Annpit Quarry
scheme, which includes Maryfield Road. MARYFIELD PLACE first appears in the
Valuation Roll for 1961-62. Mary has not been identified.

MASONHILL PLACE   See MASONHILL ROAD

MASONHILL ROAD
Also MASONHILL PLACE.[4] Old-established farm name transferred to a housing estate and
to two of the roads within the estate. Masonhill Road was formally approved in March
1963.[5] 'Mason' is probably the surname: John Mason was the name of successive Town
Clerks of Ayr in the 17th Century.

MATHEW HALL'S VENNEL   See HALL'S VENNEL

MAXWELL'S CORNER
In February 1851, at the Ayr Police Board, a Mr Cuthbertson referred to the nuisance of
loungers collecting at street corners. He said one gentleman had lately counted some 23
persons lounging about Maxwell's corner.[6] Contemporary Directories indicate that Peter
Maxwell, draper, (d.1850) traded from 2 High Street, so that Maxwell's Corner would have
been at the corner of High Street and New Bridge Street. This is still a popular spot for
'loungers'.

MAYBOLE ROAD
The main road south from Ayr into Carrick and Galloway leads to Maybole, the 'capital' of
Carrick, and is naturally called the Maybole road. An alternative route to Maybole, via
Culroy, is called HIGH MAYBOLE ROAD on Nicolson's Street Plan, while mid 19th
Century Directories distinguish between the NEW MAYBOLE ROAD (i.e., Maybole Road,

---

1   SAL, Ayr Town Council Minutes 1959-60, 118, Works Committee 24th September 1959.
      The name is spelled as one word on street signs at one end, and as two words at the other.
2   Noted in a card index formerly in the Carnegie Library, Ayr, but now mislaid.
3   SAL, Ayr Town Council Minutes 1957-58, 126, Works Committee 26th September 1957.
4   SAL, Ayr Town Council Minutes 1963-64, 43, Works Committee 20th June 1963.
5   SAL, Ayr Town Council Minutes 1962-63, 268, Works Committee 21st March 1963.
6   Ayr Advertiser, 13th February 1851, 4b.

which began as a new turnpike road authorised in 1774)[1] and OLD MAYBOLE ROAD (the Culroy route, formerly the main or only route south from Ayr). New Maybole Road is now represented by St Leonard's Road and Maybole Road, while Old Maybole Road is represented by Carrick Road, Monument Road and Alloway.

MEADOW PARK
Also MEADOWPARK DRIVE. These names appear to have been chosen purely for their pleasant quality. Meadow Park, suggested by the householders, was approved by the Town Council in October 1936,[2] and Meadowpark Drive was approved in September 1956.[3]

MEADOWPARK DRIVE   See MEADOW PARK

MERKLAND ROAD
Name approved in June 1969.[4] Merkland (a piece of land valued at 1 merk or mark) is a common Scottish farm name, here borrowed for its pleasant quality.

MEUSE LANE   See MEWS LANE

MEWS HOUSE   See MEWS LANE

MEWS LANE
Name given to the service lane which runs from Fort Street to Cassillis Street. Chambers' Dictionary defines a mews as 'a street or yard of stabling'. The name was formerly spelled MEUSE LANE, which has a more Scots look to it: the present spelling is influenced by its widespread use in London. MEWS HOUSE is the name given to the adjacent block of shops and flats at 55-63 Fort Street, built in 1966.

MID STREET   See WEST STREET

MIDSANDS ROAD   See MIDTON ROAD

MIDTON ROAD
The road that led through the centre of the Mid Sands, roughly equidistant from the Maybole Road and the Racecourse or Doonfoot Road was informally known as the MIDSANDS ROAD. In September 1845, as it became increasingly residential in character, Ayr Town Council formally conferred on it the name MIDTON ROAD, which was presumably considered to have more éclat, and to be more genteel.[5]

MILITIA COTTAGES
Name given to four cottages in Seabank Road in the 1871 Census. They were occupied by sergeants in the Royal Ayr Militia, and probably correspond to 5-8 Seabank Road, demolished in 1964.[6]

---

[1]   David McClure, Tolls and Tacksmen, [Ayr], 1994, 52.
[2]   SAL, Ayr Town Council Minutes 1935-36, 318, Corporation 12th October 1936.
[3]   SAL, Ayr Town Council Minutes 1956-57, 129, Works Committee 20th September 1956.
[4]   SAL, Ayr Town Council Minutes 1969-70, 68, Works Committee 16th June 1969.
[5]   SAL, B6/18/30, Ayr Town Council Minutes 1841-48, 11th September 1845.
[6]   AA, Ayr Dean of Guild Court plans, box no.156, plan no.41.

MILLBRAE
This road leads to the DUTCH MILLS in Alloway. The Dutch Mill, properly the Waulk Mill of Alloway, was in operation before 1535. The name is said to have been derived from a company of Dutch miners who worked a lead mine on Brown Carrick Hill. It is also worth noting that in 1582 the Scots parliament passed laws to encourage groups of Flemings to come to Scotland to improve the Scottish woollen industry.[1]

MILL BRAE
Name in informal use for the riverside slope leading to the Town or Nether Mills of Ayr: adopted for formal use c.1903 when D.H. & F. Reid established their engineering works here. MILL STREET, part of which was formerly known as MILL VENNEL, leads to the same mills from the heart of the town, leaving the High Street at the Wallace Tower. A newer name, MILL WYND, was approved in July 1968 for a residential development off Mill Street.[2]

MILL STREET	See MILL BRAE
MILL VENNEL	See MILL BRAE
MILL WYND	See MILL BRAE
MILLAR'S LAND	See CRAIGMILLAR BUILDINGS

MILLER ROAD
Built from 1852 to improve communications between the Railway Station and the Racecourse Road area. It was reported in February 1852 that terms for its construction had been agreed between the Town Council and the landowner, Mrs Nicholson of Barns House.[3] The name honours Hugh Miller, (b.1792, d.1858), who was Provost of Ayr from 1841 until 1855.[4]

MILLER'S COURT
Houses at 35 Carrick Street are so named in the 1871 Census, but the reason for the name has not, to date, been discovered.

MILLIKEN PARK
Terrace built c.1891, which was subsequently incorporated in the official names of streets as 2-20 Hunter's Avenue.[5] Built by John Milliken, builder (b.c.1852, d.1912): there is no connection with Milliken Park, between Johnstone and Kilbarchan, though the one may have influenced the other.

---

[1]   See Alastair Hendry, The Barony of Alloway 1324 - 1754, [Ayr], [1992], 18.
[2]   SAL, Ayr Town Council Minutes 1968-69, 82, Works Committee 15th July 1968.
[3]   Ayr Advertiser, 19th February 1852, 4c. The creation of Miller Road opened up a large part of the Barns estate for feuing.
[4]   Miller was a cloth merchant. See his obituary in Ayr Observer, 29th June 1858, 5b. According to J M Ferguson he was 'a decent High Street merchant' who 'held office for a long time more on account of the way he pulled the municipal strings than for any great merit he had ... but he has had one of the finest roads named after him'. Quoted in John Strawhorn, The History of Ayr, Edinburgh, 1989, 163.
[5]   1910-1911 Directory, 247, List of Erased Terraces, Etc.

MILRIG PLACE
Terrace of c.1878, built on the site of Templeton's Mill, destroyed in a tragic fire in 1876. It was subsequently incorporated in the official names of streets as 2-8 Charlotte Street.[1] It adjoined Milrig House, 18 Charlotte Street (built c.1805 for Major John Webster and demolished in 1970). The name is borrowed from Milrig, a mansion house (also now demolished) and estate near Galston, but no direct links have been discovered.

MILTON PARK   See BRADAN DRIVE

MOIRA ANDERSON DRIVE   See MURDOCH'S LONE

MOIR'S SQUARE
Name noted in 1841 Census, apparently on the north side of Taylor Street. This property appears to have belonged to Alexander Moir, builder (b.c.1771, d.1863).

MONKWOOD PLACE
Name approved in June 1969.[2] Monkwood is a mansion house and estate near Maybole: it is said to have belonged to the Monks of Melrose.[3] One of a number of names in this area chosen from south Ayrshire farms and the like: cf Kerse Park.

MONTGOMERIE TERRACE   See EGLINTON TERRACE

MONTGOMERIESTOUN TERRACE   See EGLINTON TERRACE

MONUMENT ROAD
An informal name which was used formally from c.1889 as the road began to be developed for residential use. This is the main road between Ayr and Alloway: its name refers to the fact that it leads not only to Alloway, but also to the Monument to Burns erected in 1823 close to the Brig o' Doon.

MOOR PLACE   See MOOR ROAD

MOOR ROAD
Also MOOR PLACE. The name Moor Road was approved in May 1935[4]; Moor Place in July 1939.[5] Built on a remote part of what had been the common land of the Newton Freemen. The name presumably reflects its character prior to development.

MORRISON GARDENS
This name was approved in May 1952.[6] Miss Helen Morrison, of Carrick Avenue, who died in May 1940, left £5,000 to Ayr Town Council to be put towards the erection of a hostel ('sheltered housing' in modern parlance) for elderly people.[7] Morrison Gardens is

---

[1]   1910-1911 Directory, 247, List of Erased Terraces, Etc.
[2]   SAL, Ayr Town Council Minutes 1969-70, 68, Works Committee 16th June 1969.
[3]   James Paterson, History of the County of Ayr, vol.II, Paisley, 1852, 369.
[4]   SAL, Ayr Town Council Minutes 1934-35, 165, Works Committee 8th May 1935. The name was suggested by the builders, William Paton & Sons Ltd.
[5]   SAL, Ayr Town Council Minutes 1938-39, 213, Finance Committee 6th July 1939.
[6]   SAL, Ayr Town Council Minutes 1952-53, 25, Works Committee 23rd May 1952.
[7]   SAL, Ayr Town Council Minutes 1939-40, 161-162, Finance Committee 6th June 1940.

the result of her generosity. She also gave £1,000 to be invested to provide an annual treat for the old people of the burgh.

MORTON AVENUE
Also MORTON ROAD. Names approved in January 1948.[1] These roads are built on land which formerly belonged to the Belmont estate, which for many years was the property of the Morton family. In 1867 the estate passed to John Morton Mathie-Morton (b.c.1850, d.1935), who became a doctor, and was Provost of Ayr from 1918 to 1922,[2] and the name may have been chosen, in part, in his honour.

MORTON ROAD   See MORTON AVENUE

MOSS ROAD
Name approved by Ayr Town Council in October 1933 for a road in Castlehill.[3] It appears never to have been used.

MOSSGIEL PLACE
Also MOSSGIEL ROAD. Mossgiel Road was approved in August 1948,[4] and Mossgiel Place in June 1988.[5] The names are part of the Burns theme in Forehill. Burns, with his brother Gilbert, tenanted Mossgiel Farm near Mauchline from 1784 until 1786.

MOSSGIEL ROAD   See MOSSGIEL PLACE

MOSSHILL COTTAGES
Name given to 4-6 Cambuslea Road, built in 1894 by John Milliken, builder. The name may have been a local name for this part of the Common Lands of Newton.

MOSSIDE ROAD
Name approved in September 1928.[6] The name reflects the nature of this land prior to its development.

MOTE, THE
Name approved in February 1976.[7] This street is close to Alloway Mote, at the entrance to Doonholm, the remains of an early defensible site.[8]

MOUNT, THE
Name approved in October 1955.[9] The Mount was the informal local name for this, the highest point on Belmont estate. On the draft Town Planning map of 1938 it was to be

[1]   SAL, Ayr Town Council Minutes 1947-49, 88, Corporation 12th January 1948.
[2]   Ayrshire Post, 31st May 1935, 8e.
[3]   SAL, Ayr Town Council Minutes 1932-33, 290, Works Committee 4th October 1933.
[4]   SAL, Ayr Town Council Minutes 1947-49, 333, Works Committee 27th August 1948.
[5]   SAL, Kyle and Carrick District Council Minutes 1988-89, 102, Planning & Building Control Committee 15th June 1988.
[6]   SAL, Ayr Town Council Minutes 1927-28, 338, Housing Committee 3rd September 1928.
[7]   SAL, Kyle and Carrick District Council Minutes 1975-76, 519, Planning and Building Control Committee 25th February 1976.
[8]   See Alastair Hendry, The Barony of Alloway 1324-1754, [Ayr] [1992], 7.
[9]   SAL, Ayr Town Council Minutes 1955-56, 167, Works Committee 27th October 1955.

reserved for woodland, but the Town Council agreed that it should be zoned for housing, with a belt of trees retained.[1] Cf Hilltop Place.

MOUNT CHARLES CRESCENT
Name approved in October 1969.[2] It is derived from Mount Charles House, which was divided into flats c.1948 and still exists as 36-44 Mount Charles Crescent. This was one of the small estates which came into existence after the sale of the Alloway Lands in 1754. The house sits in a raised position above the river Doon: it was named by and for its first owner, Charles Dalrymple of Orangefield (b.1721, d.1781).

MOUNT OLIPHANT CRESCENT
Also MOUNT OLIPHANT PLACE. Names which were approved in August 1948,[3] and which are part of the Burns' theme in Forehill. Burns' father tenanted Mount Oliphant, a farm close to Alloway, from 1766 until 1777. The farm name was chosen by William Fergusson of Doonholm in honour of his wife, Elizabeth Oliphant.

MOUNT OLIPHANT PLACE   See MOUNT OLIPHANT CRESCENT

MUNGO TERRACE
Recorded in the 1892/93 Directory as the house address of William Cowan, grocer, Russell Street. It appears to be an error for Mungo Cottage, 12-14 Hawkhill Avenue.

MURDOCH'S LONE
'The Depute Chief Building Control Officer reported that the access roadway to the Burns Interpretation Centre at Alloway now required to be named and stated that after consultation with the Hon.Secretary of the Burns Federation and the local member, he recommended that the name be "Murdoch's Lone". The Assistant Director of Administration reported that he had received a letter from Councillor Shirley suggesting that the street be named "Moira Anderson Drive" in acknowledgment of the fact that Miss Anderson's interpretation of Burns' songs on television had helped to popularise the poet's songs at home and abroad. After a full discussion, the Committee recommended that the street be named "Murdoch's

---

[1]   SAL, Ayr Town Council Minutes 1937-38, 330, Housing and Town Planning Sub Committee 19th October 1938.

[2]   SAL, Ayr Town Council Minutes 1969-70, 186, Works Committee 20th October 1969. The naming of this development was not without its difficulties. On 15th September 1969 the Works Committee had recommended the names BELLEISLE VIEW, FIELD BANK, MARSH BANK and STRATHDOON DRIVE, but the Town Council on 14th October asked for further consideration. On 20th October the Committee recommended Mount Charles Crescent for the longest street: the other two streets to be named from the previously submitted list. In the event only one name was required: STRATHDOON PLACE. [*ibid*, 150, 174 and 186].

[3]   SAL, Ayr Town Council Minutes 1947-49, 333, Works Committee 27th August 1948.

Lone"'.[1] The decision was discussed further at the subsequent full meeting of the District Council, but ratified by the Planning Committee in July 1976.[2]

MURRAY PLACE
Unauthorised or obsolete name which was incorporated in the official names of streets as 82-88 Allison Street.[3] This terrace of 4 houses was built c.1876 on land feued from James Murray Ferguson, publisher, politician and landowner. See Ferguson Street.

MURRAY PLACE   See ALLAN PLACE

MURRAY STREET
Name approved in May 1935.[4] Thomas Murray (b.1879, d.1959), was a Town Councillor from 1929 until 1949, and Provost of Ayr from 1943 to 1949. He was an ice merchant, having a cold storage business in Mill Street and an ice factory at the Dutch Mills, Alloway.

NELSON PLACE   see NELSON STREET

NELSON STREET
Name dates from c.1861. It is occasionally spelled 'Neilson', but appears to be in honour of Britain's naval hero, Admiral Lord Nelson (b.1758, d.1805): it is close to Wellington Street. The street was demolished as part of the comprehensive redevelopment of Wallacetown in the 1960s; a new street in this area is called NELSON PLACE, a name approved in February 1973.[5]

NETHER MILLS
In 1940 the Town Council agreed to have the Nether Mills "which are in bad condition" demolished as soon as convenient.[6] The Mill of Ayr, on this site (just above the present Victoria Bridge) since at least the 13th Century, became known as the Nether Mill when a second mill - the Over Mill - was put into operation in the late 16th Century.

NEW BRIDGE   See NEW BRIDGE STREET

NEW BRIDGE STREET
This street links the New Bridge with the junction of Sandgate and High Street, and was built on the site of the Water Vennel (q.v.), which had previously led down to the river at this point. The first NEW BRIDGE was begun in 1786, and completed in 1788. By 1876 it had become unsafe, was demolished and replaced by the present New Bridge, opened in 1878.

---

[1]   SAL, Kyle and Carrick District Council Minutes 1976-77, 81, Planning and Building Control Committee 9th June 1976. Murdoch is probably for John Murdoch (b.1747, d.1824), who was one of Burns's teachers at Alloway, hired in 1765 by William Burnes and his neighbours. Moira Anderson, b.1938 in Kirkintilloch, is a well-known Scottish singer and TV personality who grew up in Ayr.

[2]   SAL, Kyle and Carrick District Council Minutes 1976-77, 125, District Council 6th July 1976; *ibid*, 177, Planning and Building Control Committee 21st July 1976.

[3]   1910-1911 Directory, 247, List of Erased Terraces, Etc.

[4]   SAL, Ayr Town Council Minutes 1934-35, 179, Corporation 13th May 1935.

[5]   SAL, Ayr Town Council Minutes 1972-73, 301, Works Committee 20th February 1973.

[6]   SAL, Ayr Town Council Minutes 1939-40, 196, Works Committee 7th August 1940.

NEW MAYBOLE ROAD   See MAYBOLE ROAD

NEW ROAD
This new road was in the process of being built in 1830 to improve the northern approach to
Ayr from Prestwick and Kilmarnock.[1] Previously, traffic from the north followed the street
presently known as Weaver Street.

NEW YARDS   See NEWMARKET STREET

NEWARK BUILDINGS   See NEWARK CRESCENT.

NEWARK CRESCENT
Name approved in January 1973.[2] It is derived from the neighbouring Newark Castle, a
mansion house of considerable age which is prominent on the hillside to the south of Ayr.
The name is a corruption of 'new-wark', meaning "new work" or "new building".
NEWARK BUILDINGS, with a similar derivation, was the name used from its erection in
c.1892 until c.1910 for 25-29 Burns Statue Square: it is included in the 1910 list of erased
terraces.

NEWLANDS ROAD
One of the roads through the Newton Lands: as the Newton Lands were developed
Newlands Road became Hunter's Avenue. The name suggests that a part of the Newton
Lands was brought into cultivation at a latter date than the rest, hence the 'new lands'. See
also Wandgate Road.

NEWMARKET STREET
This new road between High Street and Sandgate was first laid out in 1767. It was
originally known as New Yard, or New Yards, but the name was changed after the erection
of the Butter Market, which opened in 1814.[3]

NEWTON PARK   See NEWTON PARK COURT

NEWTON PARK COURT
Name approved in October 1991.[4] This is a sheltered housing complex built on the site of
the demolished Newton Park School. The school, in its turn, had been built on the southern
part of the original Public Park in Newton: land which the Town Council offered to the Ayr
Burgh School Board in January 1902.[5] The common lands of the Freemen of Newton, of
which this piece of land was once a part, were generally known as the Newton Park. The
name NEWTON PARK is now restricted to the replacement open space, in Hunter's
Avenue, with bowling greens, &c., which was also, initially, part of the common land.

---

[1]   Air Advertiser, 22nd July 1830, 4c.
[2]   SAL, Ayr Town Council Minutes 1972-73, 264, Works Committee 15th January 1973.
[3]   James Howie, An Historical Account of the Town of Ayr, Kilmarnock, 1861, 14.
[4]   SAL, Kyle and Carrick District Council Minutes 1991-92, 1402, Planning Applications Sub
        Committee 1st October 1991.
[5]   SAL, Ayr Town Council Minutes 1901-02, 30, Works Committee 22nd January 1902.

NEWTON ROW
Appears to be an earlier name for part of North Harbour Street. In 1832 an advertisement for Mrs Miller, the local agent for Morison's Vegetable Pills, gives her address as 'Newton Row, land above Lottery Hall House'.[1]

NEWTON TERRACE
Name appears on Wood's Plan, 1818, attached to the seaward end of Green Street Lane. It was absorbed into Green Street Lane during the 19th Century, and was also affected by the expansion of the original Ayr Station, later the Goods Station, in North Harbour Street.

NILE COURT
The name was approved in 1894 by Ayr Town Council, for the 'New Court in High Street behind the "improvement" buildings'.[2] The name 'holds in its memory a worthy son of Ayr who spent many years of his life by the great river that is Egypt, and without which the ancient land of the Pharaohs would be a waste, howling wilderness'.[3] This son of Ayr has not yet been identified.

NOLTMIRE ROAD
Name approved in September 1928.[4] There was previously a farm in this area known as Knoltmire or Noltmire. 'Nolt' is a Scots word for 'cattle'.

NORTH QUAY
This name presumably had been in use ever since development of the Newton side of the river took place; from c.1895 it was gradually displaced as a street name by North Harbour Street. The properties listed as Front Street in the 1841 Census appear in the 1845-46 Directory as North Quay.

NORTH STREET
Name given on the Armstrongs' map of 1775 to that part of Cross Street (modern King Street) east of the Four Corners. An advertisement in 1806 sought contractors to pave 'North Street, and that part of Cross Street of Wallacetown which reaches the head of Garden Street'.[5]

NORTH VENNEL   See HALL'S VENNEL

NORTHDOON PLACE
Name approved in 1969.[6] Presumably so named because it is north of the mouth of the River Doon.

NORTHFIELD AVENUE
Name dates from c.1900. Also NORTHFIELD PLACE, approved in November 1958,[1] and NORTHFIELD GARDENS, approved in November 1995.[2] The name Northfield was

---

[1]   Ayr Observer, 24th July 1832, 1c.
[2]   Ayr Advertiser, 19th April 1894, 5a.
[3]   Ayrshire Post, 9th June 1911, 4f.
[4]   SAL, Ayr Town Council Minutes 1927-28, 338, Housing Committee 3rd September 1928.
[5]   Air Advertiser, 3rd April 1806, 4b.
[6]   SAL, Ayr Town Council Minutes 1969-70, 256, Works Committee 15th December 1969.

initially applied, from 1887, to the house now 46 Prestwick Road, built for the carpet manufacturer William C. Gray (b.1853, d.1915); there was also an earlier NORTHFIELD PLACE, built c.1887 and absorbed into Northfield Avenue. This area was part of the common lands of Newton: presumably a field or enclosure within those lands known as the 'north field'. A neighbouring street is called NORTH PARK AVENUE for the same reason.

NORTHFIELD GARDENS   See NORTHFIELD AVENUE

NORTHFIELD PLACE   See NORTHFIELD AVENUE

NORTH HARBOUR STREET
Name dates from c.1875, and gradually replaced the original North Quay.

NORTH NEWTON PLACE
Terrace of c.1889, subsequently incorporated in the official names of streets as 2-8 Falkland Park Road.[3]   It is, unsurprisingly, in the northern part of Newton, and close to North Newton Church (now St James), opened in 1885.

NORTH PARK AVENUE   See NORTHFIELD AVENUE

NORTH PARK TERRACE
Terrace of c.1890, subsequently incorporated in the official names of streets as 10-16 Prestwick Road.[4]   See Northfield Avenue: the field appears to have been called indifferently the 'north field' or 'north park'.

NURSERY GROVE   See NURSERY ROAD

NURSERY ROAD
Name approved in October 1955.[5] The name presumably reflects the previous use of the site. A late 1990s development off Nursery Road has the names NURSERY GROVE and NURSERY WYND.

NURSERY WYND   See NURSERY ROAD

NURSERYHALL
Name dates from c.1972. The name was previously used for a house on this site, which in 1845 was occupied by David Gairdner, land steward or factor on the Auchincruive estate.

OAKLEY AVENUE   See ENGLEWOOD AVENUE

OAKWOOD AVENUE
This name was approved in December 1954.[6] Close to Thornwood Avenue, approved at the same meeting, and probably chosen purely for its euphony and similarity to Thornwood Avenue.

---

[1]   SAL, Ayr Town Council Minutes 1958-59. 191, Works Committee 20th November 1958.
[2]   SAL, Kyle and Carrick District Council Minutes 1995-96, 369, Planning Applications Committee 28th November 1995.
[3]   1910-1911 Directory, 247, List of Erased Terraces, Etc.
[4]   1910-1911 Directory, 247, List of Erased Terraces, Etc.
[5]   SAL, Ayr Town Council Minutes 1955-56, 167, Works Committee 27th October 1955.
[6]   SAL, Ayr Town Council Minutes 1954-55, 240, Housing Committee 28th December 1954.

OLD BRIDGE END   See RIVER STREET

OLD BRIDGE ROAD
Name approved in 1983. This is a former part of Heathfield Road, including a bridge over
the Ayr to Mauchline railway, which has now been by-passed by a new stretch of road. Old
Bridge Road was the original suggestion, but following comments from proprietors in the
road, Old Heathfield Road was approved by the District Council; this was quickly dropped
and Old Bridge Road finally approved.[1]

OLD BRIDGE STREET
Name dates from late 18th Century, when the opening of the New Bridge in 1786-88
necessitated a distinction to be made between routes leading to the old and new bridges.
For the old bridge see Auld Brig. See also Brig Vennel.

OLD FARM ROAD
Name dates from c.1976. An industrial estate road on the line of the former road to South
Sanquhar Farm.

OLD FOUNDRY ROAD
Unidentified: named in a list of streets in the Air Advertiser in 1834.[2], and as Old Foundry it
is found in the Censuses for 1841 and 1851. It appears to have been close to John Street and
Church Street.

OLD HEATHFIELD ROAD   See OLD BRIDGE ROAD

OLD HILLFOOT ROAD   See HILLFOOT CRESCENT

OLD MAYBOLE ROAD   See MAYBOLE ROAD

OLD NEWTON
In the 1830 Directory three entries are given as Old Newton.[3] Presumably part of Newton
on Ayr, but not convincingly identified.

OLD RACECOURSE ROAD   See RACECOURSE ROAD

OLD RACECOURSE VIEW   See RACECOURSE ROAD

ORANGE ROW
Name given to cottages at c.172-180 Prestwick Road, in use from at least 1841, and still
found in 1892. The cottages date from c.1807. The name may reflect the political
affiliations of the proprietor or tenants.

ORCHARD AVENUE
Also ORCHARD PLACE. Orchard Avenue was approved in August 1948,[1] and Orchard
Place in June 1988[2]. The name presumably reflects the previous use of the site.

---

[1]   SAL, Kyle and Carrick District Council Minutes 1983-84, 132, Planning & Building
         Control Committee 20th July 1983; *ibid*, 387, Planning & Building Control Committee 9th
         November 1983; *ibid*, 469, Planning & Building Control Committee 7th December 1983.
[2]   Air Advertiser, 9th October 1834, 3f.
[3]   These are Hugh Muir, joiner and cabinetmaker; Hugh Park, agent, grocer and spirit dealer;
         and Andrew Smith, blanket manufacturer.

ORCHARD PLACE   See ORCHARD AVENUE

OSBORNE TERRACE
Terrace of c.1900, subsequently incorporated in the official names of streets as 47-53 Prestwick Road.[3] Pretension by association with the royal residence on the Isle of Wight, bought in 1845, and where Queen Victoria died in January 1901.

OSWALD COURT   See OSWALD ROAD

OSWALD LANE   See OSWALD ROAD

OSWALD PLACE   See OSWALD ROAD

OSWALD ROAD
Also OSWALD COURT, OSWALD LANE and OSWALD PLACE. From 1764 until 1925 the estate of Auchincruive, just to the east of Ayr, was the property of the Oswald family.[4] The estate and the family played an important part in the life of the town, especially through the exploitation of the coal under the estate. Oswald Lane and Oswald Road are roads which follow the line of the waggonway which brought coal from the Auchincruive collieries to Ayr Harbour. Oswald Road was approved as a street name by the Town Council in 1905;[5] for much of its length it was rebuilt along a new line in 1913.[6] Oswald Court (approved in 1983)[7] and Oswald Place (approved in 1924)[8] are close to Oswald Road. [Oswald Lane is marked on Nicolson's Street Plan, but its closure was recommended by Ayr Town Council in November 1935]. In George Street the names OSWALD PLACE, from c.1880, and OSWALD TERRACE, from c.1866, were used for, respectively, 13-23 and 31-43 George Street, but both names had fallen out of use by c.1892.

OSWALD TERRACE   see OSWALD ROAD

OVERMILLS BRIDGE   See OVERMILLS CRESCENT

[1]   SAL, Ayr Town Council Minutes 1947-49, 333, Works Committee 27th August 1948.
[2]   SAL, Kyle and Carrick District Council Minutes 1988-89, 102, Planning and Building Control Committee 15th June 1988.
[3]   1910-1911 Directory, 247, List of Erased Terraces, Etc.
[4]   David J Martin, Auchincruive, Edinburgh, 1994, 133.
[5]   SAL, Ayr Town Council Minutes 1904-05, 159, Works Committee 17th April 1905. According to a minute of the Works Committee of 3rd July 1905 (*ibid*, 246) Oswald Road was originally feued by Richard Oswald of Auchincruive from Newton Town Council in 1765, for use as a waggon road between his coal pits and his coalyard at the North Harbour.
[6]   See, for instance, SAL, Ayr Town Council Minutes 1913, 159, Works Committee 5th March 1913. The reason for rebuilding Oswald Road appears to have been a need to achieve separation of road and rail traffic. The work was paid for by the Glasgow and South Western Railway.
[7]   SAL, Kyle and Carrick District Council Minutes 1982-83, 650, Planning and Building Control Committee 16th February 1983.
[8]   SAL, Ayr Town Council Minutes 1924-25, 64, Housing Committee 22nd December 1924.

OVERMILLS CRESCENT
Also OVERMILLS ROAD. Names approved in June 1979 (Overmills Road)[1] and July
1990 (Overmills Crescent).[2] The Over Mills of Ayr stood near here on the river Ayr, just
upstream from the modern by-pass bridge, which is called OVERMILLS BRIDGE. The
Over Mills were in existence by 1594, and were demolished in 1963.[3] Also here are the
Stepping Stones across the Ayr, which were reset and levelled in 1938-1940.[4]

OVERMILLS ROAD   See OVERMILLS CRESCENT

PARK CIRCUS
Originally known as *PARK CIRCUS EAST* and *PARK CIRCUS WEST*, but in 1894 the
Town Council approved the name Park Circus for the whole street, with a full renumbering.[5]
Part of Arthur Lang's development of Bellevue, and originally to be called Lang Street: see
Bellevue Crescent.   Park Circus appears to be a direct homage to the mid Victorian
development in the west end of Glasgow.   PARK CIRCUS LANE is the service lane
between Park Circus and Miller Road.

PARK CIRCUS EAST   See PARK CIRCUS

PARK CIRCUS LANE   See PARK CIRCUS

PARK CIRCUS WEST   See PARK CIRCUS

PARK ROAD   See EAST PARK ROAD

PARK TERRACE   See ALLOWAY PARK

PARK VIEW
Name approved in March 1956.[6] The houses in Park View overlook a playing field.   At the
other end of the town, PARK VIEW TERRACE, which became 34-48 Hunter's Avenue,
overlooking Newton Park, was built by J & W Drinnan, builders in 1903, and renumbered
c.1910.

PARK VIEW TERRACE   See PARK VIEW

PARKHOUSE STREET
Name approved by the Town Council in July 1938,[7] when this new route between the
station and Beresford Terrace was built on the site of the football ground used by Ayr

---

[1]   SAL, Kyle and Carrick District Council Minutes 1979-80, 149, Planning and Building
        Control Committee 20th June 1979.
[2]   SAL, Kyle and Carrick District Council Minutes 1990-91, 209, Planning and Building
        Control Committee 11th July 1990.
[3]   John Strawhorn, The History of Ayr, Edinburgh, 1989, 32 and 249.
[4]   SAL, Ayr Town Council Minutes 1937-38, 125, Works Committee 9th March 1938; Ayr
        Town Council Minutes 1939-40, 157, Works Committee 5th June 1940.
[5]   Ayr Advertiser, 19th April 1894, 5a.   The original Park Circus East, numbered
        consecutively 1-13, became 3-27 Park Circus, while 1-4 and 10-15 (also consecutive) Park
        Circus West became 4-10 and 22-32 Park Circus.
[6]   SAL, Ayr Town Council Minutes 1955-56, 327, Works Committee 22nd March 1956.
[7]   SAL, Ayr Town Council Minutes 1937-38, 247, Works Committee 6th July 1938.

Parkhouse Football Club This football team had been formed in 1883, and had merged with
Ayr Football Club in 1910. Park House is an early 19th Century house which still stands at
the corner of Bowman Road and Ballantine Drive; it is first recorded in the 1837 Directory,
when it was occupied by the Misses Latimer.

PARKLAND   See SHIELING PARK

PARLIAMENTARY CLOSE
Name given to the close at 175 High Street, and still in use in the 1920s. No obvious reason
for the name can be suggested, unless it was at one time the place where local worthies were
wont to meet and discuss the issues of the day.[1]

PATERSON STREET
Name approved in September 1928,[2] at which time Thomas Paterson (b.1887, d.1971) was
Housing Convener. He was a Town Councillor from 1918 to 1953, being for much of that
time Housing Convener. An engine driver, Paterson worked on the railways for 43 years.
His interest in housing issues led to a prominent role in the post-war development of public
housing in Scotland. He was appointed chairman of the Scottish Housing Advisory
Committee in 1948, and was later a director of the Scottish Special Housing Association.
Paterson's contributions in this field were recognised by an OBE in 1965, and by the award
of the Freedom of Ayr in December 1963.[3]

PATTLE PLACE
Adopted as a public road December 1999.[4] In 'To a Mouse' Burns addresses the mouse
thus: 'I wad be laith to rin an' chase thee,/ Wi' murd'ring pattle!'. A pattle is 'a small
spade-like tool, used especially for clearing the mould-board of a plough'.[5]

PAVILION ROAD
This name was approved in February 1956.[6] The road leads from Wellington Square past the
Pavilion, an entertainment centre originally built by Ayr Town Council and opened in 1911.

PEEBLES LANE   See PEEBLES STREET

PEEBLES STREET
Names dates from at least 1830. The street is a continuation of Main Street, Newton, and
led from the town of Newton to its Manse and Glebe. These were built for, and long
occupied by, Newton's first minister, Dr William Peebles (b.1753, d.1826); the name
preserves his memory:[7] according to Gray he was "a stout, short-sized person, with a

---

[1]   See Ayrshire Post, 2nd December 1921, 2c. Stuart Harris, The Place Names of Edinburgh,
        Edinburgh, 1996, 485, can find no particular reason for the name of Parliament Close, Leith.
[2]   SAL, Ayr Town Council Minutes 1927-28, 338, Housing Committee 3rd September 1928.
[3]   Ayrshire Post, 14th May 1971, 13abc.
[4]   SAL, South Ayrshire Council Minutes 1999-2000, 941, Strategic Services Committee, 7th
        December 1999.
[5]   Mairi Robinson, ed., The Concise Scots Dictionary, Aberdeen, 1987 ed., 478.
[6]   SAL, Ayr Town Council Minutes 1955-56, 298, Works Committee 23rd February 1956.
[7]   Wood's Plan, 1818, gives the surely erroneous name Pebble Street to the road now known as
        Waggon Road.

countenance which was not easily forgotten".[1] Howie says that Peebles Street was known in the early 19th Century as "the Bay", because it was principally inhabited by fishermen".[2] A back lane has the formal name BACK PEEBLES STREET, and probably represents the PEEBLES LANE recorded in the 1841 Census Enumerators' Returns.

PEGGIESHILL PLACE
First found in the 1963-64 Valuation Road. Also PEGGIESHILL ROAD, which was approved in October 1955.[3] Parts of the Belmont South estate, which was built on the lands of Peggieshill Farm. It was presumably, for some now obscure reason, Peggy's hill.

PEGGIESHILL ROAD   See PEGGIESHILL PLACE

PEMBERTON VALLEY
Name approved in June 1969.[4] In 1967 the Town Council's Naming of Streets Sub-Committee recommended that "because of the association of the Hamiltons of Rozelle with the West Indies the names of the islands be listed by the Burgh Surveyor so that those which are suitable might be used for streets to be formed on Rozelle Estate".[5] Many of Ayr's wealthy people in the years around 1800 had made their fortunes in the West Indies - the Hamiltons more successfully than others. In May 1969 the Council decided to drop this policy, perhaps due to a perceived lack of *suitable* names.[6] Pemberton Valley was a sugar cane estate in Jamaica which belonged to the Hamiltons. Other names which reflect this short-lived policy are LEEWARD PARK, ST VINCENT CRESCENT and WINDWARD PARK, named after two island groups, and an island which is part of one of those groups.[7]

PETER BOYLE'S CLOSE
Obsolete name for the close at 226 High Street. Peter Boyle (b.1865, d.1954) was a jeweller and pawnbroker; born in Ayr, he spent some years in Australia before returning to Ayr to establish his business. He was a Councillor, Burgh Treasurer for 20 years and a director of both the Ayrshire Post and the Orient Cinema.[8]

PHILIP SQUARE
Philip Square existed in the 1850s, and appears on the 1st edition of the 1:500 scale Ordnance Survey plans of Ayr; the name is not otherwise recorded, and no reason for it has been established. The name was resurrected by the Town Council in January 1962 for part

---

[1] H C Gray's lecture on Old Ayr, reported in Ayr Advertiser, 1st February 1872, 6a.
[2] James Howie, An Historical Account of the Town of Ayr, Kilmarnock, 1861, 43.
[3] SAL, Ayr Town Council Minutes 1955-56, 167, Works Committee 27th October 1955.
[4] SAL, Ayr Town Council Minutes 1969-70, 68, Works Committee 16th June 1969.
[5] SAL, Ayr Town Council Minutes 1966-67, 340, Works Committee 20th February 1967.
[6] SAL, Ayr Town Council Minutes 1969-70, 26, Works Committee 19th May 1969. My italics.
[7] St Vincent Crescent was approved in September 1968 [SAL, Ayr Town Council Minutes 1968-69, 116, Works Committee 16th September 1968]; Leeward Park and Windward Park in June 1969, at the same time as Pemberton Valley, and after the 'West Indian' policy had been dropped. [SAL, Ayr Town Council Minutes 1969-70, 68, Works Committee 16th June 1969]
[8] Ayrshire Post, 17th December 1954, 15c.

of the redevelopment of Wallacetown.[1] PHILIP WYND also dates from this period of redevelopment.

PHILIP WYND   See PHILIP SQUARE

PHYSICWELL LANE
Named on the 1858 Ordnance Survey plan, north west of Content Farm. It presumably led, at one time, to a now-forgotten curative well.

PINE BRAE   See ALDER BANK

PIPERHILL
Name approved in June 1969.[2] Piperhill is a farm, and in the 1990s an open cast coal site, in Ochiltree parish. Chosen purely for its euphonious sound.

PLACE D'AURAY BUILDINGS
Unauthorised or obsolete name which was incorporated in the official names of streets as 54-62 Alloway Street and 71-85 Dalblair Road. These buildings had been built c.1898 by Louis le Clair, hairdresser and perfumer (b.c.1847, d.1909) who had been born at Auray, a small port in Brittany, and came to Ayr c.1873.[3]

PLACE DE ST. GERMAIN-EN-LAYE
Name approved in October 1986.[4] It honours Ayr's French twin town, an honour intensified by the French name form. The twinning had been formally initiated in 1984.[5]

PLOUGH INN CLOSE
Obsolete name for the close at 239-41 High Street. The Plough Inn stood here for many years, until it closed c.1934.

POPLAR CRESCENT   See ALDER BANK

POPLAR WAY   See ALDER BANK

PORTMARK AVENUE
Name approved in January 1973.[6] The name of an old-established settlement site on the east side of Loch Doon, chosen for its pleasant sound. Compare Lamford Drive.

PRESTWICK ROAD
The main road north from Newton leads, via Prestwick, Monkton and Kilmarnock, to Glasgow. It day-to-day parlance it would have been indifferently referred to as the 'road to

---

1   SAL, Ayr Town Council Minutes 1961-62, 223, Works Committee 25th January 1962. The Council felt obliged to stress that the name was adopted from old maps, and was not a reference to Prince Philip, Duke of Edinburgh. [Ayrshire Post, 2nd February 1962, 14d]

2   SAL, Ayr Town Council Minutes 1969-70, 68, Works Committee 16th June 1969.

3   Le Clair's obituary is in Ayr Advertiser, 12th August 1909, 4b. Auray is given as his birthplace in the 1881 Census [Registration District 612, Enumeration District 2, no.6].

4   SAL, Kyle and Carrick District Council Minutes 1986-87, 427, Planning & Building Control Committee 8th October 1986. An alternative suggestion, MANDELA GARDENS, was defeated by 7 votes to 2.

5   John Strawhorn, The History of Ayr, Edinburgh, 1989, 267.

6   SAL, Ayr Town Council Minutes 1972-73, 264, Works Committee 15th January 1973.

Kilmarnock', 'road to Glasgow', and the like. Once houses began to appear along the road, especially after the Freemen of Newton began to feu land along the road, c.1810, Prestwick Road appears to have become the generally agreed name. In July 1837 the Rev Alexander Cuthill wrote 'Not many years ago, the Glasgow road, for upwards of three miles in the vicinity of Ayr, ran on both sides, through accumulated wreaths of barren sand, which gave the traveller a very unfavourable impression of the approach to the county town. Now, however, nearly all this has vanished from the sight, and the eye is gratified with small well-cultivated inclosures, neat cottages and gardens, and handsome villas with ornamented avenues and shrubberies'.[1]

PRIMROSE PARK   See BRACKEN PARK

PRINCES COURT   See PRINCES STREET

PRINCES STREET
Name dates from c.1872, but which particular Prince is honoured is not known. The street was demolished in the 1960s as part of the Wallacetown Redevelopment. PRINCES COURT was built on part of the site: the name was approved in February 1973.[2]

PRINTING OFFICE CLOSE
Referred to in 1806,[3] and presumably the close in the High Street wherein stood the premises of J & P Wilson.

PURGATORY   See FORT STREET

QUAIL ROAD
Name dates from 1903.[4] Presumably for the bird, but the reason for the choice remains unexplained.

QUARRY ROAD   See RUSSELL STREET

QUARRY STREET   See RUSSELL STREET

QUARRYGATE
Street name recorded in use before 1348. Possibly a name for the upper part of the High Street. Compare Woodgate, and see also reference under Sandgate.

QUEEN STREET
Name from c.1860, and presumably honours Queen Victoria. A small development off Queen Street has been given the alliterative name QUEEN'S QUADRANT, though it bears no physical resemblence to a quadrant: this name was approved in February 1988.[5]

QUEEN MARY'S AVENUE   See GEORGE'S AVENUE

---

[1]   The New Statistical Account of Scotland, vol.V, Edinburgh, 1845, 2.
[2]   SAL, Ayr Town Council Minutes 1972-73, 301, Works Committee 20th February 1973.
[3]   Air Advertiser, Thursday 27th February 1806, 4c.
[4]   SAL, Ayr Town Council Minutes 1902-03, 168, Works Committee 3rd June 1903. See also note to Ardlui Road, above.
[5]   SAL, Kyle and Carrick District Council Minutes 1987-88, 878, Planning and Building Control Committee 24th February 1988.

QUEEN'S COURT
Name given to the former County Club premises in January 1953, during a period of
national anticipation of the coronation of Queen Elizabeth.[1]

QUEEN'S HEAD CLOSE
This close off the High Street (precise location unknown) is referred to in 1838.[2]

QUEEN'S QUADRANT   See QUEEN STREET

QUEEN'S TERRACE
This name was approved by Ayr Town Council in September 1845.[3] The honour is
presumably intended for Queen Victoria. The service lane on the seaward side is known as
QUEEN'S TERRACE LANE.

QUEEN'S TERRACE LANE   See QUEEN'S TERRACE

RACECOURSE ROAD
Horse-racing took place on the burgh lands from an early date. By the 18th century the area
between the town and Belleisle, close to the road to the bridge at Doonfoot, had become the
regular venue, and through the 19th Century, became increasingly regularised, especially
when the grandstand or viewhouse was built in 1867. The course was however, in the early
20th Century, deemed to be unsuitable for modern racing needs, especially because of the
tight corners, and a new racecourse was built in Whitletts. Racecourse Road gradually came
into use as the name for that part of the Doonfoot road between Ayr and the (old)
racecourse, and is now used formally for that road between Barns Terrace and the junction
with Seafield Road and RACECOURSE VIEW, which runs round two sides of the old
racecourse, offering views of the footballers and dog exercisers who use this part of the
Belleisle park. For Racecourse View see also Seafield Road. In early 1957 the Ayr Hotel,
Boarding House and Caterers' Association suggested to the Town Council that the name
should be changed to the more accurate OLD RACECOURSE ROAD, but the Council
agreed to take no action on this.[4] A similar suggestion, for both Racecourse Road and
Racecourse View (OLD RACECOURSE VIEW), was put before the District Council by a
resident in Racecourse View in March 1984, with a similar result.[5]

RACECOURSE VIEW   See RACECOURSE ROAD

---

[1]   SAL, Ayr Town Council Minutes 1952-53, 282, Works Committee 23rd January 1953.
        Spelled without the apostrophe in this reference: current nameplates have the grammatically
        correct apostrophe.
[2]   Air Advertiser, 7th June 1838, 1b.
[3]   SAL, B6/18/30, Ayr Town Council Minutes 1841-1848, 11th September 1845.
[4]   SAL, Ayr Town Council Minutes 1956-57, 274, Works Committee 21st February 1957, and
        303, Works Committee 21st March 1957.
[5]   SAL, Kyle and Carrick District Council Minutes 1983-84, 741, Planning and Building
        Control Committee 28th March 1984.

RAITHHILL
Name approved in June 1969.[1] Name chosen for its euphony. There are three farms called Raithhill in Ayrshire, one in Fenwick, and two in Coylton parish. The element 'Raith' appears to be related to the Irish, 'rath', which means a fortified hill.

RALSTON PLACE
Unauthorised or obsolete name which was incorporated in the official names of streets as 1-3 West Sanquhar Road.[2] Built in 1897 for Robert Carson, mineral water manufacturer: his wife was Agnes Ralston (b.1832, d.1906).

RAMSAY GARDENS
Formally opened in June 1955[3], this small public garden in River Terrace is named as a token of respect for Johnny Ramsay (b.1877, d.1962), a local grocer with an international reputation as a magician and conjuror.[4]

RAMSAY ROW
Howie refers to Ramsay and Boghall Rows (q.v.) as lying at the back of Elba Street.[5] Ramsay Row has not been found otherwise.

RANDOLPH TERRACE
Terrace built c.1893-94 by Robert Hutchison, builder. It was subsequently incorporated in the official names of streets as 18-28 Prestwick Road.[6] A name which conveys pretension, and probably influenced by the prominent Conservative politician, Lord Randolph Churchill (b.1849, d.1895), who 'owed much of his success to his gift for popular oratory which embraced a remarkable aptitude for the telling phrase'.[7]

RECAWR PARK   See BRADAN DRIVE

RED ROW
Found in the 1861 Census, and appears to be the name given to a row of cottages in Prestwick Road. The name may reflect construction of red stone, but compare Orange Row.

REID'S SQUARE
On south side of Russell Street. A renaming of Wilson's Square. A factory was built here c.1870 by John Reid (b.c.1800, d.1879), cloth manufacturer.[8] The factory employed about 30 to 40 people weaving wincey and flannel cloth.

---

[1]   SAL, Ayr Town Council Minutes 1969-70, 68, Works Committee 16th June 1969.
[2]   1910-1911 Directory, 247, List of Erased Terraces, Etc. This part of West Sanquhar Road subsequently became Somerset Road, and what had been Ralston Place became 2-12 Somerset Road when that road was, itself, renumbered c.1934.
[3]   Ayrshire Post, 24th June 1955, 13cd. The decision regarding the name is reported in Ayr Advertiser, 14th April 1955, 7a.
[4]   See Ramsay's obituary in Ayrshire Post, 19th January 1962, 11ab.
[5]   James Howie, An Historical Account of the Town of Ayr, Kilmarnock, 1861, 49.
[6]   1910-1911 Directory, 247, List of Erased Terraces, Etc.
[7]   John E Tyler, in Chamber's Encyclopedia, revised edition, vol.III, 1970, 560.
[8]   The description of Enumeration District St Quivox no.4 in the 1871 Census refers to 'Wilsons or Reids Square'.

RIGWOODIE PLACE
Adopted as a public road in December 1999.[1] The lines 'But wither'd beldams, auld and droll,/ Rigwoodie hags wad spean a foal,/ Lowping and flinging on a crummock,/ I wonder didna turn thy stomach' occur in 'Tam o' Shanter'. The dictionary defines 'rigwoodie' as 'wizened, gnarled, tough and rugged looking, mis-shapen'.[2]

RINGUINEA PLACE
Houses at 45-49 Church Street. The name is first found in the 1888-89 Directory. Ringuinea is a farm on the Wigtownshire coast about six miles south-east of Portpatrick. No connection has yet been found.

RITCHIE SQUARE
Houses at 12 Church Street, so called from at least 1881; the name was still in use in 1924.[3]

RIVER STREET
Also RIVER TERRACE. Names date from c.1837 (River Street) and c.1858 (River Terrace). The streets are on the Newton bank of the river Ayr. One of the most prominent properties in River Street is the Black Bull, or Simpson's Inn, where Burns stayed and gained the inspiration for the 'Twa Brigs'. In the 18th and 19th Centuries the Black Bull is described as being in OLD BRIDGE END, Wallacetown.

RIVER TERRACE   See RIVER STREET

RIVER VIEW
Name, first found in the 1985-86 Valuation Roll, for the flats above British Home Stores, which have spectacular views of the river and the bridges.

RIVERSIDE PLACE
Name approved in September 1968.[4] The only properties in Riverside Place are the three multi-storey blocks of flats close to Turner's Bridge: an alternative proposal that these be called CUMBRAE COURT, BUTE COURT and ARRAN COURT was turned down by the Council in October 1968.[5] The wheel turning full cycle, in the mid 1990s the three blocks were given the equally unimaginative names SCOTT COURT, STEVENSON COURT and BURNS COURT, for the Scots authors Sir Walter Scott, Robert L Stevenson and Robert Burns.

ROBERTSON AVENUE   See ROBERTSON CRESCENT

ROBERTSON CRESCENT
This name was approved in February 1951, though the Town Council did not decide between Robertson Crescent and Robertson Avenue. They had previously rejected an earlier proposal - Tennant Street - though their hint that some commemoration of Dr Taylor

---

[1]   SAL, South Ayrshire Council Minutes 1999-2000, 941, Strategic Services Committee, 7th December 1999.
[2]   Mairi Robinson, ed., The Concise Scots Dictionary, Aberdeen, 1987 ed.
[3]   SAL, Ayr Town Council Minutes 1923-24, 390, Public Health Committee 1st September 1924.
[4]   SAL, Ayr Town Council Minutes 1968-69, 116, Works Committee 16th September 1968.
[5]   SAL, Ayr Town Council Minutes 1968-69, 146, Corporation 15th October 1968.

of Blackhouse would be appropriate appears to have been ignored.[1] The honour is for the Rev. John Robertson (b.1813, d.1894), who had been the Original Secession minister in Ayr for 51 years; his commemoration in this manner was, in part, suggested by the closure (and hence the loss of the name) of the Robertson Memorial Church, and its re-opening as the Civic Theatre.[2]

ROBERTSON PLACE
'Robertson Place, George Street' is recorded in the 1870-1871 Directory. No reason for the choice of name has been found.

ROBSLAND AVENUE
Name approved in 1907.[3] Andrew, James and John Rob are all recorded as having possessions in the Burrowfield of Ayr in 1691.[4]

ROCKROSE PARK   See BRACKEN PARK

ROMAN ROAD
Close to Dalmellington Road, which has long been traditionally considered to be a Roman Road, leading from the presumed Roman fort at Castlehill, via the Doon Valley, into Galloway. This name was approved by the Works Committee on 24th September 1959, and confirmed by the Town Council on 12th October 1959, despite opposition, based on its historical dubiety, by Councillor Hewitson.[5]

RONALDSHAW PARK
Name dates from 1850s, and is directly borrowed from the field or park on which the houses were built. This field was acquired in 1852 by Robert Boyle (b.c.1804, d.1866), potter, and his wife Margaret Ronald,[6] and the field name may have been chosen in her honour.[7] The road through the field was proposed to be named ALBERT ROAD, presumably in honour of the Prince Consort (see Albert Terrace), but this never caught on: in 1879 it is described as a new road "which is being opened up from the ... Racecourse Road leading up to the Midton Road at Ronaldshaw Park".[8] Occasionally recorded as Ronaldshaw Park Road.[9]

1	SAL, Ayr Town Council Minutes 1950-51, 236, Works Committee 22nd December 1950; *ibid*, 262, Corporation 8th January 1951; *ibid*, 302, Corporation 12th February 1951.
2	Ayrshire Post, 16th February 1951, 7cd. Robertson's obituary is in Ayr Advertiser, 7th June 1894, 4g.
3	SAL, Ayr Town Council Minutes 1907, 87, Works Committee 6th February 1907.
4	R H J Urquhart and Rob Close, eds., The Hearth Tax for Ayrshire 1691, Ayr, 1998, 31.
5	SAL, Ayr Town Council Minutes 1959-60, 118 and 138. The subject of the Romans and Ayr is one which is hotly debated: it is not the intention of this treatise to enter into it.
6	Ayrshire Sasine Abridgement no.1505 of 1852.
7	In 1858 Boyle was advertising a 'recently erected villa' in Ronaldshaw Park for sale or let. [Ayr Advertiser 22nd April 1858, 1d]
8	Ayr Advertiser 26th June 1879, 4e.
9	For example in SAL, Ayr Town Council Minutes 1910, 164, Footpaths Committee 6th April 1910.

ROSEBANK CRESCENT
Name approved in May 1926.[1] It is borrowed from Rosebank House, which still stands in
the street. This is a house of c.1820, built for John Johnstone, watchmaker (d.1829).

ROSEBAY PARK   See BRACKEN PARK

ROSELEA COTTAGES
Original name for 12-14 Carrick Road. A fanciful name for cottages built c.1876 by David
Milligan, joiner.

ROSEMOUNT TERRACE
Terrace built c.1893, which was subsequently incorporated in the official names of streets as
31-41 Northfield Avenue.[2] A fanciful name.

ROSS STREET
Name approved by the Town Council in February 1932,[3] at which time William Henry Ross
(b.1886, d.1948) was a member of the Town Council. Ross was an engine driver and
worked on the railways for 40 years. He was a Town Councillor from 1928 to 1937.[4] He
had a son, William Ross, who became an MP, Secretary of State for Scotland and, finally, a
Life Peer.

ROSSLYN PLACE
Name approved by Town Council in November 1935;[5] development was slow and the road
was only taken over by the Town Council in September 1942.[6] Apparantly a fanciful
meaningless name.

ROWAN CRESCENT   See ALDER BANK

ROZELLE TERRACE
Part of the Burgh Lands of Alloway was acquired in 1754 by Robert Hamilton of
Bourtreehill, an Ayrshire man who had made his fortune in Jamaica. He built a house, and
named it Rozelle after one of his estates in Jamaica. Circa 1926, part of the Hamilton lands
was sold to Ayr County Council, who built a small development of houses, which they
named Rozelle Terrace.

RUSH HILL   See BRACKEN PARK

RUSSELL DRIVE   See RUSSELL STREET

RUSSELL STREET
This name was adopted c.1832.[1] Previously this road had been known as QUARRY
STREET[2] or QUARRY ROAD, as it led to the quarry in Allison's Parks, and subsequently

---

[1]   SAL, Ayr Town Council Minutes 1925-26, 237, Works Committee 5th May 1926.
[2]   1910-1911 Directory, 247, List of Erased Terraces, Etc. The terrace was subsequently
       renumbered as 59-69 Northfield Avenue.
[3]   SAL, Ayr Town Council Minutes 1931-32, 115, Works Committee 3rd February 1932.
[4]   See Ross's obituary in Ayrshire Post, 16th April 1948, 7d.
[5]   SAL, Ayr Town Council Minutes 1934-35, 315, Works Committee 1st November 1935.
[6]   SAL, Ayr Town Council Minutes 1941-42, 242, Works Committee 9th September 1942.

as BURNSIDE STREET, as it ran alongside the burn which discharged from Newton Loch. Russell presumably honours Lord John Russell (b.1792, d.1878), the champion of parliamentary reform. In 1907 David Allan, builder, sought to call his tenements in Limond's Wynd RUSSELL TERRACE, but this was not sanctioned by the Town Council.[3] Russell Street was demolished during the comprehensive redevelopment of Wallacetown. Part of the subsequent redevelopment is called RUSSELL DRIVE, a name which was approved in February 1973.[4]

RUSSELL TERRACE   See RUSSELL STREET

ST ANDREW'S CLOSE
A room used for dancing classes, down St Andrew's Closs, is referred to in 1821.[5]

ST ANDREW'S PLACE
St Andrew's Place, Wellington Street, is referred to in a Sasine Abridgement of 1882.[6]

ST ANDREWS STREET
This name dates from c.1890,[7] and was presumably chosen to honour Scotland's patron saint.

ST CATHERINES ROAD
Name dates from c.1999. There appears to be no particular reason for the choice of this name.

ST GEORGE'S ROAD
Name dates from 1904.[8] This name was presumably chosen to honour England's patron saint, though it should be noted that the application to the Town Council came from George Wyburn, for whom see Wyburn Place.

ST JAMES SQUARE   See JAMES STREET

ST JAMES STREET   See JAMES STREET

ST JOHN STREET
Long established lane or street leading from the town to the old church of St John's. It is so named on Nicolson's Street Plan, but common usage favours ST JOHN'S LANE. Howie notes that Collectors' Vennel is now named John Street.[9] It was reported to the Police Commissioners in June 1893 that the proprietors in St John Street were willing for the street to be closed to through vehicular traffic.[10]

---

1   In 1832/33 Directory it appears as address of Thomas Reid, accountant.
2   For example on Wood's Plan, 1818.
3   SAL, Ayr Town Council Minutes 1907, 89, Works Committee 6th February 1907.
4   SAL, Ayr Town Council Minutes 1972-73, 301, Works Committee 20th February 1973.
5   Air Advertiser, 11th January 1821, 4b.
6   Ayrshire Sasine Abridgement no.2033 of 1882.
7   Ayrshire Sasine Abridgement no.9796 of 5th July 1890 records the sale in April 1890 of a building plot bounded 'by proposed road or street to be called St Andrews Street'.
8   SAL, Ayr Town Council Minutes 1904-05, 24, Works Committee 7th December 1904.
9   James Howie, An Historical Account of the Town of Ayr, Kilmarnock, 1861, 14.
10   SAL, B6/22/9, Ayr Police Commissioners, Committee Minutes 1892-93, 201, Works Committee 8th June 1893.

ST JOHN'S LANE   See ST JOHN STREET

ST JOHN'S PLACE
Terrace built in c.1893-95, and subsequently incorporated in the official names of streets as 26-36 Fort Street. Named for its proximity to St John's Tower.

ST LEONARDS COURT   See ST LEONARDS ROAD

ST LEONARDS ROAD
Name given, from c.1896, to that part of the New Maybole Road between St Leonard's Church and Belmont Crossing. St Leonard's Church was built c.1886, taking its name from the long-vanished pre-Reformation chapel and hospital of St Leonard, which had been situated in the nearby lands of Slaphouse. ST LEONARDS COURT, off St Leonards Road, was approved in March 1995,[1] while ST LEONARDS WYND, also off St Leonards Road, dates from c.1999.

ST LEONARDS WYND   See ST LEONARDS ROAD

ST PHILLANS AVENUE
Name approved by Ayr Town Council in October 1933.[2] St Phillans, a house near Skelmorlie (now the Manor Park Hotel) belonged at this time to Leslie Hamilton Wilson of Castlehill, who suggested the name. See Leslie Crescent.

ST VINCENT CRESCENT   See PEMBERTON VALLEY

SALT STREET
Name used on Wood's Plan, 1818, for what appears to be contemporary York Street.

SALTFIELD   See SALTFIELD LANE

SALTFIELD LANE
Also SALTFIELD.[3] The name suggests a field which suffered from salt, due to its proximity to the sea. The original Saltfield Lane was lost during redevelopment of Newton Green in the 1930s,[4] but the name was reborn in February 1975 for a new street between Green Street and Green Street Lane.[5]

SALTPANS ROAD
Old-established name. The road originally led through the Newton Common lands to the Saltpans which used to be situated here. In January 1873 'the ruins of the old saltpans ... were nearly all levelled with the sand' by an especially large tide.[6]

---

[1]   SAL, Kyle and Carrick District Council Minutes 1994-95, 545, Planning Applications Committee 22nd March 1995.
[2]   SAL, Ayr Town Council Minutes 1932-33, 290, Works Committee 4th October 1933.
[3]   At a auction in November 1869 of properties of J T Gordon of Blackhouse, the 'extensive buildings, with ground attached, on the North Quay, called Saltfield' were unsold. [Ardrossan and Saltcoats Herald, 13th November 1869, 4f]
[4]   Its closure was recommended by the Town Council in November 1935. [SAL, Ayr Town Council Minutes 1935-36, 32, Housing Committee 16th November 1935]
[5]   SAL, Ayr Town Council Minutes 1974-75, 310, Works Committee 18th February 1975.
[6]   Ardrossan and Saltcoats Herald, 11th January 1873, 5b.

SANDGATE
'Very early records reveal that, by 1348, the principal thoroughfares in Ayr were the Woodgait, the Cambergait, the Seagait, the Doongait and the Quarrygait. Early street-naming was completely practical, the name having to show where the street was leading. Since 'gait' was simply 'the way to', then in Ayr there were the way to the wood, the way to the chamber, the way to the sea, the way to the Doon, and the way to the quarry. In later days, Doongait became the Sandgate, Seagait changed to Boat Vennal, and - if the Chamber was the Tolbooth - the Cambergait became merely the lower end of High Street'.[1] In 1690 a convicted thief was to be scourged through the town 'to begin at the Sandgate, there to receave six whips by the lockman, six at the Mercat Cross, six at the Brigend, six at the Meall-mercat, six at the old Tower, six at the Barnns gate and to be returned back to the Bridge Port and there to receave other six'.[2] The Victorian and tautological SANDGATE STREET is last used in the 1922-23 Valuation Roll.

SANDRINGHAM TERRACE
Terrace built c.1893, and subsequently incorporated in the official names of streets as 2-14 Bellevue Road.[3] Sandringham estate in Norfolk was bought for the Prince of Wales (later Edward VII) in 1861.

SANNOX PLACE
Also SANNOX VIEW. Names approved in May 1952 (Sannox View),[4] and November 1967 (Sannox Place).[5] Sannox View has a view of the north end of Arran, which is the location of the village of Sannox.

SANNOX VIEW   See SANNOX PLACE

SAVOY COURT   See SAVOY PARK

SAVOY PARK
The name SAVOY ROAD is first found in the 1896-97 Directory, but SAVOY PARK is used in the 1898-99 Directory. SAVOY COURT was approved in July 1973,[6] and is built on the site of Savoy Cottage, a house of c.1844, built for William Rose (b.1795, d.1862), who had been a plantation owner in Jamaica. The house was named after Rose's estate in Clarendon parish, Jamaica; in turn, it gave its name to these streets.

SAVOY ROAD   See SAVOY PARK

SCAUR O' DOON ROAD
Name approved in July 1954,[7] but probably a long-established informal name for the track, now a road, leading along the south side of the Doon near its mouth. The ground here, being sandy, would have been prone to scouring ('scauring') away by spates on the river.

---

[1]   William J Dillon, The Streets in Early Times, in Annie I Dunlop, ed., The Royal Burgh of Ayr, Edinburgh, 1953, 69-70.
[2]   Quoted in John H Pagan, Annals of Ayr in the Olden Time: 1560 - 1692, Ayr, 1897, 80.
[3]   1910-1911 Directory, 247, List of Erased Terraces, Etc.
[4]   SAL, Ayr Town Council Minutes 1952-53, 25, Works Committee 23rd May 1952.
[5]   SAL, Ayr Town Council Minutes 1967-68, 220, Works Committee 20th November 1967.
[6]   SAL, Ayr Town Council Minutes 1973-74, 93, Works Committee 17th September 1973.
[7]   SAL, Ayr Town Council Minutes 1954-55, 103, Works Committee 30th July 1954.

SCHOOL VENNEL   See ACADEMY STREET

SCOTT COURT   See RIVERSIDE PLACE

SEA LANE
Recorded in the 1870-1871 Directory, and also found in Kennedy's index to the 1861 Census. It appears to have been near Green Street.

SEABANK ROAD
In use by c.1858. This street lies on the seaward defences of the Cromwellian citadel, and this may have suggested the name.

SEAFIELD CRESCENT
Also SEAFIELD DRIVE and SEAFIELD ROAD. Seafield was one of the small estates on the south side of Ayr, and the present Seafield House still stands, after serving from 1921 to 1991 as a children's hospital: the name is accurately descriptive of its position close to the sea. The first Seafield House was built for Colonel George McKenzie,[1] and was described as 'elegant [and] new' in 1809'.[2] Seafield Road was adopted in 1894 as the name of the road or lane separating the estates of Blackburn and Seafield.[3] The other names say something of attitudes to various suffixes. In October 1933 the County Council (as owners of Seafield) suggested the names SEAFIELD STREET and Seafield Crescent: the Town Council approved of Seafield Street, but rejected Seafield Crescent, substituting SEAFIELD TERRACE. In March 1934, 'having considered protests from persons living on the streets', SEAFIELD CRESCENT replaced Seafield Terrace, and the name-plates for Seafield Street and Carnochan Street were taken down,[4] and in July of that year it was agreed that these short streets should be numbered as parts of Seafield Drive.[5] Seafield Road and Racecourse View were known informally as Double Dykes Road.[6]

SEAFIELD DRIVE   See SEAFIELD CRESCENT

SEAFIELD ROAD   See SEAFIELD CRESCENT

SEAFIELD STREET   See SEAFIELD CRESCENT

SEAFIELD TERRACE   See SEAFIELD CRESCENT

SEAFORTH CRESCENT   See SEAFORTH ROAD

---

[1]   Thomas Limond, The Enclosure of the Town's Common of Ayr, in Annie I Dunlop et al, eds., Ayrshire at the Time of Burns, [Ayr], 1959, 205. McKenzie was b.c.1747 and died in Ayr in 1840. [Ayr Advertiser, 16th April 1840, 4f]
[2]   Air Advertiser, 3rd August 1809, 1b.
[3]   Ayr Advertiser, 19th April 1894, 5a.
[4]   SAL, Ayr Town Council Minutes 1933-34, 118, Works Committee 7th March 1934. SEAFIELD CRESCENT had, however, already been approved some years earlier: SAL, Ayr Town Council Minutes 1925-26, 237, Works Committee 5th May 1926.
[5]   SAL, Ayr Town Council Minutes 1933-34, 230, Works Committee 4th July 1934.
[6]   In September 1892, the National Telephone Company were given permission to carry a telephone line, inter alia, from Shalimar to the Double Dykes Road at the Knowe. [SAL, B6/22/9, Ayr Police Commissioners, Committee Minutes 1892-93, 42, Works Committee 9th September 1892.] See also Ayr Advertiser, 26th June 1879, 4e.

SEAFORTH PLACE   See SEAFORTH ROAD

SEAFORTH ROAD
Loch Seaforth, which separates Harris from Lewis, has given its name to a noble family, the Mackenzies, Earls of Seaforth, and to a regiment, the Seaforth Highlanders, first raised in 1778.[1] A direct connection with Ayr has not been discovered. 120-122 Prestwick Road, built c.1890, at the junction with Seaforth Road, were known as SEAFORTH PLACE, and represent the initial use of the name in this area. In 1914 Seaforth Road was described as being 'one of the old Newton Freedom roads, has never been formed, and has not been taken over or been maintained at any time by the Corporation, and in terms of the Police Act it is a private street'.[2] The name SEAFORTH CRESCENT was approved in September 1929.[3]

SEA TOWER COURT
Also SEA TOWER GARDENS. The names were approved by the Town Council in December 1973.[4] Seatower is a house built c.1872, for David Hunter (b.c.1830, d.1896), merchant and ship-owner: the name a fanciful invention for a tall Baronial house with sea views. It was subdivided into flats, named Sea Tower Court, and the stables and outbuildings also converted, and named Sea Tower Gardens.

SEA TOWER GARDENS   See SEA TOWER COURT

SEAVIEW   See SEAVIEW TERRACE

SEAVIEW TERRACE
Built in 1896-1898, and subsequently incorporated in the official names of streets as 100-108 Prestwick Road.[5] It presumably had a sea view. SEAVIEW was also the original name of part of New Road: the ironmonger James Highet (b.c.1784, d.1873) retired 'to the seclusion of Seaview, where he lived contented with a moderate share of the good things of Providence'.[6]

SHALLOCH PARK
Name approved - as Shalloch Place - in January 1973:[7] during the development of the Burton estate *Park* must have acquired a better image than *Place*, hence the change. Common farm and land name in south west Scotland: the best known perhaps being Shalloch-on-Minnoch, the highest hill in Ayrshire.

SHALLOCH PLACE   See SHALLOCH PARK

---

[1]   Antony Makepeace-Warne, Brassey's Companion to the British Army, London, 1995, 321.
[2]   SAL, Ayr Town Council Minutes 1915, 28, Works Committee 9th December 1914.
[3]   SAL, Ayr Town Council Minutes 1928-29, 362, Housing Committee 5th September 1929.
[4]   SAL, Ayr Town Council Minutes 1973-74, 239, Works Committee 17th December 1973.
[5]   1910-1911 Directory, 247, List of Erased Terraces, Etc.
[6]   Ayr Advertiser, 25th September 1873, 4d.
[7]   SAL, Ayr Town Council Minutes 1972-73, 264, Works Committee 15th January 1973.

SHANTER WAY

This name was approved in August 1939.[1] The reference is obviously to Burn's epic poem, Tam o Shanter, which is set, in large part, in Alloway. Although now a short cul-de-sac, Shanter Way was initially envisioned as part of a proposed arterial road or bypass for Ayr. This project was presumably aborted by the Second World War. In June 1940, when Shanter Way, was being made up prior to adoption as a public road, the Town Council, who had insisted that it be 50 feet wide instead of the normal 40 feet, agreed to pay £86 10s 4d, the additional costs caused by this decision.[2]

SHANTER'S WYND

SHAVIN BRAE

In December 1971 the Town Council considered, and approved, a suggestion from the County Clerk that that part of Macnairston Road, which was inside the new Ayr By-pass and consequently cut off from the remainder of the road, should be renamed Shavin Brae. MacKenzie[3] notes that this part of Macnairston Road was, for 'some unaccountable reason' known as Shavings Brae; he also relates that the foot of the neighbouring Sandyhill road, at Old Toll 'was called Shaving's (sic) Brae because the shavings from the joiner's shop at [Old Toll] were blown across the main road and gathered here. It was a common prank of the youngsters in those days to set them alight'.

SHAWFIELD AVENUE

Name approved in 1963.[4]   Shawfield was a small property close to the site of Shawfield Avenue: it is shown on the 1858 1st edition Ordnance Survey map. It appears to have belonged, from at least c.1780, to a John Shaw, who may be the John Shaw, Finikland (i.e. Fenwickland), whose daughter Agnes died in October 1772. Jean Curle, wife of John Shaw at Shawfield, died, aged 91, in 1819.[5]

SHIEL HILL

Name approved in November 1965.[6]   No particular reason for the name has been established.

SHIELING PARK

Approved in September 1968, after the Town Council had rejected the initial suggestion, PARKLAND.[7] The name is borrowed from the house here, The Shieling. A shieling is a

---

[1]   SAL, Ayr Town Council Minutes 1938-39, 257, Works Committee 9th August 1939. The Ayrshire Post of 18th August 1939, 9b, noted that 'at last Ayr Town Council has risen to the occasion. On the recommendation of the owners of Cambusdoon estate they have agreed that the new street off Monument Road near Alloway's auld haunted kirk should be named 'Shanter Way'. Enough said'.

[2]   SAL, Ayr Town Council Minutes 1939-40, 161, Finance Committee 6th June 1940.

[3]   Rev A MacKenzie, In the Wake of the Years, in Ayrshire Post, 14th March 1955, 15e.

[4]   SAL, Ayr Town Council Minutes 1963-64, 139, Works Committee 24th October 1963.

[5]   Jean B Kennedy, Old Parish Records Ayr (598) Voume 9 Deaths March 1766 to May 1820, [Ayr], 1996.

[6]   SAL, Ayr Town Council Minutes 1965-66, 172, Works Committee 15th November 1965.

[7]   SAL, Ayr Town Council Minutes 1968-69, 81, Works Committee 15th July 1968, and 116, Works Committee, 16th September 1968. These minutes spell the name Sheiling.

summer residence, often associated with occupations carried on at a distance from the permanent house, such as peat-cutting or shepherding. The use of the name for houses is not uncommon, though it terms of comfort and durability, these 'summer residences' are far removed from the basic shelters found in places such as the peat moors of Lewis. The first house on this site, Frankville, was built c.1802 for Mrs John Kelso; it was renamed as The Shieling, c.1891, for Frederick E Villiers, and a new house was built c.1934.

SHORE ROAD
The road leading into the north harbour from the north. The name, given on Nicolson's map, appears never to have been formally adopted. It is one of a number of names which appear to have been adopted by the Harbour Authorities.

SKATE LANE
Cast iron name plates were ordered for Skate Lane in 1894, but the order was quickly cancelled. The location of this unalluring street is not known, but a location west of the Barracks is suggested by a reading of the Burgh's Roll of Superiorities.[1]

SLOAN PLACE
Also SLOAN STREET. Names date from 1945 (Sloan Street)[2] and 1965 (Sloan Place).[3] Although not specifically stated, the original name appears to honour the South Ayrshire MP, Alexander Sloan (b.1879, d.1945), who had died shortly before the name was approved. Sloan was a miner from Rankinston who succeeded James Brown (see James Brown Avenue) in the seat in 1939.[4]

SLOAN STREET   see SLOAN PLACE

SMITH PLACE
A property in Prestwick Road, noted between the 1840s and 1890s. It was probably built c.1810 by Adam Smith (d.1814), one of the Newton Freemen.

SMITH STREET
Formerly known as SMITH'S ROAD, which name was formally adopted by the Town Council in 1845 for the road running past the endowed free school known as Smith's Institution.[5] Over the years the name has changed to SMITH STREET. The name of the school honours Captain John Smith (d.1817), who left £2000 in his will to endow and maintain a school for the poor: it was in operation by 1825 and a purpose-built school was opened in 1842.[6]

SMITH'S ROAD   See SMITH STREET

---

[1]   SAL, Ayr Burgh Records, Roll of Superiorities Belonging to Provost, Magistrates and Council of Royal Burgh of Ayr, folio 209.

[2]   SAL, Ayr Town Council Minutes 1945-46, 16, Works Committee 26th November 1945.

[3]   SAL, Ayr Town Council Minutes 1965-66, 145, Works Committee 15th October 1965.

[4]   See Sloan's obituary in Ayrshire Post, 23rd November 1945, 6cde. It is interesting to note that neither James Brown nor Alexander Sloan was MP for Ayr Burghs, and that none of town's own parliamentary representatives have, to date, been similarly honoured.

[5]   SAL, B6/18/30, Ayr Town Council Minutes 1841-1848, 11th September 1845.

[6]   James McClelland, Schools, in Annie I Dunlop, ed., The Royal Burgh of Ayr, Edinburgh, 1953, 226-227.

SNOWDROP SQUARE   See BRACKEN PARK

SOLITUDE PLACE
Original name for a house in New Road. This was presumably considered a remote and quiet spot when the house was built c.1855. The house became Newtonhead Villa, c.1864, and was probably demolished c.1890 when Elmbank Street was developed.

SOMERSET PARK   See SOMERSET ROAD

SOMERSET PARK ROAD   See SOMERSET ROAD

SOMERSET PLACE   See SOMERSET ROAD

SOMERSET ROAD
In 1909 Ayr Town Council received a petition from householders in the southern part of West Sanquhar Road, asking that that part be renamed SOMERSET PARK ROAD: the Council approved the principle of a separate name but approved the shorter Somerset Road.[1] In the absence of meaningful alternatives, it must be considered that the road has been named after the English county: the name chosen for its pleasant sound and associations. Prior to this the name had been used, as SOMERSET PLACE, for the houses, now 4-10 Hawkhill Avenue, built c.1877, and was then adopted for the Ayr United football ground, SOMERSET PARK, which was opened in 1888.

SORREL DRIVE   See BRACKEN PARK

SOUTER PLACE
Name approved in November 1955.[2] Another of the Forehill Burns names, taken from one of the protagonists of 'Tam o' Shanter', Souter Johnny, the Kirkoswald shoemaker. A souter or soutar is a shoemaker; the Council approved the name as Soutar, a spelling which annoyed a sketch writer in the local press.[3]

SOUTH BEACH ROAD
This name was approved in June 1972 for the new road running between Ayr Baths and the Citadel Wall.[4] The name had previously been in use in the early 20th Century, and probably since c.1883 when the Slip Dock and Esplanade were built.

SOUTHFIELD PARK
Name dates from 1972, and is presumably an old-established informal name for the field on which the road is now built. In June 1972 the Council suggested COMMONHEAD PLACE as the name for this street, but this was rejected; in July a new suggestion - CAIRNRYAN WAY - was made, but this too was turned down, and the decision was left in the hands of the Convener of the Works Committee and the Burgh Surveyor. They presumably decided on Southfield Park.[5] Of the alternative names, Cairnryan may have been suggested by

---

1   SAL, Ayr Town Council Minutes 1909, 290, Works Committee 6th October 1909.
2   SAL, Ayr Town Council Minutes 1955-56, 202, Works Committee 24th November 1955.
3   Ayrshire Post, 16th December 1955, 14f.
4   SAL, Ayr Town Council Minutes 1972-73, 59, Works Committee 19th June 1972.
5   SAL, Ayr Town Council Minutes 1972-73, 59, Works Committee 19th June 1972, and *ibid*, 95, Works Committee 17th July 1972.

proximity to the Stranraer railway, while Commonhead was a farm which stood where the original Ayr Technical College now stands on the far side of the railway from Southfield Park.

SOUTH HARBOUR STREET
Formerly known as HARBOUR STREET, an old and obvious name for the road along the south (Ayr) side of the river. It became South Harbour Street during the 1880s, to distinguish it from North Harbour Street.

SOUTH LODGE COURT
Name approved in 1990.[1] South Lodge is the house on whose grounds this development was built. It is one of the villas which sprang up along Racecourse Road in the early 19th Century, and was built c.1834 for William Cunningham (b.c.1787, d.1838), a major in the East India Company's army: it opened as an Old Peoples Home in March 1954.[2] Its rather unimaginative name refers to its position relative to Ayr, coupled with a contemporary epithet for a suburban villa.

SOUTHPARK ROAD
South Park was the name given to one of the fields created in the Mid Sands. Southpark Road is the street that was created through the centre of the park to open it up for development, probably in the 1860s. In 1894 Southpark Road absorbed the short-lived Avondale Road.[3] Southpark House, 37 Racecourse Road, was in existence by 1847, being advertised for sale, and 'new', in the Ayr Advertiser of 4 February 1847.

SOUTH PLACE
Terrace of four houses, built c.1852, which was incorporated in the official names of streets as 30-36 Midton Road.[4]

SOUTH QUAY
A long-standing name for the Ayr side of the harbour. As a street name it was used in the 19th Century, and probably earlier, but was superceded by South Harbour Street.

SPEEDWELL SQUARE   See BRACKEN PARK

SPION KOP
Informal name bestowed on Craigmillar Buildings (q.v.), King Street. Spion Kop was a hill near Ladysmith, South Africa, the site of a battle between the British and the Boers on 24th January 1900, from which the Boers emerged victorious. The name was very much in the news in early 1900, and became attached to these flats, for obscure reasons which may reflect the grim humour of life in Ayr's poor northern suburbs.[5] The 'Kop' at Liverpool

---

[1]   SAL, Kyle and Carrick District Council Minutes 1989-90, 925-926, Planning and Building Control Committee 21st February 1990.
[2]   Ayrshire Post, 26th March 1954, 10.
[3]   Ayr Advertiser, 19th April 1894, 5a.
[4]   1910-1911 Directory, 247, List of Erased Terraces, Etc.
[5]   That grim humour may be related to the comments of reporters, including a young Winston Churchill, on the 'astounding ineffeciency' of the British artillery, calling Spion Kop that 'acre of massacre, that complete shambles'. Quoted in Simon Inglis, The Football Grounds of Great Britain, 2nd ed., London, 1987, 363. Inglis dates Liverpool's Kop to 1906, and

F.C.'s Anfield Football Ground was also originally called Spion Kop, and other examples are known throughout Britain.

SPRINGBANK ROAD
In 1911 the Works Committeee recommended 'that names Bellrock Road and Springbank Road respectively be given to the roads presently known by these names'.[1] Springbank Road was built from 1906: no particular reason for the name has been identified.

SPRINGVALE
Springvale was the name of a house in Midton Road built c.1807: it is now called Dolphin Cottage. SPRINGVALE ROAD was in existence by 1865, while in June 1883 the sports of Ayr Academical Club were held in Springvale Park, and 'if Springvale Park did not impress one as being a model athletic arena, its claims to the picturesque could not be overlooked'.[2]
SPRINGVALE PARK was approved as a street name in February 1925.[3]

SPRINGVALE PARK   See SPRINGVALE

SPRINGVALE ROAD   See SPRINGVALE

SPRUCE PARK   See ALDER BANK

SPUR ROAD
A modern name given by the Harbour Authorities to a spur road within the harbour.

STANLEY PLACE
Original name, from c.1873, of 30-34 Dalblair Road. A name conveying pretension, though it may honour Henry Morton Stanley (b.1841, d.1904), who found David Livingstone at Ujiji in November 1871.

STATION BRIDGE   See STATION BRIDGE ROAD

STATION BRIDGE ROAD
Name used in Valuation Rolls from 1981 for the address of the filling station opposite the south gable of the Station Hotel. The name STATION BRIDGE had been approved by the Town Council in 1927 for the road between Burns Statue Square and the junction of Holmston and Castlehill Roads.[4]

STATION COTTAGES, Alloway
Built by the Glasgow and South-Western Railway for staff at Alloway Station, on the Maidens and Dunure Light Railway, opened in 1906.[5]

STATION ROAD
Road close to Ayr station, a new road made when Victoria Bridge was opened in 1898.

STEVENSON COURT   See RIVERSIDE PLACE

---

          says that a terrace built in 1904 at the Manor Ground (Woolwich Arsenal FC - a team with a
          strong military following) was christened Spion Kop.
[1]   SAL, Ayr Town Council Minutes 1911, 284, Works Committee 9th August 1911.
[2]   The Field, vol lxi, no.1590, 16th June 1883, 816.
[3]   SAL, Ayr Town Council Minutes 1924-25, 126, Works Committee 4th February 1925.
[4]   SAL, Ayr Town Council Minutes 1926-27, 258, Works Committee 4th May 1927.
[5]   Ayr Advertiser, 17th May 1906, 4f.

STEWART ROAD
Name approved in September 1928.[1] Named after John Stewart (b.1867, d.1944), who was Provost of Ayr from 1927 to 1930. He was a farmer's son from Lugton, and from 1898 had a joiner's business in Ayr.[2]

STEWARTLEA
Name marked on Nicolson's Street Plan. Stewartlea was a large villa that has now been subdivided. The flats, and houses in the grounds, are formally numbered as 72-82 Midton Road. The villa was built c.1871 for David Campbell (b.1803, d.1879), banker in Ayr.[3] The name seems to be a fanciful invention.

STOBHILL CRESCENT   See BLACKHILL STREET

STONECROP PLACE   See BRACKEN PARK

STONEFIELD PARK
This name approved in February 1968,[4] is presumably an old-established local name for the field here. There is at the junction with Dunure Road a large boulder, which may be a standing stone or glacial erratic, and this may have suggested the name.

STRATHAYR PLACE
Name approved in May 1974.[5] A fanciful invention, based on genuine place names such as Strathclyde and Strathdon. A 'strath' is a broad valley.

STRATHDOON DRIVE   See MOUNT CHARLES CRESCENT

STRATHDOON PLACE
Name dates from 1969. A fanciful invention, using the same template and format as Strathayr Place. See Mount Charles Crescent.

STUART PLACE
Houses built and named c.1881, and subsequently incorporated in the official names of streets as 7-11 Carrick Road.[6] Commemorates the Scots royal family, in exile after 1690.

SUMMERFIELD COTTAGES
Group of four local authority houses in Monument Road, erected in 1938. Summerfield is probably a local field name.

SUN INN CLOSE
Former name of close at 219-223 High Street, named for the public house which used to be here.

---

1   SAL, Ayr Town Council Minutes 1927-28, 338, Housing Committee 3rd September 1928.
2   Ayrshire Post, 20th October 1944, 4ab.
3   From c.1826 until 1864 Campbell had been factor on the Auchincruive estate. His obituary
         is in Ayr Advertiser, 4th December 1879, 4e.
4   SAL, Ayr Town Council Minutes 1967-68, 337, Works Committee 19th February 1968.
5   SAL, Ayr Town Council Minutes 1974-75, 19, Works Committee 20th May 1974.
6   1910-1911 Directory, 247, List of Erased Terraces, Etc.

SUNNINGDALE AVENUE
Name approved in 1963.[1]   The name of the Surrey village and golf course appears to have
been chosen purely for its pleasant sound.

SUNNYSIDE
The four houses between Park Terrace and the Low Green are officially in Park Terrace, but
unnumbered. They are occasionally listed in Directories and other sources under the name
Sunnyside, the name of one of the houses, built c.1856. An appropriately euphonious name
for houses with wide views across the Low Green to Arran and the setting sun.

SYCAMORE CRESCENT   See ALDER BANK

SYMS LANE
This lane is referred to in 1910 as the 'new private lane running through Sym's property
from Wallace Street to Limond's Wynd'.[2]   The lane was created by the redevelopment of
32-34 Wallace Street by the Trustees of Henry Sym (b.1809, d.1871), a builder in Ayr.

TAM O' SHANTER CLOSE
Close or Vennel at 232 High Street, to the right of the Tam o' Shanter Inn. The Tam o'
Shanter Tavern is first mentioned in the 1841-42 Directory, but it was Andrew Glass, who
became the licensee in 1857, who first vigourously promoted the house as being that in
which Tam and the Souter drank the night away. There is no evidence to support the
identification.[3]

TAM'S BRIG
Bridge by which the Ayr to Prestwick road crosses the main railway line. It was first built
about 1852 and named, partly facetiously, after a local character, Thomas McCreath, farmer
of Bellesleyhill.[4]   In 1925 the Town Council confirmed its existence as a street name.[5]

TAYBANK DRIVE
This name was approved by the Works Committee on 24th September 1959.[6]   The name,
which appears to be a fanciful invention, was initially applied in the late 19th Century to a
cottage in Maybole Road. This gave its name to a commercial laundry here, which in turn
appears to have suggested the name for this street.

TAYLOR COURT   See TAYLOR STREET

TAYLOR STREET
This name was in use by 1845, but is probably earlier. The family of Taylor owned
Blackhouse estate from 1787 until 1870, and were very active in the industrial development
of Ayr, being among the first to mine coal in a modern and systematic manner. They were

[1]   SAL, Ayr Town Council Minutes 1963-64, 139, Works Committee 24th October 1963.
[2]   SAL, Ayr Town Council Minutes 1910, 120, Lighting Committee 4th March 1910.
[3]   The story of the Tam o' Shanter is well told in Joseph D Shearer, The Dwelling House of
       James Shearer, Ayr, c.1980.
[4]   William McKill recounts the full story in the Ayrshire Post, 12th February 1904, 3c.
[5]   SAL, Ayr Town Council Minutes 1924-25, 126, Works Committee 4nd February 1925.
[6]   SAL, Ayr Town Council Minutes 1959-60, 118.

leading partners in the Ayr Coal Company, and in George Taylor & Co. The family involved themselves heavily, as did their neighbours the Oswalds of Auchincruive, in the development of Ayr Harbour. There were persistent, but unsuccessful efforts in the early 1950s to incorporate a name honouring Dr John Taylor (b.1805, d.1842), a member of this family and a prominent Chartist, in the names chosen for the local authority housing at Craigie.[1] The old peoples' hostel at 17 Taylor Street, built in 1937,[2] was renamed, c.1981, as TAYLOR COURT.

TENNANT STREET   See ROBERTSON CRESCENT

TERRY'S CLOSE
Close at 26-30 High Street, demolished c.1914, when the former YMCA Hall was built. Supposedly the former town house of the Neills of Swinridgemuir (Dalry), it was sketched by Robert Bryden in 1887. From at least 1867 until c.1912 the shop at the head of the close was that of James Terry & Son, locksmiths and bellhangers. This business was established by James Terry (b.c.1819, d.1894) and continued by his son, Isaac Terry (b.c.1844, d.1931)

TEVIOT DRIVE   See ETTRICK PLACE

TEVIOT STREET   See ETTRICK PLACE

THEATRE LANE
Recorded in the 1841 Census Enumerators' Returns, this name appears to have been given to that part of Mew Lane adjacent to Ayr Baptist Church, which was originally Ayr's Theatre.

THISTLE WALK   See BRACKEN PARK

THOMSON STREET
Name approved in November 1945.[3] It honours the solicitor Peter Allan Thomson (b.1866, d.1951), who was Town Clerk of Ayr for over 40 years, from August 1905 until he retired in May 1946. The son of Peter Thomson, who was for more than 40 years gardener at Rozelle, P A Thomson was an enthusiastic amateur gardener and 'at all times a staunch supporter of the allotments movement in Ayr'.[4]

THORNWOOD AVENUE   See THORNYFLAT DRIVE

THORNYFLAT CRESCENT   See THORNYFLAT DRIVE

THORNYFLAT DRIVE
Also THORNYFLAT ROAD[5] and THORNYFLAT STREET.[1] These streets are part of a local authority development on Laigh Thornyflat Farm. Thornyflat Maternity Home was

---

[1]   See, for instance, Ayrshire Post, 19th March 1954, 15e. The leading pro-Taylor protagonist was Councillor Hewitson.
[2]   AA, Ayr Dean of Guild Court plans, Box no.70, plan no.41.
[3]   SAL, Ayr Town Council Minutes 1945-46, 16, Works Committee 26th November 1945.
[4]   See Thomson's obituary in Ayrshire Post, 19th January 1951, 8ef.
[5]   Thornyflat Drive and Thornyflat Road were approved in February 1947. [SAL, Ayr Town Council Minutes 1946-47, 121, Housing & Town Planning Committee 24th February 1947]

opened in July 1948[2] and closed c.1992: subsequent residential development on its site includes THORNYFLAT PLACE and THORNYFLAT CRESCENT. This name appears to mean a flat piece of land with thorn bushes. The adjacent name, THORNWOOD AVENUE, approved in December 1954,[3] appears to be a fanciful invention, based in part on its being in the Thornyflat development.

THORNYFLAT PLACE See THORNYFLAT DRIVE

THORNYFLAT ROAD See THORNYFLAT DRIVE

THORNYFLAT STREET See THORNYFLAT DRIVE

TIG ROAD
Name dates from c.1890. It was originally the private road or drive leading to Tig Cottage, built c.1880 for James Drennan (b.1825, d.1882), a farmer turned slater. Drennan was born in Ballantrae parish, where one of the main rivers is the Water of Tig.

TODD'S CLOSE
On the west side of Main Street, but not precisely located. Howie, in referring to the alterations wrought in public rights of way in Newton by the arrival of the railway says that 'a road or footpath which passed through what is called Todd's Close, across the"“riggs” into Newton Green, and thence to the Shore, was formerly used daily by all'.[4] The name is found in the 1871 Census Enumerators' Returns.

TOLLPARK ROAD
Former name of Fairfield Road, which is built through the field in the Laigh Sands known as Toll Park, from its situation close to the toll bar at the southern end of Alloway Place.

TOWNHEAD
The head of the town, now represented by the area around Kyle Street, Burns Statue Square and the Station. The Station is approximately on the site of Townhead Quarry, which provided much of the stone from which Ayr is built.

TRAMWAY HOUSES See ALDERSTON AVENUE

TREEBANK CRESCENT
Name approved in 1965.[5] A street in Masonhill, close to the many tree names there (see Alder Bank). A fanciful invention.

No formal approval date has been found for Thornyflat Street: it first appears in the 1950-51 Valuation Roll.

1 In the minutes of February 1947 (see above) the name is spelled Thorneyflat. In July 1952 the Town Council confirmed that the correct spelling was THORNYFLAT, i.e with no E before the Y, and a single T at the end. [SAL, Ayr Town Council Minutes 1952-53, 89, Housing Committee 21st July 1952. The Ayrshire Post, 26th September 1952, 7b, reported that 'there has been a variation of the spelling of “Thornyflat” which is now to be regarded as the correct spelling for official purposes']

2 Formally opened on 3rd July 1948, two days before inception of National Health Service. [Ayrshire Post, 9th July 1948, 7ef]

3 SAL, Ayr Town Council Minutes 1954-55, 240, Housing Committee 28th December 1954.

4 James Howie, An Historical Account of the Town of Ayr, Kilmarnock, 1861, 47.

5 SAL, Ayr Town Council Minutes 1964-65, 358, Works Committee 19th April 1965.

TREFOIL PLACE   See BRACKEN PARK

TRYFIELD PLACE
This name dates from c.1890. Tryfield Cottage is found in the 1884-85 Directory, but the derivation is obscure.

TURNER'S BRIDGE
Footbridge crossing the river Ayr between Mill Street and John Street. It was built at his own expense by the Ayr brewer Andrew Muir Turner (b.c.1842, d.1912) in 1899-1900, and was formally handed over to the Town Council on 12th September 1900.[1]

TWEED STREET   See ETTRICK PLACE

TWINNINGHAM PLACE
Houses at the junction of Prestwick Road and McCall's Avenue, dating from c.1841, and demolished c.1890. The name honours Elizabeth Twinningham (b.c.1793, d.1840), the wife of Alexander McCall.

UNION ARCADE
Alternative name for BURNS STATUE ARCADE. The properties which back onto the Arcade (31-45 Burns Statue Square and 24-60 Smith Street), were known as UNION BUILDINGS. All were built c.1890 on or close to the former site of Ayr Cattle Market. See also Union Avenue for discussion of the name.

UNION AVENUE
Name approved in 1890 as UNION STREET.[2] The union commemorated is presumably that between the parliaments of Scotland and England in 1707; the union was seen as a cornerstone of the development of Britain and the British Empire. Its commemoration in street names, pub names and the like is widespread, north and south of the border, throughout the 19th Century.

UNION BUILDINGS   See UNION ARCADE

UNION STREET   See UNION AVENUE

UPPER CROFTS
Name approved in October 1966, 'as this name had a local connection and was to be found on earlier maps of the district'.[3] Alloway Upper Crofts were part of the Barony lands of Alloway, and were sold by Ayr Town Council in 1754 to John Crawford of Doonside for £310.[4]

UPPER LOANING   See LOANING, THE

---

[1]   Ayr Advertiser, 13th September 1900, 5b.
[2]   Ayr Advertiser, 12th June 1890, 6e, reporting decision of Ayr Police Commissioners.
[3]   SAL, Ayr Town Council Minutes 1966-67, 181, Works Committee 14th October 1966.
[4]   Thomas Limond, The Roup of the Lands of Alloway, in Annie I Dunlop et al, eds., Ayrshire at the Time of Burns, [Ayr], 1959, 202-203.

VICTORIA BRIDGE
A road bridge over the Ayr at this point, and a new road linking Holmston Road and Whitletts Road, were first suggested in May 1896.[1] The foundation stone of the bridge was laid in June 1897,[2] on the day of Queen Victoria's Diamond Jubilee, and it was formally opened in April 1898.[3] It was reconstructed in 1961, as the plaque on the bridge testifies, and widened in 1977. VICTORIA COURT Is a sheltered housing complex, opened c.1983, in Mill Street, close to Victoria Bridge.

VICTORIA COURT   See VICTORIA BRIDGE

VICTORIA CRESCENT
The Sasine Abridgements for 46-48 Park Circus, built c.1886, describe them as being bounded by a proposed road to be called Victoria Crescent.[4] The name appears never to have been used, and absorbed into Park Circus.

VICTORIA PARK
Name given to one of the fields created out of the Mid Sands, and presumably chosen to honour Queen Victoria. Villas were being erected in Victoria Park by 1850,[5] including those which are now numbered in Racecourse View, and the road through the field appears to have been originally known as VICTORIA ROAD, becoming Victoria Park Road, and ultimately Victoria Park.

VICTORIA PLACE
This name dates from c.1881, but seems in the 1890s to have been incorporated into Princes Street, as nos 58-62. However c.1905, these houses became 1-5 VICTORIA ROAD, and this short but grandly named road persists until the 1969-70 Valuation Roll, when it was lost as part of the re-development of Wallacetown.

VICTORIA ROAD   See VICTORIA PARK

VICTORIA ROAD   See VICTORIA PLACE

VICTORIA STREET
Formerly known as BOGHALL ROW. first mentioned in the 1851-1852 Directory. Boghall was a farm on the eastern edge of Ayr, swallowed up in the 19th Century development of the Content area. The name is self-explanatory, and Boghall Row was close to the site of the farm steading. In April 1896 it was agreed to rename it VICTORIA STREET, honouring Queen Victoria.[6]

---

[1]   Ayr Advertiser, 21st May 1896, 5g.
[2]   Ayr Advertiser, 24th June 1897, 5a.
[3]   Ayr Advertiser, 21st April 1898, 5def. Photographs of the opening ceremony appear in the Scots Pictorial, vol.III, no.58, 7th May 1898, 4.
[4]   Ayrshire Sasine Abridgements nos.1335 and 1345 of 1886.
[5]   In the Ayr Advertiser, 14th November 1850, 1c, a 'recently erected' villa in Victoria Park was advertised for sale or let.
[6]   Ayr Advertiser, 16th April 1896, 6c.

VICTORIA TERRACE
Terrace of c.1879, which was subsequently incorporated in the official names of streets as 26-36 Viewfield Road.[1]

VIEWFIELD ROAD
Name dates from c.1881. It was formerly considered as part of Waggon Road, and shares the origin of that road. The name is borrowed from Viewfield Farm, which formerly stood near here, and which presumably had a slightly raised position, offering views.

VIRGINIA GARDENS
Name dates from c.1905. Built to the rear of 100-106 New Road, which were originally named VIRGINIA PLACE. The name seems to be derived from the American state: a name chosen to suggest cosmopolitan attitudes. Compare Allegheny Terrace, Florida Terrace and Havannah Place. Here, probably, and certainly at Havannah Place, the developer was James M Ferguson who was, amongst many things, a tobacco manufacturer, and this may have suggested these names.

VIRGINIA PLACE   See VIRGINIA GARDENS

VOLUNTEER BUILDINGS
Obsolete name for 1-7 Burns Statue Square, which were built c.1903 for the 2nd Volunteer Battalion of the Royal Scottish Fusiliers, with a drill hall above and shops below.

WAGGON ROAD
Name dates from c.1855: it is called Pebble Street on Wood's Plan, 1818. Waggon Road is built on the line of one of the late 18th Century waggonways which brought coal from the coalfield of Auchincruive to the north harbour. These were superceded by the railway, and the pits became exhausted, and the waggon ways converted to non-railed traffic.[2] Viewfield Road (which was formerly considered as part of Waggon Road) and Oswald Road are also conversions of old waggonways. WAGGON WAY was approved in December 1981[3] for the small industrial estate off Green Street Lane, built on the site of the original Ayr railway station, latterly Ayr's goods station.

WAGGON WAY   See WAGGON ROAD

WALKER ROAD
Name approved in September 1925 for a new road, between Whitletts Road and the bridge at the end of McCall's Avenue, built as a unemployment relief project.[4] The road passed through land owned by John Walker, a member of the family which owned the Hawkhill Chemical Works, W G Walker & Sons.

---

[1]   1910-1911 Directory, 247, List of Erased Terraces, Etc.
[2]   See Harry Broad, Rails to Ayr, revised edition, [Ayr], 1989 for a history of these waggonways.
[3]   SAL, Kyle and Carrick District Council Minutes 1981-82, 582-583, Planning & Building Control Committee 23rd December 1981.
[4]   SAL, Ayr Town Council Minutes 1924-25, 434, Works Committee 9th September 1925.

WALLACE STREET
Long established name for part of the main north-south street through Wallacetown: it is so named on the Armstrongs' map of 1775. It refers to the landowners and feu superiors, the Wallaces of Craigie. Initially Wallace Street extended from the Auld Brig to the Four Corners, but c.1875 Kilmarnock Street was absorbed into Wallace Street. One entry in the 1830 Directory is listed, presumbably erroneously, as WALLACETOWN STREET.[1]

WALLACETOUN HOUSE
In January 1960 Ayr Town Council approved this name, suggested by the Ministry of Works, for the new government offices then being built in John Street.[2] A consciously archaic spelling for an aggressively modern building, which is now the local Department of Social Security offices.

WALLACETOWN STREET   See WALLACE STREET

WANDGATE ROAD
This name is used in the early 19th Century for one of the roads or tracks through the lands of the Newton Freemen, roughly equivalent to the modern West Sanquhar Road. The meaning is obscure.

WARD COURT
Also WARD ROAD. Names date from the 1990s. This is a housing development built on the site of Heathfield Hospital, leading to the word, 'ward', with its many meanings.

WARD ROAD   See WARD COURT

WATER VENNEL
In 1785 Ayr Town Council resolved 'to build a new bridge from the Water Vennell to the street of the old Newton'.[3] The upgraded Water Vennel, which had connected Sandgate with Newton via a ford, was widened and became New Bridge Street.[4]

WATTFIELD ROAD
Name dates from c.1884. This small development was built on land belonging to Wattfield Cottage in Midton Road, which was the property of James Watt and his family from 1811 until 1865.

WEAVER STREET
Long-established name, though the street itself now exists in little more than name. It was once one of the main routes north from Newton. It was a street in which many hand-loom weavers lived. Recorded only once in the 1830 Directory, as WEAVERS ROW,[5] and on Wood's Plan, 1818, as WEAVERS STREET.

---

[1]   Mrs C Mitchell, innkeeper, 13 Wallacetown Street.
[2]   Ayr Advertiser, 14th January 1960, 6b.
[3]   David M Lyon, Ayr in the Olden Times, Ayr, 1928, 40, quoting from the minutes of Ayr Town Council.
[4]   Ayr Advertiser, 6th January 1955, 8d.
[5]   Directory for Ayr, Newton & Wallacetown, &c., Macarter, 1830, entry for John Ewing, innkeeper.

WEAVERS ROW   See WEAVER STREET

WEAVERS STREET   See WEAVER STREET

WEBSTERS VENNAL
Ayrshire Sasine Abridgement 6500 of 1879 records a Dispostion, made in 1850 by Hugh McWhinnie RN to his wife, of a fauld of land "on the west side of Websters Vennal of the burgh of Ayr". This name has not otherwise been noted.

WEIR ROAD
This name refers to Alexander Weir (b.1821, d.1880) who founded the Ayr Chemical and Manure Works here, c.1859, in the old foundry of James Miller.[1] The street is first referred to in 1919 as WEIR'S ROAD.[2]

WEIR'S ROAD   See WEIR ROAD

WELLINGTON CHAMBERS   See WELLINGTON SQUARE

WELLINGTON LANE   See WELLINGTON SQUARE

WELLINGTON SQUARE
The square is named in honour of Arthur Wellesley, created 1st Duke of Wellington in 1809, military hero and politician (b.1769, d.1852). The service lane behind the south side of Wellington Square is known as WELLINGTON LANE, though this name was not used originally: an 1856 minute of the Town Council refers to the 'Meuse lane behind the south side of Wellington Square'.[3] The impressive commercial block at the north east corner of Wellington Square, at the junction of Fullarton Street and Fort Street, built c.1897, is known as WELLINGTON CHAMBERS.

WELLINGTON STREET   See DUKE STREET

WELLPARK
Name approved in July 1954.[4] The field here presumably had a spring or well in it. One of the fields belonging to the Barns House estate through which Miller Road was built was also, for the same reason, known as Well Park, giving its name to a terrace, WELLPARK PLACE, now 29-31 Miller Road, and a villa, Wellpark, which is now the Meteor Hotel, 5 Racecourse Road.

WELLPARK PLACE   See WELLPARK

WELL'S COURT
This name is found in the 1851 Census Enumerators' Returns for a court off Isle Lane (Hope Street), but no explanation for the name has been found.

---

[1]   "Miller's Foundry" is marked on the 1858 1st edition Ordnance Survey map. Weir's obituary is in Ayr Advertiser, 29th April 1880, 4e.
[2]   SAL, Ayr Town Council Minutes 1918-19, 365, Works Committee 3rd September 1919.
[3]   SAL, B6/18/31, Ayr Town Council Minutes 1849-1856, 448, 12th March 1856.
[4]   SAL, Ayr Town Council Minutes 1954-55, 103, Works Committee 30th July 1954.

WEST PLACE
Name approved in January 1973.[1] Perhaps the least imaginative of all Ayr's street names, it contained two houses and one shop. In February 1984 it was agreed to incorporate West Place into Belmont Road.[2]

WEST STREET
An 1834 reference to West Street of Newton Green is coupled with references to Mid Street of Newton Green and Green Street or Dander Row.[3] They appear to be, respectively, York Street, York Street Lane and Green Street. West Street and Mid Street refer to their position within the planned development of Newton Green.

WESTFIELD ROAD
Name approved in May 1927.[4] Presumably based on a local name for the westmost of the fields that belonged to Blackburn Farm.

WESTON PLACE
Obsolete name for 7-9 Miller Road, also found as WISTON PLACE. The houses were built c.1876, but the derivation is obscure.

WEST SANQUHAR AVENUE   see WEST SANQUHAR ROAD

WEST SANQUHAR PLACE   see WEST SANQUHAR ROAD

WEST SANQUHAR ROAD
Name formalised in 1905,[5] to prevent fragmentary naming in terraces. This was the lane or path, known as Wandgate Road, that led from the town towards West Sanquhar Farm. In 1908 that part of West Sanquhar Road between the railway bridge and Back Hawkhill Avenue was renamed Somerset Road. Sanchar or Sanquhar is an old variant on the name of St Quivox parish.[6] WEST SANQUHAR AVENUE and WEST SANQUHAR PLACE are late 1990s developments off West Sanquhar Road.

WESTWOOD AVENUE
Also WESTWOOD CRESCENT. The so-called 'Swedish timber houses' in Westwood Avenue were built in 1946, as part of the national post-war policy of quickly building as many houses as possible. They were formally opened on 30th November 1946 by Joseph Westwood (b.1884, d.1948), who was Secretary of State for Scotland between 1945 and 1947, and the street named in his honour. Westwood Avenue was approved in December 1946,[7] and Westwood Crescent in February 1947.[1]

---

[1]   SAL, Ayr Town Council Minutes 1972-73, 264, Works Committee 15th January 1973. The name was necessary to prevent an entire renumbering of the odd-numbered side of Belmont Road.

[2]   SAL, Kyle and Carrick District Council Minutes 1983-84, 673, Planning & Building Control Committee 29th February 1984.

[3]   Air Advertiser, 9th October 1834, 3f.

[4]   SAL, Ayr Town Council Minutes 1926-27, 258, Works Committee 4th May 1927.

[5]   SAL, Ayr Town Council Minutes 1905-06, 231, Works Committee 4th July 1906.

[6]   James Paterson, History of the County of Ayr, vol II, Paisley, 1852, 414.

[7]   SAL, Ayr Town Council Minutes 1946-47, 39, Corporation 9th December 1946.

WESTWOOD CRESCENT   See WESTWOOD AVENUE

WHEATFIELD ROAD
Name dates from c.1897, and used for development of the grounds of Wheatfield House (1 Wheatfield Road). This was built c.1790 by Hugh Cairncross, mason, and is either a fanciful invention of his own or a formalisation of an older local name for a part of the Low Green particularly suited to the growth of wheat

WHIN HILL ROAD
Name approved, as WHIN HILL, in September 1961.[2] A local name for a hill on which whins (gorse, broom) flourished.

WHITE STREET
Name approved by Ayr Town Council in May 1936.[3] It honours Dr Alexander White (b.1869 in Galston, d.1954), who had practiced in Ayr since 1895, and retired in 1948. Councillor Peyton said to the Council, 'it was only right and proper that the name of a good man like Dr. White should be perpetuated in the town'.[4]

WHITEFORD AVENUE
Name approved, as WHITEFORD VIEW, in October 1988.[5] No reason for the choice has been discovered.

WHITEFORD VIEW   See WHITEFORD AVENUE

WHITEHILL STREET
Name dates from c.1907: the developer was John McIntyre. The street was demolished in 1961 to make way for an extension to the Neptune Works of the Scottish Stamping and Engineering Co Ltd.[6] No reason for the name has been discovered.

WHITFIELD ROAD
Name approved in February 1978,[7] superceding original proposal of Crooksmoss Drive. No particular reason for this choice has been found.

WHITLETTS
Village, predominantly a mining community, about a mile and a half out of Ayr on the road to Mauchline. It has now been absorbed into Ayr, and most of the old village demolished and replaced with local authority housing. The village developed from c.1800, and was

---

[1] SAL, Ayr Town Council Minutes 1946-47, 121, Housing & Town Planning Committee 24th February 1947. Joseph Westwood was a Fife miner and union official who was MP for Stirling and Falkirk from 1935 until his death.

[2] SAL, Ayr Town Council Minutes 1961-62, 110, Works Committee 21st September 1961. The same meeting also approved CHERRY HILL. These may represent sloppy minuting, or the developer may have decided unilaterally to add the 'Road' suffix.

[3] SAL, Ayr Town Council Minutes 1935-36, 192, Housing Commitee 14th May 1936.

[4] Ayrshire Post, 12th June 1936, 10e. See also obituary in Ayrshire Post, 5th February 1954, 9b.

[5] SAL, Kyle and Carrick District Council Minutes 1988-89, 421, Planning and Building Control Committee 5th October 1988.

[6] Demolition was approved by a Dean of Guild Court Warrant, Box no.134, no.82, of 1961.

[7] SAL, Kyle and Carrick District Council Minutes 1977-78, 547, Planning and Building Control Committee 1st February 1978.

noted as the 'thriving village of Whitelets' in 1837. WHITLETTS ROAD, first recorded c.1890, leads here from Wallacetown. WHITLETTS COURT, sheltered housing, was approved in January 1985.[1] The meaning of the name remains obscure.

WHITLETTS COURT   See WHITLETTS

WHITLETTS ROAD   See WHITLETTS

WHITTLE ROAD   See ALLAN PLACE

WILLIAM STREET
Ayrshire Sasine Abridgement 3251 of 1882 contains an 1814 reference to a William Street in Content which appears to refer to property in Elba Street.

WILLIAM GRANT PLACE
This was in George Street, and is mentioned twice in the 1880-81 Directory.[2] It is not otherwise recorded, and it has not been possible to locate this street accurately.

WILLOW PARK   See ALDER BANK

WILLS ROAD
Name approved by Ayr Town Council in November 1935.[3] James Wills (b.1877, d.1940) served as Provost from 1936 to 1940, dying while in office. He was the managing director of Afflecks Ltd, which was a long-established Ayr firm of house furnishers.[4]

WILSON STREET
Name approved in February 1932:[5] Thomas Wilson (b.1868, d.1942) was Provost of Ayr from 1930-1933, and was a councillor for 20 years. A miner's son from Tongue Row near Rankinston, he was the head of Thomas Wilson & Son, warehousemen, King Street, Glasgow.[6]

WILSON'S SQUARE
This name, recorded in 1841 and 1861, is an earlier name for Reid's Square. The reference is to Peter Wilson (b.c.1803, d.1865), a builder in Ayr, who sold the property to John Reid in 1855.[7]

WIMPEY BUNGALOWS
Temporary houses in Whitletts belonging to the house builder, George Wimpey & Co. Ltd. Erected during the Second World War, they were demolished c.1949.

---

[1]   SAL, Kyle and Carrick District Council Minutes 1984-85, 652, Planning & Building Control Committee 9th January 1985.
[2]   It is given as the address of James McKissock, flesher, 3 William Grant Place, and of James Thomson, mason, 8 William Grant Place.
[3]   SAL, Ayr Town Council Minutes 1935-36, 33, Housing Commitee 16th November 1935.
[4]   See Wills's obituary in Ayrshire Post, 17th May 1940, 6de.
[5]   SAL, Ayr Town Council Minutes 1931-32, 115, Works Committee 3rd February 1932.
[6]   Ayrshire Post, 18th December 1942, 6d.
[7]   Ayrshire Sasine Abridgement, no.3681 of 1855.

WINDSOR TERRACE

Terrace of c.1899 which was subsequently incorporated in the official names of streets as 55-69 Prestwick Road.[1] Additionally WINDSOR VILLAS was the original name for 25-27 Miller Road, built c.1871. In both cases, pretension is bestowed by association with the royal castle.

WINDSOR VILLAS	See WINDSOR TERRACE
WINDWARD PARK	See PEMBERTON VALLEY

WINTON BUILDINGS

'Mr McTaggart's new Buildings, on the site of the Old Meal Market ..., which are a great embellishment to our town, have been named Winton Buildings, in honour of the Lord Lieutenant of the County, the Earl of Eglinton and Winton'.[2] The earldoms of Eglinton and Winton had been united in 1840 when Archibald William, the 13th Earl of Eglinton, succeeded additionally as the 6th Earl of Winton. Winton is an estate near Pencaitland in East Lothian.

WISTON PLACE	See WESTON PLACE

WOLSELEY PLACE

Appears to be the original name for 19-27 Church Street, built c.1888, though the name was obsolete by 1896. Sir Garnet Wolseley, 1st Viscount Wolseley (b.1833, d.1913) was a notable army leader whose chief successes were the defeat of the Ashanti in 1874, and the victory at Tel el Kebir in 1882.

WOOD PARK

Name dates from c.1960, though never apparently approved by the Town Council. It is close to WOODLANDS CRESCENT, approved in October 1955.[3] The reason for these names remains obscure.

WOODEND ROAD

This name was approved in October 1962,[4] and is presumably a formalisation of an earlier local name for an area at the end of a neighbouring wood.

WOODFIELD AVENUE	See WOODFIELD ROAD
WOODFIELD CRESCENT	See WOODFIELD ROAD
WOODFIELD HOUSE	See WOODFIELD ROAD

WOODFIELD ROAD

Also WOODFIELD AVENUE, WOODFIELD CRESCENT and WOODFIELD ROAD. These names all date from the 1910s and 1920s, and are given to developments built on land formerly part of the grounds of a house called WOODFIELD HOUSE, latterly 127

---

[1] 1910-1911 Directory, 247, List of Erased Terraces, Etc.
[2] Ayr Advertiser, 22nd February 1844, 4b.
[3] SAL, Ayr Town Council Minutes 1955-56, 167, Works Committee 27th October 1955.
[4] SAL, Ayr Town Council Minutes 1962-63, 140, Works Committee 25th October 1962.

Prestwick Road. In later years this became part of the Dalblair Motors[1] garage, and was finally demolished c.1995. In contrast to Ayr's other '--field' names this house gained its name from its builder, William Wood, grocer, (b.c.1798, d.1880), who presumably concocted the name in his own honour. Wood first acquired land in this area in 1833,[2] and is recorded as living at Woodfield House in the 1841-1842 Directory. WOODFIELD TERRACE is a former name for 5-21 Woodfield Road, listed in the 1910 list of suppressed names. Woodfield Avenue was approved in June 1922;[3] Woodfield Crescent in June 1926,[4] but Woodfield Road seems never to have received official sanction.

WOODFIELD TERRACE   see WOODFIELD ROAD

WOODGATE
'This was the way to the wood. The venerable old name disappeared early from the records, and we can not be sure of the wood or the street. Certainly the Woodgait was above the old tower at the Townhead Port, on the east side of the King's Street, so that it could have been Mill Street, or a branch of the High Street, perhaps the one blocked by the Overport. ... A man called David Reid had a tenement in the Woodgait, between another tenement and the Cow Vennel, so that it does look as if the Woodgait was the other division of High Street, leading to Maybole. Perhaps the wood was Carcluy Wood which belonged to the town, is referred to in old records, and is situated along this route'.[5]

WOODLANDS CRESCENT   See WOOD PARK

WOODLEA PLACE
Name approved in November 1965.[6] A fanciful invention, chosen for its pleasant sound.

WOOD'S CLOSE, High Street
Recorded in 1838, approximately at 168 High Street.[7] Wood is William Wood, noted under Woodfield Road.

WOOD'S CLOSE, Main Street
Recorded in the 1871 Census Enumerators' Returns at 17 Main Street. It was the property between 1857 and 1875 of Robert Wood (b.c.1801, d.1875), a dyer.

WORKMEN'S DWELLINGS
Formal name for 57 King Street, a philanthropic development of 63 houses in a tenemental square, built c.1899 by the Ayr Workmen's Dwellings Ltd. The houses were demolished in 1956.

WRIGHTFIELD COTTAGES   See WRIGHTFIELD PLACE

---

[1]   So called because their first premises were in Dalblair Road, where they remained from 1939 until c.1975.
[2]   Ayrshire Sasine Abridgement no.1216 of 1833.
[3]   SAL, Ayr Town Council Minutes 1921-22, 271, Housing Committee 2nd June 1922.
[4]   SAL, Ayr Town Council Minutes 1925-26, 265, Housing Committee 3rd June 1926.
[5]   William J Dillon, The Streets in Early Times, in Annie I Dunlop, ed., The Royal Burgh of Ayr, Edinburgh, 1953, 73-74, quoting Mason's *Protocol Book*, no.53.
[6]   SAL, Ayr Town Council Minutes 1965-66, 172, Works Committee 15th November 1965.
[7]   Air Advertiser, 12th April 1838, 1f.

WRIGHTFIELD PLACE

This name was approved in February 1989,[1] but WRIGHTFIELD COTTAGES is an earlier name for the cottages which stood in Greenfield Avenue. In the 1829-30 Directory, these are occupied by David Wilson; in directories of the 1840s to 1860s, the occupier is Hugh Muir, cartwright.

WYBURN PLACE

Name approved in February 1973.[2] This somewhat belated honour appears to be for Councillor George Wyburn (b.1858, d.1942), who was 'a well-known figure in the town, and a generous patron of swimming'.[3] He was a joiner and funeral undertaker, and is also remembered in St George's Road.

YORK STREET

Also YORK STREET LANE. These names date from the early 19th Century, and presumably honour a contemporary Duke of York.[4] William McGachie, mason, is recorded at York Street in the 1832/33 Directory, while Ayrshire Sasine Abridgement no.2699, of December 1835, refers to a property 'on the west side of the new designed street called York Street'. Perhaps inaccurately, Wood's Plan, 1818, gives the names Salt Street and Green Street to contemporary York Street and York Street Lane. See also West Street.

YORK STREET LANE   See YORK STREET

YOUNG STREET

Name approved in October 1930.[5] It appears to commemorate John Young (b.1862, d.1950) who was the Burgh Surveyor of Ayr from 1899 until 1939, and oversaw all of Ayr's council houses built during that period.

---

[1] SAL, Kyle and Carrick District Council Minutes 1988-89, 809, Planning and Building Control Committee 8th February 1989.

[2] SAL, Ayr Town Council Minutes 1972-73, 301, Works Committee 20th February 1973.

[3] Ayrshire Post, 19th June 1942, 3b. See also Ayrshire Post, 6th November 1931, 14cd.

[4] Probably Frederick, Duke of York (b.1763, d.1827), the second son of George III. He was the Commander-in-Chief of the British Army from 1798 until 1809, and again between 1811 and 1827.

[5] SAL, Ayr Town Council Minutes 1929-30, 442, Works Committee 31st October 1930.

Notes